T0243367

THE DIGITAL TRANSFORMATION ROADMAP

"David L. Rogers's work has both affected and validated our digital transformation efforts at Acuity. He's provocative and pragmatic, teaching us a different way to think about and stand out from our competitors. His insight and advice continue to have lasting impacts on our digital journey."

—Melissa Winter, president, and Ben Salzmann, CEO, Acuity Insurance

"Essential reading for leaders seeking to thrive in a rapidly evolving digital landscape. Embark on your digital transformation journey with Rogers as your guide and gain the tools to ensure success amid constant technological shifts."

—Sami Hassanyeh, chief digital officer, AARP

"Rogers provides a powerful blend of strategy and tactics to help large companies move smarter and faster into the digital world. Featuring real-world lessons and a pile of hands-on tools, this book is your essential roadmap to get any firm moving at startup speed."

—Bob Dorf, coauthor of *The Startup Owner's Manual* and lifelong entrepreneur

"Digital transformations all too often go badly wrong because those leading the change have not taken the time to work through the organizational and human barriers that keep things locked into old patterns. Armed with this terrific book, you can enter the transformational space with your eyes wide open. It will be your guide to what the future holds."

—Rita McGrath, Columbia Business School, and author
of *Seeing Around Corners* and *Discovery-Driven Growth*

"After over a decade of digital transformations, if we've learned one thing, it is that the battle to generate business value is won through breaking down organizational barriers and aligning people, processes, and metrics. With *The Digital Transformation Roadmap*, Rogers offers powerful insights to maximize the chances of transformation success."

—Didier Bonnet, professor of strategy and digital transformation at
IMD Business School and author of *Leading Digital* and *Hacking Digital*

"We've been undergoing digital transformation now for several decades, and it's only accelerating. The continuous change approach outlined in this book is the only way for organizations to thrive in the long run. It's 'go digital' or 'go out of business.'"

—Thomas H. Davenport, President's Distinguished Professor
of Information Technology and Management, Babson College

THE DIGITAL

TRANSFORMATION

ROADMAP

Rebuild your organization for continuous change

DAVID L. ROGERS

Columbia University Press
Publishers Since 1893
New York   Chichester, West Sussex
cup.columbia.edu

Library of Congress Cataloging-in-Publication Data
Names: Rogers, David L., 1970– author.
Title: The digital transformation roadmap : rebuild your organization for
continuous change / David L Rogers.
Description: New York : Columbia University Press, [2023] | Includes index.
Identifiers: LCCN 2023014410 | ISBN 9780231196581 (hardback) |
ISBN 9780231551731 (ebook)
Subjects: LCSH: Technological innovations—Management. |
Information Technology—Management. | New products. | Strategic planning.
Classification: LCC HD45 .R6337 2023 | DDC 658.4/062—dc23/eng/20230418
LC record available at https://lccn.loc.gov/2023014410

Printed in the United States of America

Cover design: Noah Arlow

For Karen, my beloved partner in creative mucking around

CONTENTS

PREFACE

This is my fifth book and my first sequel. The prequel, *The Digital Transformation Playbook*, which I published with Columbia University Press in 2016, was the first book on digital transformation. It put the topic on the map, becoming a global bestseller in more than a dozen languages. It also defined the discipline by arguing that digital transformation is not about technology; it is about strategy, leadership, and new ways of thinking. That book has helped thousands of business leaders rethink their business around new strategies and embark on transformations for the digital era.

In many of these transformations, I had a front row seat as an adviser in boardrooms and leader of workshops with executives at many different companies, including Google, Microsoft, Citibank, HSBC, Procter & Gamble, Merck, General Electric, and dozens more equally ambitious enterprises. I have taught over 25,000 business leaders through my classes at Columbia Business School's Executive Education programs in New York City, in Silicon Valley, and online. Through this work and my one-to-one advising of CEOs and chief digital officers (CDOs), I have delved into the inner workings of digital transformation efforts in diverse industries and around the world.

Today, every leading organization is pursing some kind of digital transformation (DX). The question is no longer, "Should we pursue DX?" but rather, "How do we ensure DX's impact and business value?"

Answering that question is not easy. Established businesses that have embarked on DX may be ready to rethink their strategy, but across all industries, *these businesses are struggling with the challenges of organizational change*: How do we align digital efforts across our silos? How do we balance future growth versus our current core business? How do we overcome the inertia that plagues large, complex organizations?

This book presents an approach based on a decade of evidence of DX attempts, successes, and failures. It shows that, to lead an established business today, you don't just need to *rethink your business* with strategy for the digital era. You need *to rebuild your organization* for a world of constant digital change. As daunting as that may sound, let me assure you it is possible—and it is the only way to sustain and grow your business for the future.

In *The Digital Transformation Roadmap*, I provide a practical roadmap for any leader attempting to transform their organization for the digital era. Like all my books, this one includes practical tools and frameworks to apply while driving change in your organization. I road-tested these tools in my work with executives pursuing digital change in a wide range of organizations. In the process, I have refined each tool to answer the needs of firms of different sizes, industries, geographies, and strategic challenges.

My goal is to help you, the reader, to maximize your DX success in any organization you are leading or helping to grow, now and in the future.

Acknowledgments

No book is possible without the help of many generous contributors. I want to thank all the many business leaders whose work and insights are reflected in the book. You were immensely generous in sharing your experiences and lessons with me, whether in my consulting engagements, classrooms, or interviews.

This book is indebted to the continued support of my longtime agent, Jim Levine, and my publisher, Myles Thompson. My editor Brian Smith helped guide the text through every stage, in and out of pandemic disruptions. My dear and brilliant friends Bob Dorf and Lucy Kueng each graciously read my entire first draft and offered critical feedback. The final text owes much to the aid of my peerless manuscript editor, Karen Vrotsos. Her incisive queries clarified my thinking at every turn, trimming the excess and bringing focus, buoyancy, and economy to the final text.

Throughout the book's development, Columbia Business School has sustained the development of my work and ideas and has been an invaluable home base, where I've taught and conducted research for over twenty years. I especially want to thank Mark Roberts, Pierre Yared, Dil Sidhu, and Mike Malefakis for their leadership of our Executive Education division and support of my teaching and research. I also want to thank the thousands of executive students I've had the pleasure to teach while writing this, in both my live and online programs on digital transformation, strategy, and leadership. The questions they've shared and the personal stories from their careers contributed to the evidence I probed in developing this book's key insights. Thanks also to Ashwin Damera and Chaitanya Kalipatnapu at Emeritus for an incredible journey in online education, and to Clark Boyd for sharing the virtual stage in my online courses for countless ask me anything's (AMAs) with students.

Thanks also to Tom Neilssen and his team at BrightSight Speakers for their advice and support, from the proposal stage to ideas for the book's cover. Heather Hinson contributed expert and wide-ranging research with great cheer, and Mindy Bowman designed the book's illuminating graphics. Amy Kazor and Pat Curtis were indispensable, as always, in keeping me focused on the book amid countless competing projects.

Last, I thank my wife, Karen, and son, George. Their support, companionship, and good humor kept me writing and smiling throughout the long journey. Their love is the inspiration behind all my work.

David Rogers
www.davidrogers.digital

THE DIGITAL TRANSFORMATION ROADMAP

1

The DX Roadmap

In the early days of the digital revolution, as the World Wide Web emerged as a mass platform for global communication, the New York Times Company embarked on a bold new project to reimagine its business for a new era. The project was what we would call today a digital transformation (DX).

The digital transformation of the Times Company began with the mandate of its chief executive: publisher Arthur Ochs Sulzberger Jr. was the driving force and put his full authority behind it. He established a separate division to champion the company's digital efforts, a subsidiary called the New York Times Electronic Media Company. He hired Martin Nisenholtz, an expert in digital media and advertising, as president of the division, which went on to hire new digital talent to drive the project forward.

In the years that followed, the Times undertook a wide range of projects aimed at showcasing new forms of digital journalism. Pieces like the stunningly beautiful Pulitzer Prize–winning multimedia feature "Snow Fall" promised exciting new possibilities for interactive media in journalism.[1] But such projects seemed to stand apart from the daily output of the paper. The Times's technology teams built digital versions of the legacy product (the print newspaper), and they even digitized the archive of articles going back to 1851. But editors lacked the data to understand readers' online behaviors in real time or to connect readers to past articles on topics of interest. The Times showed a willingness to try every new technology trend—from email and the Web to social media, tablet editions, virtual reality, and chatbots. But it lacked clear strategic priorities and the discipline to grow what worked and quickly close pilots that failed to achieve results.

Over time, serious problems began to emerge in the organization. Creating a separate division for digital initiatives established a pattern: a few people were tasked with driving all things digital, and the rest of the organization stuck to their old ways of working. Meanwhile, the legacy organizational structure—with its historic separation of the business side from the journalism side—remained untouched. Despite Sulzberger's initiative, the Times's leadership clearly prioritized the old line of business (the print edition) over new digital ones. For example, every new hire was invited to attend the daily Page One meeting to observe the most senior editors choose which articles would go on the front page of the physical paper.[2] Meanwhile, editors refused to use data to make decisions about matters of content—even when choosing between two options for an article's headline.

Equally serious problems appeared on the business side. From the start, the vision of digital transformation at the Times was all about "digitizing" the core business—literally, taking the same articles produced every day for the print edition and using new technologies to deliver them to readers. When he hired Nisenholtz, Sulzberger pledged to deliver the *New York Times* by website, CD-ROM, or any other new digital medium to come. "The internet? That's fine with me. Hell, if someone would be kind enough to invent the technology, I'll be pleased to beam it directly into your cortex."[3] This thinking—seeing technology as just a new means of delivering the old product—persisted for years, defining the Times's future in terms of its past business. Meanwhile, the Times failed to reckon with the fundamental shift in the economics of advertising wrought by the internet. In the long term, no news media business could survive if it clung to the old ad-based business model.

As the digital revolution continued, the Times's transformation looked more and more inadequate. Despite the Pulitzer and Peabody awards for celebrated digital articles, some of the best digital talent the Times had hired was moving to other publishers. New digital-native publishers like Vox, BuzzFeed, and the Huffington Post—with interactive formats, social media savvy, content optimized for search engines, and feisty style—surged past the *Times* in attracting young readers. For some stories, they even beat the *Times* by repackaging content from its own archives. As one Huffington

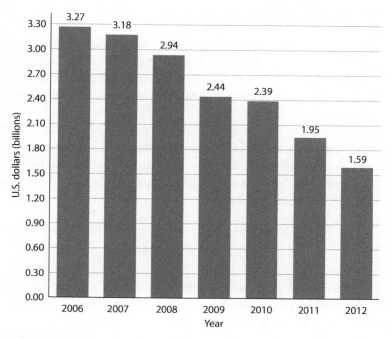

Figure 1.1.
New York Times Company revenue, 2006 to 2012

Post executive confessed, "You guys got crushed . . . I'm not proud of this. But this is your competition."[4]

Most seriously, the financial performance of the Times continued a long slide (see figure 1.1). Revenue from print advertising dropped precipitously, and digital advertising failed to deliver on its promise. Total revenue dropped every year from 2006 to 2013, declining 52 percent in just seven years.[5]

In 2014, a bombshell dropped. Buzzfeed published a secret report, commissioned by the Times's top leadership and leaked from the inside after a months-long investigation. The "Innovation Report" described the New York Times Company as an organization at war with itself over its digital future. Older employees clung fiercely to the status quo. Departmental silos were organized around old traditions rather than the changing needs of the business. Perfectionism prevented experimentation with new digital models. Resources were poured into one-off digital projects rather than digital tools and skills to change everyday work. Senior leaders clung to an outdated focus on the old print business, and digital talent decamped, seeing no future at the paper. As the report explained, the constant focus on the company's legacy business became "a form of laziness because it is work that is comfortable and familiar to us, that we know how to do. And it allows us to avoid the truly hard work and bigger questions about our present and our future: What shall we become. How must we change?"[6]

The story of the Times does not end there. But the questions and crisis it faced are facing every legacy business attempting to transform today. Like so many organizations that have struggled or lost ground in the new era, the Times spent years of wasted effort because it lacked a digital transformation roadmap for the future.

The Crisis of DX Failure

In the past several years, as the digital revolution has expanded from media into every other industry, nearly every established business has embarked on some kind of effort at digital transformation. But in sector after sector, the large majority of these firms have failed to achieve the results they hoped for. Multiple global studies, including surveys by BCG and McKinsey, have found that 70 percent or more of digital transformations fall short of their objectives or fail to achieve any sustained benefit.[7] The results of this institutional failure can be seen everywhere. Famous companies and global brands (Kodak, Blockbuster, etc.) have gone bankrupt in the face of digital challengers. Market leaders rushed to exit businesses where they had once dominated (Nokia phones). Entire categories of traditional companies are in steep decline (movie theaters, department stores, news publishers, etc.).

In other cases, established businesses have managed to hold onto their existing business, but they watch helplessly as new digital entrants swoop in to capture massive growth opportunities in their sector. In the auto industry, legacy automakers watched as Tesla made the first move into electric vehicles and quickly soared past them in market value. In financial services, legacy banks focused mainly on adapting their existing lines of business to the digital era, while fintechs like Stripe, Block, Paypal, and Ant Financial defined entire new categories of financial services and reaped phenomenal growth.

Faced with this glaring trend, business leaders have struggled in their efforts at digital transformation. Famous examples include General

Electric (GE), which launched a hugely-ambitious DX effort in 2015 called GE Digital. It was championed by CEO Jeffrey Immelt, who announced that GE would become a "top 10 software company" in five years. Three years later, after disappointing results, GE Digital was scaled back and spun out by the next CEO.[8]

I have spoken to executives in countless companies who tell me that a chief digital officer (CDO) has been hired, but no one in the business knows what the strategy for digital is supposed to be. Others have pointed to complacency and unwillingness to risk capital on new digital investments after years of success with their old business. One large retailer I advised had hired senior-level talent from Google and Amazon to turn their business into a data-driven organization but confessed that their managers lacked the real-time data to experiment and make decisions.

Failure to transform is fatal. Every year, digital technologies have a deeper impact on business in every industry. The COVID-19 pandemic accelerated many of these shifts, compressing several years of change into weeks in areas like telemedicine, streaming media, online learning, e-commerce, and remote work. These shifts are not slowing down. They are continuing and accelerating. As shown by a global study of senior executives I conducted with HCL, today's leaders know that digital transformation is no longer a question of "if" but of "how fast?"[9]

DX is on the agenda for every board in every industry. We cannot afford to keep getting it wrong.

DX Defined

Before we go further, let's clarify the definition of DX because the term, now widely adopted, has become clouded in the confusion that envelops all buzzwords. Having researched, practiced, and taught the topic for many years, I define digital transformation as a very particular activity:

Transforming
an established business
to thrive in a world of constant digital change.

Three ideas are worth noting. First, DX is about business, not technology. Too often, DX efforts are defined in terms of the technologies they intend to harness (artificial intelligence [AI], blockchain, robotics, cloud computing, etc.). Of course, technology will be part of the implementation of any digital strategy you develop. But any DX effort should be framed around your business, your employees, and your customers—not around a list of technologies to adopt.

Second, DX is about changing an existing organization, not creating a start-up. A start-up's mission is to search for a profitable business model and then scale up a new organization to support its growth. But an established business already has both a business model and an organization—with employees, customers, products, distribution channels, partners, and an established culture and way of working. Thus, DX is fundamentally about changing an organization that is already in motion. In physics, the tendency of a body in motion to keep moving in the same direction and at the same speed is called inertia. The more massive the body, the harder it is to change course. This is true in business as well, where your biggest enemy of transformation is inertia—the organization's resistance to change.

Third, DX is a continuous process; it is not a project with start and end dates. This is because the digital revolution is not a single change that has happened (the birth of the internet, the shift to mobile, or cloud computing) that you must adapt to. The digital revolution is an *ongoing acceleration of change* being driven by successive waves of new technologies. It will continue to reinvent customer behaviors, business models, and economic systems far into the future. Buckle up for the ride.

How DX Goes Wrong

Over the years, I have heard countless commentators on DX proclaim that the single most important factor in success is a clear CEO mandate for change. And yet, in GE, the New York Times Company, and countless other cases, I have witnessed the opposite. In these cases, the chief executive declares their full-throated commitment to a DX effort. They even commit substantial financial and human capital. And yet years go by, and the results fail to live up to what was expected or to what is desperately needed for the future.

Why is DX failing? What have so many companies done so wrong?

Let's start by recognizing that DX is hard. In many ways, it involves a kind of balancing act. DX cannot simply be an effort to "digitize" the legacy business—that is, to upgrade existing technology, cut costs, and improve the customer experience of your current offerings. To stay relevant, survive, and grow in the digital economy, every business must be ready to digitize its core *and* grow beyond it, to maximize its current cash flow *and* invest for the future, to pursue both incremental innovations *and* more radical ones. But you cannot rebuild your current business and build your next business with the same people, processes, and organizational structures. You cannot use the same approach to rebuild the past and to build the future.

The DX challenge is particularly hard for complex organizations. Today, organizational complexity is driven by three primary factors: the number of employees (measured in head count), lines of business (with different offerings to different customers), and geographies of operation (each with different regulations imposed). As any of these factors increases, the complexity of managing the organization compounds dramatically. Simply put, if you have an established business with just 500 employees and a single line of business operating in one geography, transformation will be much easier to achieve. For such a business, if you define a clear digital strategy based on market and technology trends, you should be able to execute that strategy with good leadership. But if your business has 10,000 (or 100,000) employees, you operate multiples lines of business, and they straddle several geographies with differing regulations, then driving DX will be much, much harder.

The symptoms of this difficulty are seen everywhere. Talk to leaders of complex organizations, and you will hear a litany of DX troubles: Our employees are afraid of change. New ventures always lose out to the core business. Legal and compliance reject many of our promising ideas. Our digital efforts make for good press releases, but they aren't moving the needle. Risk aversion and slow decision making mean we can't keep up with digital competitors. Our legacy information technology (IT) is inflexible. Our data is trapped in silos. Our workforce lacks the skills they need.

Sound familiar? The list goes on, but these are all just symptoms of more fundamental problems in how DX is practiced. In my own research and work with a wide range of companies, I have found five root causes of failure in digital transformation. Let's review each of these barriers to DX and the problems that they bring.

Top Barriers to DX Success

1. NO SHARED VISION

One of the biggest barriers to effective DX is the lack of a shared vision. In countless large companies, I have seen "digital" declared to be a priority, but when you talk to managers, it becomes clear that there is no shared understanding of the digital future of their industry, where their business aims to compete, or what gives them a right to win in that future. Instead, there is only a generic rallying cry to "become digital."

The symptoms of this lack of shared vision are many. Employees move slowly and show fear of change, lacking a clear sense of where the firm is going and how they might contribute. Investors balk at large financial investments in digital, as do executives responsible for profit and loss statements (P&Ls). The company's digital initiatives are generic, following the moves of peers and reacting belatedly to market trends. And leaders rely on generic "digital maturity" metrics to guide their efforts because they have no clear business metrics to judge their DX progress.

2. NO GROWTH PRIORITIES

The next major barrier to DX is a lack of clear priorities for growth. This lack may arise because the company is focused only on "digitizing" its past business and not looking beyond it. Or leaders may lack the discipline to define a few strategic priorities to focus on—whether customer problems to solve or business opportunities to capture.

The symptoms of this lack of priorities are many. Without a clear set of priorities, DX lacks strategic direction. Rather than focusing on business problems, DX is defined by technologies (AI, cloud computing, blockchain, etc.) and is easily hijacked by the latest shiny new thing. Without a growth focus, DX focuses only on cutting costs and optimizing the current business. Digital efforts are run by technology specialists as the rest of the organization continues its work unchanged. As a result, DX grows disconnected from business needs and loses support over time.

3. NO FOCUS ON EXPERIMENTATION

The third major barrier to DX is an emphasis on planning over experimentation. Decision makers spend years developing their plans for DX. They demand laborious development of business cases before work begins on any new digital product or service. When work does begin, the focus is on meticulous planning and execution, following a stage-gate approach to carry each project through to a predefined solution. This approach stands in direct opposition to the model of rapid experimentation that guides digital-native businesses. And though legacy firms may adopt the trappings of experimentation—rolling out agile software teams and enrolling in design thinking classes—they squeeze these iterative methods into a planning-heavy management model.

The symptoms of relying on planning over experimentation are painful. Decision makers wait for benchmarks and best practices rather than validating new ideas directly with customers. Teams are assigned to build solutions rather than to solve problems. Projects have no flexibility to change direction, leading to costly failures and a culture of risk avoidance. Digital ventures move slowly, are beaten to the market, and struggle to make an impact on the business.

4. NO FLEXIBILITY IN GOVERNANCE

The fourth barrier to DX is the use of business-as-usual (BAU) processes and governance for all initiatives. Traditional silos, reporting lines, and budgeting dominate, stifling efforts at growth. Companies lack processes for iterative funding or for allocating resources beyond the core. They are unable to stand up multifunctional teams to move fast on new opportunities. In short, they have no repeatable process for managing and scaling growth.

The symptoms of inflexible governance can be seen everywhere. Executive sponsors must personally approve digital projects and grant waivers to company rules. Functional silos impede team collaboration and slow innovation. Resources are trapped in annual budgeting cycles, hampering efforts to scale innovation. With few projects approved, no one is willing to shut theirs down once it is started. Uncertain ventures are deemed too risky, and innovations outside the core are simply ignored.

5. NO CHANGE IN CAPABILITIES

The final barrier to DX is a reliance on preexisting capabilities, including technology, talent, and culture. Legacy technology remains in place, with only patches and cosmetic fixes to IT architecture, data assets, and the rules that govern both. Legacy talent remains undeveloped, with little investment in digital skills or in the workforce and leadership who were hired and trained for the needs of the past. Legacy culture remains unchanged, with mindsets and behaviors that are rooted in top-down, command-and-control leadership.

The symptoms of stagnant capabilities are many. IT systems are inflexible and reinforce the silos inside the organization. Managers lack the shared real-time data that they need to make decisions. Every digital project must go through a central IT division, causing bottlenecks. IT needs are outsourced to vendors because your own workforce lacks the skills for digital innovation. A top-down culture and mindset lead to cynicism and a wait-and-see attitude from disengaged employees.

How DX Goes Right

If the above scenarios sound familiar and bleak, don't be disheartened. True, surveys show that 70 percent of DX efforts are failing, but let's focus on the 30 percent that are succeeding! The DX Roadmap, which is just ahead, draws from dozens of successful DX cases. Here are just a few of the amazing stories of DX success in business-to-consumer (B2C) and business-to-business (B2B) industries:

• *The Walt Disney Co.*—The legacy media business has stood up to tech titans (Netflix, Apple, Amazon) by expanding its library of content and launching its fast-growing streaming services Disney+, ESPN+, and Hulu. Within three years of launching Disney+, the company's total number of streaming subscriptions had surpassed those of Netflix.[10] At the same time, the firm has reorganized its growth strategy, its metrics, and its organizational structure around Disney's new digital future as a direct-to-consumer business.

• *Mastercard Inc.*—The credit card processing company is now one of the world's biggest fintechs. Leveraging its tremendous data and global business network, Mastercard has built a growing business in digital commerce. The company runs one of the top accelerators for fintech start-ups, and its own innovation labs are building and scaling new business models around cybersecurity, digital identity, and analytics—while selling digital services to business customers around the world.

• *Domino's Pizza, Inc.*—The restaurant chain has achieved phenomenal growth by reinventing its core delivery business for the digital age. Domino's invested in an AI-powered mobile app (one of the first to take your order by voice); an "Anyware" omnichannel strategy that allows customers to order by emoji, tweet, Apple Watch, or Amazon Alexa; and innovations in delivery vehicles that include rolling pizza delivery bots (for narrow streets in European cities) and even flying pizza drones (first tested in mountainous New Zealand). With a relentless focus on innovation in the delivery experience, Domino's digital investments helped power a stunning growth in share price of 3,200 percent in just seven years.[11]

- *Deere & Company*—The company made its name selling John Deere farm equipment like tractors, seeders, and harvesters. Today, Deere still makes these machines, but all of them are software- and sensor-enabled and connected to the cloud. Deere is gathering data on every square foot of a customer's farmland and using that data to help them optimize how seeds are planted, fertilized, and harvested, with precision farming and data analytics.
- *Air Liquide*—The global leader in industrial gases is harnessing data to unlock new sources of value in key industries like health care and manufacturing. Today, Air Liquide is capturing data from its 400 industrial plants and its 20 million gas cylinders around the world and leveraging that data to create value in areas like predictive maintenance. Air Liquide is reshaping its customer experience for business clients across an omnichannel mix of web, phone, apps, and face-to-face interactions. And it is collaborating in new ways with large partners and digital start-ups to address new markets like home health care and urban air pollution.

The message from these and other companies from the winning 30 percent could not be clearer: DX is absolutely possible if your business embraces transformative change.

DX = Digital Strategy + Organizational Change

I wrote the first book on the topic of DX, *The Digital Transformation Playbook*. That book has become a global bestseller, published in over a dozen languages and in both print and audio formats. Its reach has led me to speak at venues around the world and advise the leadership of scores of businesses. Meanwhile, my executive teaching for Columbia Business School—both on campus and online—has brought me into close contact with thousands more business leaders.

This book is the culmination of that practical experience and years of research on DX. It draws on both the common, persistent problems I have seen companies face and the key steps I have seen lead them to success. Based on all this, I have developed a complete DX Roadmap.

At the outset, let's be clear that digital transformation is not only about adapting your strategy. True DX requires a combination of digital strategy and organizational transformation. To sum it up as a formula,

$$DX = D \text{ strategy} + \text{organizational } X$$

If you have read my previous book, you will recognize that this means rethinking strategy for the digital era across five domains: your customers, your competition, your data, your process of innovation, and your value proposition. The DX Roadmap presented in this book encompasses each of those five domains and shows how to make that kind of change happen at every level of your organization—no matter its industry, size, or complexity.

As we examine the DX Roadmap, it is important to remember that DX is not a traditional change management project with start and end dates, not a journey with a fixed destination. Instead, it is the way to rebuild your organization to be ready for continuous transformation in the digital future. As we'll see, that's precisely how digital-native businesses like Amazon, Alphabet, Microsoft, and Netflix have learned to thrive under continuous change. Your business can, too.

The DX Roadmap

Since my last book was published, I have received multiple inquiries from CEOs, essentially asking, "Dear Professor Rogers—I have read your book, I agree with it, and I am now ready to start my digital transformation. Can you please send me an article, or better yet a PowerPoint slide, that shows me the steps I should take?"

Let me be clear. What follows is not a set of IKEA instructions. There is no simple list of investments, budget allocations, and strategic steps that every company can follow for its DX. Every organization has a unique context and history, unique strengths and challenges; therefore, every organization will have its own starting point and its own path forward. But, however unique each DX path may be, I have seen that every organization faces the same barriers that must be overcome for DX to have a real and lasting impact.

Therefore, I have developed a framework of five iterative steps to navigate your own path to DX success for your business. The DX Roadmap is based on my experience advising CEOs and CDOs at more than twenty companies in varying industries and locations and with different sizes and ownership structures, and on the experience of scores of other companies that I have followed in my research.

Before we take a close look at each step, it is important to note that they are not like steps on a ladder that you climb once and leave behind.

Digital Transformation (DX) Roadmap Steps		Key Concepts
Vision	**1. Define a shared vision**	• Future landscape • Right to win • North Star impact • Business theory
Priorities	**2. Pick the problems that matter most**	• Problem/opportunity statement • P/O Matrix • Venture backlog
Experimentation	**3. Validate new ventures**	• Four Stages of Validation • The Rogers Growth Navigator • Illustrative versus functional MVPs
Governance	**4. Manage growth at scale**	• Team and boards • Iterative funding process • Three paths to growth • Corporate Innovation Stack
Capabilities	**5. Grow tech, talent, and culture**	• Tech and Talent Map • Modular architecture • Culture-Process Map

Figure 1.2.
The Digital Transformation Roadmap

Although there is a sequence to starting them (begin Step 1, then begin Step 2 . . .), the work of each step continues as you advance to the others. DX is not a finite project. Its change will be iterative and cumulative as you deepen and broaden the transformation of your organization over time. Keeping this in mind, let's take a look at each step of the DX Roadmap (see figure 1.2).

1. VISION: DEFINE A SHARED VISION

In the first step of the DX Roadmap, your goal is to define a shared vision of the digital future for your organization. This starts with describing the future landscape of your industry, shaped by digital forces. It includes defining the unique advantages that give you a right to win in this digital future. It means choosing a North Star goal for the impact your work will have on customers and others. And it means spelling out a business theory of how you will capture value and earn a return on your digital investments.

When done right, this step will enable your business to lead proactively rather than react to external trends, to invest only in digital initiatives where you have a competitive advantage, to clearly define the business impact of digital investments, and to win the backing of investors and finance chiefs as well as the support of the employees who will drive your digital agenda forward.

2. PRIORITIES: PICK THE PROBLEMS THAT MATTER MOST

In the second step of the DX Roadmap, your goal is to define the strategic priorities that will guide your digital growth agenda. This starts with looking at strategy through the twin lenses of problems to solve and opportunities to pursue. This step uses a variety of tools to identify the most valuable problems and opportunities for your business. And it uses problem/opportunity statements to define strategy and spark ideas for digital innovation at every level of your enterprise.

Done right, this step will enable you to provide direction to teams across your organization, focus digital on solving problems and not deploying technologies, ensure digital delivers growth and not just efficiency, and accelerate change with new ventures at every level and in every department.

3. EXPERIMENTATION: VALIDATE NEW VENTURES

In the third step of the DX Roadmap, your goal is to rapidly test new digital ventures in order to validate which ones will create value for your customers and the firm. The step starts with thinking like a scientist: defining your hypotheses and designing experiments to test your business assumptions. It uses iterative metrics to gather data directly from customers. It uses iterative prototypes and minimum viable products (MVPs), each designed to answer a specific question. And it uses a new model, the Four Stages of Validation, to sequence learning and guide any venture on its path from new idea to business at scale.

When done right, this step will enable your business to test many new ideas and learn which work best, make decisions based on data from customers rather than benchmarks, keep your failures cheap and your bias toward risk taking, and iterate and adapt quickly to build innovations with value at scale.

4. GOVERNANCE: MANAGE GROWTH AT SCALE

In the fourth step of the DX Roadmap, your goal is to design governance models to scale digital growth across the enterprise. This means defining rules and decision rights for small, multifunctional teams; creating structures (like labs, hackathons, and venture funds) that provide flexible pools of resources; establishing boards that green-light new ventures and oversee iterative funding; and managing three paths to growth—inside the core, partnered with the core, and outside the core—with the right rules and governance for each.

When done right, this step will enable you to empower teams to drive growth, allocate resources flexibly, quickly shut down ventures that are not working, and manage a steady pipeline of digital innovations both in your core and beyond it.

5. CAPABILITIES: GROW TECH, TALENT, AND CULTURE

In the last step of the Roadmap, your goal is to invest in the technology, talent, and culture that will be critical to your digital future. This includes investing in technology with a microservices architecture, synchronized data assets, and effective IT governance. It means growing your digital skills by managing the talent lifecycle from hiring to training, exiting, and beyond. It means defining the culture—shared mindsets and norms of behavior—that will support your digital strategy; communicating that culture with stories, symbols, and action; and enabling that culture through everyday business processes.

When done right, this step will enable your business to integrate technology across silos and with outside partners, use data to provide a single source of truth to managers, give teams the skills to build their own digital solutions, and empower employees at every level to drive bottom-up change.

The Roadmap from the Bottom Up

The importance of empowering employees brings up an essential point. As you apply the DX Roadmap, it is critical to understand that DX does not flow only from the top of the organization down. Your DX effort may begin in the CEO's office or under the direction of a change agent like a CDO. But it will never succeed if it is driven only from the top.

The defining fact of the digital era is its accelerating pace of change. Every organization must learn to adapt not once but continuously. To keep up, businesses are forced to shift away from top-down, command-and-control management and to embrace a more agile vision of the organization that prizes employee autonomy and initiative. Digital-native businesses like Amazon, Netflix, and Alphabet have all embraced this new model—achieving speed at scale by pushing decision making down to the lowest possible level.

As we will see throughout this book, applying the DX Roadmap means taking a bottom-up approach to your own organization as well. "Bottom up" does *not* mean a flat organization with no hierarchy. It means three things: decision making is pushed down, market insights flow from the bottom up, and innovation starts at every level of the organization.

Following the Five Steps: Success for the New York Times

The five steps of the DX Roadmap can ensure a strong start to any new transformation effort, but they can also turn around a DX effort that has long struggled. Among today's most impressive DX success stories is the New York Times Company. In the years since the painful self-examination and exposure of its *Innovation Report*, the Times has turned the corner to become a leading example of DX success. It did so by addressing each of the five barriers to transformation and pursuing all five steps of the DX Roadmap.

The turnaround began with a clear *vision* of the future. With the internet continuing to disrupt the advertising market, the only hope for the Times Company's survival was to reinvent its business model. Instead of a business run primarily on advertising revenue, it would become a business based primarily on subscription revenue. This was arguably the biggest strategic shift in the company's history, and it required changing nearly everything about the business. The year after the damning *Innovation Report*, the Times's leadership released a strategic document titled "Our Path Forward." It clearly spelled out the ambition to transform the Times's business model so that digital revenue exceeded print revenue. It included a target to double digital revenue in five years to reach $800 million—a figure that could sustain the paper's journalistic efforts around the world. Only then would the mission of the Times be secure from the disruption of its print business.

The document also laid out a few strategic *priorities* to focus and guide its digital efforts: transform the product experience to make a *New York Times* subscription as indispensable to readers' lives as a Netflix or Amazon Prime account. Expand the *Times*'s global reach and international readership. Grow digital advertising by creating new and compelling ad formats. Organize employees' work around digital platforms and the reader experience. Shift energy from the print edition while still maintaining quality for its audience.

With priorities in place, the Times Company accelerated its pace of digital *experimentation* and new ventures. In its core news product, this meant telling stories that were more visual and data driven, many of them pioneered by The Upshot, a new journalism desk. It meant experimenting with media like video, podcasts, virtual reality, and interactive newsbots to see which would engage subscribers on mobile devices. At the same time, the Times launched new stand-alone digital subscriptions like NY Times Cooking and Games. And it explored new business models based on licensing (a TV show on the FX network and Hulu), affiliate sales (the Wirecutter product review site), and live conference events. Several digital ventures came by acquisitions, including Wirecutter, Serial (a podcasting studio), Audm (an audio app), the Athletic (a sports site with global reach), and the hit online game Wordle. Meanwhile, advertising and technology teams developed new formats for advertising on mobile and for audio products.

Transformation at the Times Company extended to its *governance* as well. Digital was no longer placed in a separate subsidiary but at the core of the entire organization. For the first time, journalism, product, and engineering perspectives were brought together in cross-functional teams. Different governance models were established for different growth opportunities. New subscriptions like Cooking and Crosswords were placed in the Standalone Products and Ventures Group to focus on their distinct metrics for growth. And The Athletic—an acquisition with a distinct audience of sports fans—was made a separate operating unit, led by its original founders.

At the same time, the company refocused its efforts to build the *capabilities* that would be critical to its digital future. The Times's engineering teams built up its technology and data infrastructure, allowing it to capture data on every digital action by its readers, link any news articles to related stories from the *New York Times*'s century-plus archive, and target advertising with proprietary first-party data that maintained readers' privacy.

Meanwhile, new digital talent was hired and promoted into leadership positions. Reporters of all stripes were trained in the use of data-driven journalism and visualization. A. G. Sulzberger, who became publisher in 2018, boasted, "We employ more journalists who can write code than any other news organization."[12] The culture of the Times began to shift as well, from a risk-averse mindset dictated by old traditions of the newsroom to a culture focused on risk taking and learning from mistakes.

The results of this second wave of DX at the Times were breathtaking. The company reached its ambitious goal of $800 million in digital revenue a year ahead of target. An added goal to reach 10 million subscriptions by 2025 was met nearly four years early.[13] Most important, the Times achieved both its overarching goals—digital revenue exceeded print revenue, and subscriptions eclipsed advertising. Investors took notice, and in five years, from 2016 to 2021, the stock price soared by 261 percent. Looking ahead, the Times Company's annual report laid out a new vision: "We aim to be the essential subscription for every English-speaking person seeking to understand and engage with the world."[14]

Why the DX Roadmap Matters

The stakes could not be higher for businesses. The five steps of the DX Roadmap will set you on the course to achieve truly impactful DX. They will enable you to avoid the failures of organizational stagnation that stifle so many DX efforts and to join the ranks of the DX winners. Table 1.1 summarizes the difference in outcomes between DX efforts that fail or succeed in each of the five steps of the DX Roadmap.

How to Use This Book

The book is meant to be extremely practical. It is based on my own work advising firms of diverse sizes and in different industries and locations—but also on the countless questions and years-long exchanges that I have had with thousands of global executives through my programs at Columbia Business School.

Because digital transformation must happen at every level of the organization, the DX Roadmap is designed to zoom in or zoom out. Each step

Table 1.1.

Symptoms of Failure Versus Success in the Five Steps of the DX Roadmap

Symptoms of Failure	Symptoms of Success
Step 1: Vision	
• Employees fear change and lack a clear sense of where the firm is going.	• Employees at every level understand the digital agenda and push it forward.
• Backing for digital investments is weak from investors, CFOs, and P&L heads.	• Support for digital investments is strong from investors, CFOs, and P&L heads.
• Digital initiatives are generic, following the examples of peers.	• Only digital initiatives with a competitive advantage receive investment.
• Generic digital maturity metrics are used to guide efforts.	• The business impact of digital is clearly defined, with metrics to measure and track results.
• The firm follows the market, reacts to others, and is surprised by new entrants.	• The firm leads the market, alert to critical trends while there is time to choose a course.
Step 2: Priorities	
• Digital transformation is a series of scattered projects with no clear direction.	• Clear priorities provide direction to digital transformation across the organization.
• Digital efforts are defined by the technologies they use.	• Digital efforts are defined by the problems they solve and opportunities they pursue.
• Digital is focused solely on operations, cost cutting, and optimizing the current business.	• Digital is focused on future growth as well as improving the current business.
• A few people in the organization drive digital while the rest stick to old ways of working.	• Every department is pursuing its own digital ventures, with a backlog of ideas to try next.
• Transformation is disconnected from business needs and loses support over time.	• Transformation is linked to the needs of the business and gains support over time.
Step 3: Experimentation	
• Innovation is focused on coming up with a few great ideas.	• Innovation is focused on testing many ideas to learn which work best.
• Decisions are made based on business cases, third-party data, and expert opinion.	• Decisions are made based on experimentation and learning from the customer.
• Once they start a project, teams are committed to building the solution in full.	• Teams stay focused on the problem but flexible on the solution.
• Failures are costly, so the fear of risk is high.	• Failures are cheap, so there is a bias toward risk taking.
• Good ideas move slowly and don't seem to move the needle on the business.	• Good ideas grow fast and deliver business value at scale.

(continued)

Table 1.1.
(*Continued*)

Symptoms of Failure	Symptoms of Success
Step 4: Governance	
• A top executive must personally approve any new innovation.	• Established structures provide resources and governance for innovation.
• New ventures move slowly, led by traditional teams in functional silos.	• New ventures move fast, led by highly independent, multifunctional teams.
• Allocating resources to new ventures is slowed by the annual budgeting cycle.	• Resource allocation happens quickly through iterative funding.
• Innovation is limited to a few big projects, which are hard to shut down once they are started.	• A steady pipeline of innovations is managed with smart shutdowns to free up resources.
• The only ventures to gain support are low-risk innovations in the core business.	• Governance supports ventures with low and high uncertainty, both in the core and beyond.
Step 5: Capabilities	
• Inflexible IT systems reinforce silos and limit collaboration.	• Modular IT systems integrate across the organization and with outside partners.
• Data is contradictory, incomplete, and inaccessible to managers in real time.	• Data provides a single source of truth to managers across the company.
• Centralized IT governance causes bottlenecks for new projects.	• IT governance provides oversight while keeping innovation in the hands of the business.
• Employees lack digital skills, so digital projects must be outsourced.	• Employees can build and iterate digital solutions themselves.
• A top-down culture and bureaucracy stifle employees, breeding cynicism and inertia.	• An empowering culture and processes help employees drive bottom-up change.

is applicable whatever your role—whether you are CEO, CDO, directing digital for a business unit, leading a functional team like human resources (HR), or designing a new digital product.

The next chapter (chapter 2) examines the connection between DX and innovation and why established firms are failing to innovate at the pace demanded in the digital age. It explores the challenge of innovation under great *uncertainty* and the challenge of innovation *beyond your core* business. And it shows what we can learn from digital-era businesses and from digital-era methods such as agile, lean start-up, design thinking, and product management.

Chapters 3 through 7 lay out the five steps of the DX Roadmap in detail. Each step is illustrated with real-world case studies of businesses. You'll find dozens of examples from a range of industries: banking, insurance, retail, consumer goods, media, telecom, technology, automotive, energy, health care, nonprofit, industrial manufacturing, and even container shipping. Each case illustrates the strategic concepts of the book with stories of individuals and their work in the real world.

I have also included eight strategic planning tools to give you the practical means of applying the DX Roadmap with your own team:

- Shared Vision Map
- Problem/Opportunity Statements
- Problem/Opportunity Matrix
- Four Stages of Validation
- Rogers Growth Navigator
- Corporate Innovation Stack
- Tech and Talent Map
- Culture-Process Map

These tools are based on my experience advising and consulting. They are designed to pose the crucial questions that will guide you to the right answers for your particular organization. Downloadable versions of the tools, as well as additional tutorials on their application, can be found in the Tools section of my website at www.davidrogers.digital.

The book's conclusion returns to the theme of the bottom-up organization and examines the three jobs of leaders in an era of constant change. In the appendix, you will find visual summaries, a self-assessment tool, and directions to more resources online.

The DX Roadmap is designed to be started quickly so that you can learn by doing and see immediate results. Remember, real DX is iterative in nature. Once started, the five steps will repeat, overlap, and support one another. As you progress, your transformation will both deepen and broaden in scope. The main point is to get started and to learn by doing. Don't wait for a five-year plan; start *something* in ninety days! DX is not about spending months planning a multiyear process and then faithfully carrying it out. It is about starting the first steps now and learning as you go.

To thrive in the digital era, your organization must be built for continuous transformation. By the time you adapt to today's massive digital shifts, you will already need to be ready for tomorrow's. With a nod to Darwin, I suggest that it is not the strongest of businesses that will survive the digital era but those that are most adaptive to change.[15]

Onward to continuous transformation!

2

DX and the Challenge of Innovation

Before we begin the five steps of the Digital Transformation (DX) Roadmap, it is important to understand the role of innovation in DX. In this chapter, we will learn how the failure to innovate is holding legacy firms back, what the two key challenges to corporate innovation are, and how to solve each of them. We will also discover what incumbents must learn from digital-era organizations and methods to successfully innovate for the digital age.

DX Is Innovation

In the twentieth century, the goal of any company was to find a business model that worked, optimize that model, and exploit it for as many years as possible. A successful business would see many changes over the years in its product features, customer segments, technology, operations, and more. But the business model—the means by which the company created, delivered, and captured value from the market—could prosper unchanged for generations. A few long-lived firms would shift business models over many decades, such as IBM evolving from selling office machines to services, or General Electric moving from electric appliances to power plants, financial services, and broadcast television. But these rare firms were exceptions that proved the rule of business model constancy.

In the digital era, however, transformation is the rule, not the exception. The life span of a business model—from when it emerges as a viable means to run a business until its profitability begins to fade—seems to grow shorter every year.[1] Digital businesses thrive not by sustaining and excelling at a single business model but by constantly developing new models to adopt or to replace the old.

Netflix's Repeated Reinvention

Think of Netflix, the preeminent global media company born to date in the digital era. In its first twenty-four years, we can see a pattern of transformation through at least four distinct business models. Marc Randolph and Reed Hastings launched Netflix with a business model aimed at disrupting the way people watched movies at home—which, in 1998, meant renting individual VHS tapes from stores that demanded quick returns and charged punishing late fees. Netflix's first business model entered the market by offering a premium membership plan and delivering DVDs (then a cutting-edge format) by mail with no late fees.

But even as Netflix grew rapidly, its founders were already looking to their second business model. They knew the future would be streaming videos over the internet, but the technology infrastructure was not ready when they started the company. As consumers' home internet bandwidth increased, Netflix began a pilot test of streaming video, offering a tiny library for free to their DVD subscribers. After that test proved favorable, Netflix began to license a large library of movies from rights holders like Starz and Epix. When conditions were right, Netflix launched its second business model to much fanfare: Hollywood movies streamed straight to your home screen.

The company's third business model arose because the finances of its second model became unsustainable. Netflix's soaring membership numbers and revenue demonstrated the huge market for streaming video, and rights holders demanded much larger fees to renew their licenses. As streaming other people's movies became unprofitable, Netflix pivoted to its third business model—becoming its own television and film network. With hit series like *House of Cards*, Netflix began investing billions of dollars each year producing original content to keep subscribers coming back.

Demand for growth led Netflix to expand around the world, creating global content in diverse languages. With non-English-language series like *Squid Game*, Netflix proved there was profit in repurposing content from anywhere for a global audience.

Netflix's fourth business model came after years of subscriber growth finally began to slow down. From 2011 to 2021, subscribers had grown from 21 million to 220 million. But in 2022, Netflix posted a (slight) decline in subscribers for the first time in a decade. Shocked investors cut the value of the stock in half. In response, Hastings turned to a new business model, long discussed but never implemented: advertising. This fourth business model (harkening back to the older model of broadcast television), would generate a new revenue stream from advertisers. It would also allow Netflix to pursue new customers: those not willing to pay the full price of a subscription, as well as the 100 million freeloaders, by Netflix's estimate, borrowing the accounts of others. Investors responded favorably. As Netflix prepared to launch this new business model, the company's leaders stressed that it would evolve too: "Like most of our new initiatives, our intention is to roll it out, listen and learn, and iterate quickly to improve the offering. So, our advertising business in a few years will likely look quite different than what it looks like on day one."[2]

The Innovation Divide

The same pattern of business model invention can be seen in every digital-era business. Uber began by offering its customers rides, then expanded to meal delivery. Tesla began selling electric sports cars, then charging systems, then at-home batteries for a decentralized power grid. Google started with a search engine, but it has grown to include video (YouTube), a mobile operating system (Android), digital home devices (Nest), and enterprise computing. Alibaba began with an online marketplace and added search, digital payments, and a broad set of financial services, including credit scoring and the world's largest mutual fund.

For older legacy businesses, the digital era demands no less. Digital transformation cannot mean just upgrading your data and technology to optimize the business you have always run. For any established business to thrive, DX must deliver innovation and new engines of growth. But the reality is that most pre-digital-era companies are terrible at this. In every industry, we see legacy enterprises struggling to create new business models beyond their core business. For every digital innovation that succeeds in the market, there is an incumbent serving the same customers, in the same industry, saying to themselves, "We should have done that!"

Why did Nokia, the king of mobile phones, fail to launch the iPhone or a similar first-generation smartphone? Why did established book publishers (e.g., Random House) and retailers (e.g., Barnes & Noble) fail to create an e-book format before Amazon launched the Kindle? Why did hospitality chains like Marriott fail to capture the market that Airbnb saw for a digital travel experience based on a multisided market? Why did Hollywood studios and television networks wait years to follow Netflix's path into streaming? Why did global automakers wait a decade to follow Tesla into electric vehicles? Why did traditional banks wait a generation after PayPal, Alibaba, and others pioneered peer-to-peer payments, only to launch a belated copycat like Zelle?

Again and again, we see traditional companies fail to capture tomorrow's opportunities for growth. They are failing because of two fundamental challenges to innovation in established companies. I call these the challenges of uncertainty and proximity. Fortunately, both have management solutions—solutions that are at the heart of the DX Roadmap.

Innovating Under Uncertainty

The first challenge for innovation in an established company is managing innovation under great uncertainty. The topic of uncertainty has long been central to the theory and practice of innovation. Many practitioners describe business innovation as an effort to address three types of uncertainty: desirability (does the market want this?), feasibility (can we deliver this?), and profitability (can this make a profit?). But other types are critical as well—defensibility (can it fend off competitors?), scalability (can it grow?), and legality (will it comply with laws and regulations?), for example. For any specific venture, the sources of uncertainty become even more specific, such as cost structure, competitive differentiation, channel partners, user experience, and so on.

In the business environment of the digital era, uncertainty is only increasing thanks to new technologies, competition across industries, and constantly changing customer needs and expectations. The greatest uncertainty is faced by companies exploring new digital business models. Think of the questions that Airbnb's founders faced when starting their company. Which customers would be willing to try this new business model? How could Airbnb increase trust in the system? How would it collect money? How would it navigate local taxes and regulations? And how would the company scale while holding off competitors?

Established digital firms also face uncertainty as they pursue new growth ventures. Google acquired YouTube eighteen months after the video service launched, when the start-up was growing fast but had no proven business model, had no revenue, and was in possible violation of copyright law. Apple began work on the iPhone under tremendous technical uncertainty about its touchscreen design and with no notion that success would hinge on creating an app store for outside developers. Facebook bet big on mobile, enduring years with zero revenue as it first moved from the desktop to phones. Microsoft bet on Azure when a focus on cloud computing seemed incredibly risky and could cannibalize its existing enterprise Server and Tools business line.

The Inadequacy of Traditional Planning

Managing under high uncertainty is extremely hard for established businesses. As most organizations grow larger and more complex, their every function—marketing, HR, operations, financial planning—is designed for consistency and control, using methods like Six Sigma or total quality management. An aversion to risk is matched by a mindset that "failure is not an option." The whole point of management becomes to generate a predictable return on investment (ROI).

Not surprisingly, the response of such businesses to uncertainty is to manage it through planning. We can observe four steps in the classic planning process: gather third-party data, write a detailed business plan, make an expert decision, then focus on execution. In short, study > plan > decide > build.

This approach to planning that was taught for years in business schools works well with a well-known business model (which is exactly what it was developed for). But it fails dramatically when managing innovation under great uncertainty. (See the box "The Perils of Planning.") When pursuing innovation in our highly uncertain digital world, traditional planning is a recipe for disaster. Often, it leads to so-called analysis paralysis as laborious benchmarking and writing of business plans stretch on for many quarters or even years, and opportunities go to nimbler competitors. In the worst cases, traditional planning leads to incredibly costly failures in the digital realm.

The Perils of Planning

When dealing with well-known problems or when operating long-standing business, that is, when managing under relative certainty, the traditional planning approach (study, plan, decide, build) can work quite well. But in digital-era conditions of uncertainty, traditional planning fails at each stage.

Study (gather third-party data). Faced with the unknown, managers are taught to gather preexisting data, often with the help of large consulting firms. They look to competitors for benchmarking and search for established case studies that might provide them with best practices. While this is useful when facing a known problem that others have already solved, it can be a fatal distraction when pursuing innovation in a rapidly changing marketplace.

Plan (write a detailed business plan). Next, traditional managers apply their best analysis to write a business case full of detailed steps and projections on future outcomes. A major decision can lead to multiple detailed business cases— each one spelling out the implications of a different course of action. But when you are pursuing innovation under uncertainty, a business plan is a work of pure fiction! (My colleague Bob Dorf has said for years that the practice should be moved from business schools to creative writing departments.)

Decide (make an expert decision). Having analyzed the options, a decision must now be made about what course of action to take. Traditional practice is to rely on the opinions of experts—those with the most seniority and experience. When the future looks a lot like the past, the intuition of experienced leaders may prove an excellent guide. But when dealing with great uncertainty, expert opinion based on past experience can be highly misleading. In Silicon Valley, this practice is called management by "HIPPOs"—the highest-paid person's opinion.

Build (focus on execution). After a course of action has been chosen, the traditional enterprise becomes entirely focused on execution. "You scope it, we build it!" is the mantra of traditional IT and operations teams. Companies begin making large investments that lock them into a multiyear plan for a particular solution. Instead of starting small and proceeding with humility about whether a planned innovation is the right one, companies rush to start building at scale.

THE PLAN FOR CNN+

The failure of CNN+, launched in 2022 as a new digital business model for news, is a perfect example. In it, we can see all four stages of traditional planning at work:

- **Study:** CNN began this initiative by surveying the booming market for streaming video with the help of consulting firm McKinsey. Netflix and Amazon Prime continued to dominate, with hundreds of millions of customers, but Disney+ had recently launched and gained 10 million subscribers on its first day. Meanwhile, CNN's sister network HBO was making a big push for streaming as well.
- **Plan:** CNN laid out a plan to launch a paid subscription news service with many of the same celebrity broadcasters as its TV channel (although contracts with cable companies prohibited streaming their live TV content). CNN and McKinsey projected that the service would attract 2 million subscribers in its first year, and at least 15 million within four years.[3]
- **Decide:** The decision to move forward with CNN+ came straight from the top. CNN president Jeff Zucker saw in it the future of news and a new era for the company. His boss Jason Kilar proclaimed, "In my opinion, CNN+ is likely to be as important to the mission of CNN as the linear channel service has been these past 42 years. It would be hard to overstate how important this moment is for CNN."[4] Not everyone agreed, but as one CNN insider put it, "It was a vanity project . . . *They* wanted to launch it."[5]
- **Build:** With the most-senior executives' decision to move ahead, the company went all in on execution, with $300 million spent developing CNN+ and hundreds of employees hired. Contracts were signed for name-brand anchors such as NPR's Audie Cornish and Fox News's Chris Wallace. Plans were made to spend over $1 billion in the first four years to grow the service.[6]

No doubt CNN+ was a bold and innovative new business model. But the biggest uncertainty it faced was this: Did anyone want to pay $5.99 a month to stream news? By one estimate, CNN+ joined more than 300 other unique streaming services operating in the United States, yet the average household paid for only four of them.[7] At a minimum, it would have been useful to know what percentage of CNN's current viewers were interested in paying for a streaming version of the brand (10 percent? 5 percent? less?). But rather than conduct a test to find out, the company plowed ahead with its plan.

As it turned out, uptake by CNN's existing customers was small. At the time, CNN's TV channel was attracting an average of 773,000 viewers per day. In its first weeks, CNN+ was watched by fewer than 10,000 people per day—about 1 percent of the TV audience.[8] Less than a month after launching, it was announced that CNN+ would shut down. Its corporate parent, Warner Bros. Discovery, concluded that customers simply didn't want to pay for another streaming service, let alone one focused on news but lacking their favorite prime-time CNN shows. Say goodbye to $300 million.

WHICH PHONE TO LAUNCH?

Even digital-native businesses can fall prey to overreliance on traditional planning, especially when innovation decisions are driven by a charismatic CEO. When Amazon decided it should enter the smartphone market to compete with Apple's iPhone and Google's Android business, two ideas were developed. One, code-named Otus, would be a low-cost handset using the same software as Amazon's popular Fire tablets. The other, code-named Tyto, would be a high-end smartphone with a 3D display that allowed users to control their phone by gesture. Which idea would succeed in the market? No one knew, but apparently a test was never conducted. Otus was shelved and Tyto planned for launch based on the founder's decision. Reportedly enthralled with its 3D display, Jeff Bezos maintained a personal commitment to Tyto even as the screen posed huge technical challenges and the project dragged on for four years—with 1,000 employees and more than $100 million devoted to development. By the time Bezos himself unveiled the product, dubbed the Fire Phone, the smartphone market had evolved considerably. Amazon's phone was out of touch with customer demand and too expensive for what it offered (it lacked compatibility with popular apps like Gmail and YouTube). In a year when new iPhones sold 4 million units in their first twenty-four hours, the Fire Phone sold just tens of thousands of units in its first six weeks.[9] The product was heavily discounted and cancelled soon after.

How do digital start-ups like Airbnb and Netflix innovate successfully in the face of such uncertainty? How do venture capitalists invest in these kinds of ventures from the start without going bankrupt? And how do large firms like Google and Apple continue to innovate new business models? We will see the solution to the challenge of uncertainty shortly. But first, let's take a look at another challenge.

Innovating Beyond the Core

The second challenge for innovation in an established company is managing innovation outside its core business. (This is a challenge not faced by start-ups.) I call this the challenge of proximity. Managing growth beyond the core is one of the key difficulties that executives tell me they struggle with amid digital change. Once a company becomes successful, there is an inherent tension between growing the existing business model and pursuing innovations that stretch beyond it. In too many firms, this tension is always resolved in favor of staying close to the core.

But for any organization to grow in the rapidly changing digital era, it is essential that DX include innovation both in and beyond the core. New ventures beyond the core may serve different customers than the current business does. They may earn revenue in different ways, and they may carry a different cost structure. They may require new capabilities and partnerships. All these differences mean that innovation beyond the core requires the organization to learn and adapt to new management challenges—and this work is essential. Every business needs to place bets on innovative ventures outside its core if it hopes to achieve sustainable long-term growth. As its existing business model matures and loses the potential for growth, innovation of this kind is critical.

The Lessons of Amazon Web Services (AWS)

Amazon poses a powerful example of the importance of innovation beyond your core business. The company began with a retail business model, taking orders online and shipping physical goods to consumers. This core business started with books and expanded into other product categories. Amazon extended its business model by adding a marketplace to include third-party sellers on its website. And it added a hugely successful retail membership model, Amazon Prime, based on free shipping. But Amazon also pursued growth far beyond its core business of retailing—including streaming media (music, TV, and movies) and electronic devices (Kindle e-readers, smart home devices, and its Alexa assistant). Most important, its innovation beyond the core included Amazon Web Services (AWS).

The idea for AWS was floated in a 2003 paper by network engineer Benjamin Black and his boss Chris Pinkham. The paper proposed building a new computing architecture for the Amazon.com website that would be more flexible, stable, and scalable. At the end of the paper, Black and Pinkham added the suggestion that the company could even sell the use of this architecture to other companies as a B2B cloud-computing service.[10]

That idea, to enter the cloud-computing market, was far from Amazon's core business. At the time, Amazon was a purely consumer-facing retail business. Cloud computing was radically different. It would serve a completely different customer (enterprises rather than shoppers), require a completely different sales process, and interface with a completely different ecosystem of IT partners.

Bezos approved work on the new venture, and over time AWS became not just a hugely successful venture but the most profitable part of Amazon. By the time the company publicly broke out the unit's financials for the first time in 2015, AWS was already a $5 billion business, which stunned investors.[11] Six years later, with AWS representing 63 percent of all company profits, its head, Andy Jassy, succeeded Bezos as Amazon CEO.[12]

Other digital-era businesses have thrived by innovating beyond their core. Think of Apple, which started as a computer maker and extended into other hardware businesses—MP3 players, smartphones, tablets, and watches. But Apple grew beyond its core of hardware. It enriched its ecosystem and its profits by venturing into the sale of music, games, and apps. It launched its own television and movie studio. It even created a data-driven fitness service.

We will see the same pattern in successful examples of DX throughout this book. The New York Times Company's digital innovation includes apps and emails for its news subscription but also includes ventures in podcasting, live events, and digital subscriptions beyond news. Walmart's transformation has extended its physical retail into the world of e-commerce, but it also includes data-driven ventures in health care and financial services. And Mastercard has not simply extended its core credit card business into digital wallets and online payments; it has found new growth in cybersecurity and digital identity services.

Struggling Beyond the Core

Despite these examples, most established businesses find it extremely hard to pursue innovation beyond their core. This is almost inevitable. *Incumbents are designed and managed for the primary goal of optimizing their current business model.* As a result, employees who come up with great ideas outside the current business may find it impossible to bring those ideas to market. Consider these famous examples:

- *Cisco*—Cisco was already a market leader in videoconferencing technology with its Webex product when employee Eric Yuan proposed innovating in a new direction. To complement its success in the enterprise market, Yuan conceived of plans for a more consumer-oriented videoconferencing tool. But within Cisco, this idea was shot down as too far afield from the enterprise focus of the core. Frustrated, Yuan quit to start his own company and brought his innovation to the market as Zoom.[13] When the COVID-19 pandemic sparked global quarantines and a surge in demand for videoconferencing, it could have been an enormous opportunity for Cisco. Instead, the company watched as users flock to the previously little-known Zoom platform. Daily users of Zoom rose to 200 million from just 10 million the year before.[14] Overnight, Webex became an also-ran in its own category.
- *IBM*—In 1999, IBM's strategy group reported to their CEO, Lou Gerstner, that the firm had developed 29 recent breakthrough technologies—in areas such as speech recognition, radio frequency identification (RFID), business intelligence, and the first internet router—each of which IBM had failed to commercialize because executives were focused on serving their current markets and were rewarded for delivering on short-term, predictable results. Instead, second-mover companies like Nuance, Akamai, and Cisco captured huge markets in areas that could have been IBM's to dominate.[15]
- *Xerox*—When Xerox founded its legendary lab Xerox PARC, it assembled many of the world's greatest computer scientists and engineers. Their work produced innovations close to the company's core business (photocopying), such as the laser printer, which was a commercial success for the company. But the greatest innovation by far to come out of PARC was the Xerox Alto, the world's first computer with a graphical user interface (GUI). If you've never heard of it, that's because Xerox left the Alto languishing in the lab. The company failed to realize the Alto's commercial potential because it was so far from Xerox's core business. It was Steve Jobs who saw the Alto on a visit to PARC, recognized it as a breakthrough, and brought GUI to the market with his Macintosh computer, followed soon by Microsoft's Windows operating system. Jobs later remarked, "If Xerox had known what it had and had taken advantage of its real opportunities [it could have become] the largest high-technology company in the world."[16]

Why do established companies fail to invest in their own employees' innovations and fail to bring them to market? There are many reasons why established companies find it hard to innovate beyond their core:

- *Organizational structure*—Growth opportunities outside the core do not fit easily into existing business units, so there is no power center in the company to support and sponsor them effectively.
- *Metrics*—Established business metrics are often poorly suited to judge the success of a new business model. As a result, the opportunity appears unattractive, risky, or too small to merit attention.
- *Resources*—In a typical organization, executives who generate the most revenue today control the investment of resources for the future. Ideas that are irrelevant to their business units are left with nothing but resource scraps.
- *Customer focus*—Companies are understandably focused on their existing customers. Clayton Christensen identified this paradox: most companies fail to invest in disruptive innovations because they are too focused on their current customers to see the opportunity to serve a different market.[17]
- *Cannibalization*—Promising innovations are actively resisted and even shut down if they are perceived as threats that could cannibalize the core business that generates today's profits.
- *Narrow vision*—Over time, success causes a company's vision of the future to be defined by the products of its past. Businesses develop a narrow, backward-looking view famously described as strategic myopia by Ted Levitt. Hollywood studios that thought they were in the movie business rather than the entertainment business disappeared when newer media arrived. Railroad companies that failed to focus on the broader transportation market met a dead end.[18] Levitt saw that successful companies failed during times of change because they focused on the products they built instead of the problems they solved.

The net result is a perennial challenge for established businesses: the less proximity an innovation has to the core business, the harder it is for the company to manage it to growth.

We've now seen why so many established companies struggle to innovate, faced with the twin challenges of uncertainty and proximity. But we have also seen examples of firms that overcame both these obstacles to achieve tremendous growth. Let's look at the lessons from the digital era to see how any business can solve the challenges of uncertainty and proximity.

Solving for Uncertainty

Innovating under great uncertainty is possible. This much is obvious from the growth of incredibly valuable digital businesses started around the world with venture capital (VC) investment. Every one of these businesses began under tremendous uncertainty because it was inventing a new digital business model. Each succeeded by using two levers available to every manager: experimentation and iterative funding.

Experimentation: What Start-Ups Do

It is a Silicon Valley truism that great start-ups don't start with a great idea; they start with *an* idea and then test and pivot their way to what works in the market. Instead of the traditional corporate reflex to plan, plan, plan, and then build; start-ups succeed through a constant process of experimentation. In *The Digital Transformation Playbook*, I define experimentation as "an iterative process of learning what does and does not work."[19] In both start-ups and the scientific method, the aim of experimentation is the same: to *validate* your key hypotheses or assumptions.

In a scientific experiment, you seek to validate whether condition X will lead to outcome Y (e.g., if patients take a pill versus a placebo, will their health improve?). To develop a single medicine, many hypotheses must be validated. Does the pill speed recovery? By how much? What dosage is required? How quickly does it take effect? Are there side effects?

In business experimentation, your goal is to validate the key assumptions in your business model for any new venture. Assumptions to test include: Who is the customer? What is their problem or unmet need? Are they interested in our proposed solution? How much would they pay for it? When, where, and how will they use it? How would we deliver it? What profit margin could we make? What's the total possible size of the market?

Experimentation is the defining philosophy of digital-native businesses. If you spend time with fast-growing start-ups or with titans like Google and Amazon, you will quickly pick up a whole different vocabulary around innovation: "MVP," "fail fast," "design sprint," "pivot," "lean metrics," "agile squads," "product thinking," and so on. Any business leader who aims to master the art of innovation today should be aware that these terms and practices derive from four powerful approaches to innovation that have arisen in the digital era. These four schools of thought are lean start-up, agile software development, design thinking, and product management. I think of these as the Four Religions of Iterative Innovation because each has its own rituals and passionate adherents, yet they all share the same core principles of managing innovation through iterative experimentation. To learn about each, see the box "The Four Religions of Iterative Innovation."

The Four Religions of Iterative Innovation

Despite their differences, the Four Religions of Iterative Innovation were each developed to address the same management challenge: how to innovate and solve problems under tremendous uncertainty. Each one tackles the challenge of uncertainty with an approach that is designed around learning rather than planning. And each envisions learning as a highly iterative process that seeks to spend less upfront, build something tangible as early as possible, and use that to validate assumptions and reduce uncertainty in rapid fashion.

Lean start-up, also known as customer development, arose in the world of Silicon Valley start-ups. Its goal was to replace traditional business planning when searching for new business models. The core ideas were formulated in the early 2000s by Steve Blank and his coauthor Bob Dorf and extended by Blank's student Eric Ries. Blank defines a start-up as "a temporary organization designed to search for a repeatable business model."* This search is conducted by learning directly from customers with interviews and MVPs designed to capture customer feedback through rapid experimentation.

Agile software development, often shortened to agile, originated in the world of IT developers. It was formulated in response to traditional software development practices inside large organizations that were too slow, costly, and inflexible. Agile is comprised of several different methodologies, including Scrum, Kanban, XP, and others, whose founders met in 2001 at a Utah ski lodge and produced a shared manifesto on improving the practice of software development.† Guiding principles include self-directed teams, a focus on customer needs, rapid iteration cycles, and the continuous delivery of software through incremental deployments.

Design thinking originated with designers working for large organizations; their goal was to bring principles of good design out of the last phase of product development (What should our product look like?) and into much earlier phases (What should the product be? What problem is it trying to solve?). While rooted in theories of human factors and creativity dating to the 1960s, design thinking

---

(*continued on next page*)

(continued from previous page)

was popularized in the 2000s by design firms like IDEO. Design thinking has no unifying text or framework; its core principles are framing innovation around the needs of customers, carefully studying the problem to be solved, and iterative prototyping to bring in tangible feedback early and often.[‡] In practice, it uses teams that combine expertise in different fields such as industrial design, anthropology, and data science.

Product management is a term heard most often in large digital-native companies (e.g., Alphabet, Meta) to describe how they organize teams working on new ventures and ongoing products. It has no single methodology and typically applies many tools of the other three religions (MVPs, design sprints, journey maps, etc.). Individual companies develop their own tools as well: Amazon product managers will write a "future press release" for any proposed innovation to visualize the imagined customer impact and work backward to begin development.[§] Product management is often contrasted with *project management*—a traditional practice best suited when you know the deliverable you need to build, and your goal is to meet a fixed timeline with fixed resources.[‖]

[*] Steven G. Blank and Bob Dorf, *The Startup Owner's Manual: The Step-By-Step Guide for Building a Great Company* (Pescadero, CA: K & S Ranch, 2012).

[†] Kent Beck et al., "Manifesto for Agile Software Development," 2001, http://agilemanifesto .org/. The history of the gathering that produced the manifesto is recounted at Jim Highsmith, "History: The Agile Manifesto," 2001, http://agilemanifesto.org/history.html.

[‡] Jon Kolko, "The Divisiveness of Design Thinking," 2017, https://www.jonkolko.com/writing /the-divisiveness-of-design-thinking. Kolko's article is an excellent look at the roots of design thinking, as well as a critique of its trivialization and commercialization in some quarters.

[§] Werner Vogels, "Working Backwards," *All Things Distributed*, November 1, 2006, https:// www.allthingsdistributed.com/2006/11/working_backwards.html.

[‖] Kyle Evans, "Product Thinking vs. Project Thinking," *Medium*, Product Coalition, October 21, 2018, https://productcoalition.com/product-thinking-vs-project-thinking-380692a2d4e.

Whatever methods it adopts or combines, every great digital business has used experimentation to find its way to growth. It was through constant testing and learning that Airbnb's founders validated their business model for a multisided market for travel hospitality. From their very first test of their idea (in which they themselves hosted guests on a weekend when

San Francisco's hotels were fully booked) through countless iterations in one city after another, they gradually validated what would draw users to the site, what would earn the trust of both travelers and hosts, how the company could comply with myriad local laws and regulations, and how they could leverage network effects to fend off competition and grow to a phenomenal scale.

Uncertainty in innovation can never be wished away or banished by detailed case planning. Every digital winner knows that the only way to reduce uncertainty is by learning directly through experimentation in the market to convert hypotheses into facts.

Iterative Funding: What VCs Do

The second lever that managers can use to solve the challenge of uncertainty is iterative funding. Digital start-ups use experimentation to validate their path to growth; VC investors use iterative funding to invest in those same start-ups. The whole point of VC investing is to back new, highly uncertain ventures. VC firms handle the risk by investing smaller amounts (at lower valuations) when a start-up is new and its uncertainty is high, and increasing investment in later rounds if the start-up is able to validate its business assumptions (see figure 2.1).

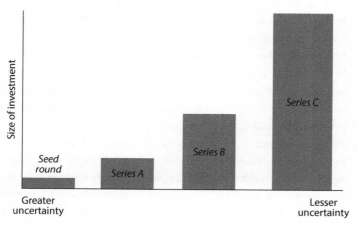

Figure 2.1.
Typical VC investment stages

This approach is the exact opposite of how most established businesses allocate capital. Recall that CNN spent a massive $300 million in its first year to launch CNN+, and it planned a similar budget for each of the next three years. The traditional approach to funding corporate innovation is to delay investment while completing as much planning and analysis as possible. Then, if a top leader decides, after much deliberation, to move ahead, the company makes a large initial investment in hopes of increasing the odds of success. Under digital-age conditions of high uncertainty, this approach is doomed. Instead, to practice iterative funding, businesses should follow four simple principles:

- *Invest less when uncertainty is higher; invest more when uncertainty is lower.* If uncertainty is low (e.g., investing in warehouses for your established e-commerce business), you can afford to make a large investment from the beginning. But the greater the uncertainty at the start of a project, the smaller your initial investment should be. With new business models and untested market ideas, you should start with as small an investment as possible.
- *Place more bets when uncertainty is high.* In the early seed stage, VC firms take stakes in many different start-ups. Later, when uncertainty is reduced, they invest in a much smaller number of ideas (those that have been validated through market testing). If your company's goal is to find a couple of big innovations that move the needle on your entire business, start by investing in a lot of high-uncertainty ideas, experiment, and winnow them down based on what you learn.
- *Know what you are spending for.* When investing with low uncertainty, you are spending money to make a financial return. You goal is to "spend to earn." But when you invest under high uncertainty, your goal should be to "spend to learn." Early investments should not be directed toward launching a product but to conduct small, cheap tests that reduce uncertainty. Even if you think you understand the customers' needs and their problem to be solved, your first goal is to test and validate.
- *Accelerate spending as uncertainty diminishes.* If experimentation reduces the uncertainty of an idea, you should ramp up quickly to much larger investments, for example, to prepare a product for market launch. But be careful. Investment increases should happen only at learning milestones, that is, when critical business hypotheses are validated. Do not release more money just because the calendar has rolled forward on your budgeting.

When Facebook received its first seed round of funding led by investor Peter Thiel, the service was just four months old, had no revenue, and had been tested in a handful of college campuses. Thiel invested $500,001 for a 10.2 percent stake, which gave the company a valuation of $4.9 million. The following year, Facebook had surpassed 1 million users and was generating revenue from major advertisers like Mastercard. In its Series A round, Facebook received $12.7 million and was valued at $98 million. The next year, as Facebook spread to colleges, high schools, and corporate campuses, its Series B round valued the company at $500 million. The following year, when Facebook had launched on mobile, started its Newsfeed, and opened to app developers, Microsoft led its Series C round, valuing Facebook at $15 billion. The core idea of Facebook did not change between its launch and its Series C round. But the market value of that idea went from $5 million to $15 billion—even though the company would still not turn a profit for two more years. What changed between 2004 and 2007? The uncertainty of Facebook's business model.

Maximum Upside, Minimum Downside

The harsh truth of innovation is that most ideas that sound good on a sketchpad turn out to be unworkable in the real world. Innovating under uncertainty can work only with the use of both experimentation and iterative funding. The two together will not give you better ideas or a crystal ball to see the future. (You will still dream up innovations, like a 3D smartphone, that seem amazing to you but will fail in the real world.) What they will do is capture the upside of every idea that works while minimizing the downside of ideas that don't work.

The problem with CNN+ was not that it failed but that it cost $300 million to fail! It was actually a good idea to test, but it could have been tested with $30,000. By combining the two levers of experimentation and iterative funding, any business can master innovation under uncertainty—cutting its losses early on ideas that prove infeasible and doubling down on those with the highest chance of success.

In the five steps of the DX Roadmap, we will learn how to tackle uncertainty with tools and frameworks that can be applied by any organization. We will introduce the Four Stages of Validation used to test the assumptions behind any business model. We will apply them with a visual tool to guide experimentation of your next innovation from notepad sketch to global execution. We will also learn how to apply iterative funding, drawing on pools of dedicated resources and allocating them quickly and flexibly while using smart shutdowns to avoid wasteful disasters.

Solving for Proximity

As we have seen, the other innovation challenge faced by every established business is proximity—how to manage innovation far from its core business. This is hard for many reasons, including structural barriers (metrics, resources, and organizational design) as well as mindset (vision, focus, and fear). Despite this, we see mature digital firms, like Amazon, Apple, and Alibaba, and legacy businesses, like Walmart, Mastercard and the New York Times, pursuing innovation successfully beyond their core. As we explore the DX Roadmap, I will provide more examples of companies that are conquering the challenge of proximity. You can do the same in your business by following a few essential principles:

- *Focus on problems that play to your strengths.* How does a business find growth ideas outside its core and escape the trap of strategic myopia? The answer is to focus on customer problems to be solved rather than your current products or industry. But once you broaden your lens in this way, how far should you stretch beyond your current business? If Ford Motors decides it is no longer a car company but rather a mobility company, should it now build airplanes? Not necessarily. Effective strategy looks not just at opportunities but at where you hold a unique advantage over competitors. How did Alibaba, as an online retail business, decide to move into digital payments? It started with a customer problem to solve: its own customers needed ways to pay each other on its marketplace. But Alibaba also had a unique ability to solve this problem by leveraging its scale, existing customer base, and rich user data.
- *Make it independent.* Many opportunities for digital innovation should be managed in your existing business units because they directly involve your core business and cannot be pursued outside it (think of Domino's Pizza reinventing the delivery experience of its restaurants). But when you pursue a new venture that diverges from your core business (with different customers, revenue, cost structure, or capabilities), that venture should be managed independently from the core—at least in its early stages. This independence may even include

physical distance, to escape interference and meddling. When Amazon decided to pursue its idea for AWS, it made sense to run the project independently from the e-commerce division. AWS was started as an independent group of fifty-seven people led by Jassy, with the majority of its hires from outside Amazon.[20] A team led by Pinkham set up shop in Cape Town, South Africa, to build EC2, one of two initial AWS products.[21] (That's about as far from Seattle headquarters as possible!)

- *Keep an umbilical cord.* As important as independence is, a growth venture beyond the core business should never be left to sink or swim entirely on its own. These ventures still need access to critical assets and resources from the parent firm. In the early days of the Web, British grocery chain Tesco launched Tesco.com, the first grocery e-commerce business to succeed in the United Kingdom. CEO Terry Leahy set up the team as a distinct operating unit because he knew Tesco's culture was ferociously competitive—even internally. He saw a real risk of a visceral organ rejection by the company of the new dot-com business unit. But despite its independence, the new venture's relationship to the core (physical store) business was critical. Employees of Tesco.com needed to pick products off the shelves for speedy delivery to nearby customers. So, retail stores were given "shadow accounting" metrics that attributed to them part of the profits from the online business. The online business also had access to the core's data sets and customer lists to mine for prospects, and it shared the same outside marketing agency. Chris Reid, who led Tesco.com at the time, explained to me that his unit was run in many ways like a start-up but with "a tight umbilical cord to the main business."

- *Manage by different rules.* New ventures outside the core need more than just separation into distinct units. These units need to be managed by different rules—even if they are housed on the same corporate campus as the core. They need to operate with their own budget and a dedicated funding source. They need their own metrics for success; their own talent pool, with many hired from outside the firm; and their own executive sponsorship, reporting, and oversight. Alphabet has used X (formerly Google X) as a "moonshot lab" to explore ventures far from its core business—like driverless cars, supply chain software, and health care. X was set up to have metrics, financing, and leadership that are all different from the core business of search and digital advertising. The New York Times established its Standalone Products and Ventures Group to develop and launch new digital products beyond the news subscription. The Group was set up on a separate floor of the Times's headquarters, with each new app or product assigned a cross-functional team that applies product management methods and works in a single conference room.

- *Plan where it will land.* Any time a team is set up to start a venture outside the core business, its sponsors should think ahead about where they expect it to land. If the venture succeeds, it should eventually either merge with the core or become its own permanent business unit—in some cases, triggering a redesign of the whole organization. AWS was set up as its own business unit before its public launch in 2006; it has continued to grow rapidly and runs as a separate unit to this day. Retailers like Tesco who started dot-com teams in the early days of e-commerce ultimately converged on an omnichannel strategy. In most companies, this meant reorganizing by product category or customer type. Online and physical store teams were combined and given unified metrics (like customer lifetime value) that prioritized total value to the firm. In managing ventures outside your core, start with a plan but be ready to adapt as you go. Efforts that need to be separate at the start may be better combined as the market and the organization mature.

In the five steps of the DX Roadmap, I will introduce tools and frameworks to manage growth beyond the core in any business. I will provide tools that will enable you to focus your strategy on problems to solve and to avoid the trap of strategic myopia. We will see how to define a future landscape and your unique right to win and how to use those perspectives to pick which opportunities to pursue. And I will introduce a model called the Three Paths to Growth to apply the right governance for ventures both within and beyond your core.

∾

No company will survive in the digital era if it ignores the challenges of innovation. Digital transformation cannot be just low-risk investments with clear benchmarks and best practices. It cannot be only about upgrading and digitizing the core. Digital transformation is first and foremost about using digital tools to solve new problems and drive new growth. This is why the DX Roadmap takes a holistic, growth-focused approach—one that is integrated with your work on strategy, innovation, governance, and culture as much as with your IT planning.

In the five chapters ahead, we will see how to link digital vision to strategy and innovation, how to focus on customers and problems to solve, how to experiment with new ventures while applying governance to grow them to scale, and how to support all of this with the right capabilities and culture.

The table is set. It's time to begin.

3

Step 1: Define a Shared Vision

VISION

At the 2011 TED conference in Long Beach, California, William "Bill" Clay Ford Jr. strode onto the stage to speak about a vision of the future of transportation. Bill Ford was the executive chair and recent CEO of Ford Motor Company. He had spent his whole life and career in the automotive industry; he was the great-grandson of the company's founder, Henry Ford. Yet he began his talk with a provocative question: what if the future of Ford Motor was not simply to make and sell more cars? The presentation that followed was not a typical TED Talk but the outline of a defining corporate vision from the chair of a leading global corporation.

Bill Ford defined two great challenges facing the automotive industry: environmental impact and a looming mobility crisis. On the first, Ford Motor was already making progress toward electrification of engines and other technologies aimed at developing zero-emissions vehicles. On the second challenge, Ford pointed to the increasing stresses of urbanization; a rising global middle class; and the threat of global gridlock, from Beijing to Abu Dhabi, that could threaten the freedom of mobility that his great-grandfather had championed in starting the business. The existing solution—selling more vehicles and building more roads—was insufficient for a future population of 8 billion people, 75 percent of whom would be living in cities. The implications were a stifling of economic growth and the inability to deliver food, health care, and essential services effectively to communities around the world.

The response Bill Ford laid out was to invest in building a smart network of vehicles, roads, fueling stations, and public transport using data and digital technologies to connect every component and create new integrated solutions around travel, parking, payment, and safety. Pointing to examples of innovation from Hong Kong to Masdar, he described a future of connected vehicles that talk to each other in an "integrated system that uses real-time data to optimize personal mobility on a massive scale." He committed to focusing Ford Motor on pursuing this vision not just as an automaker but as a digitally driven mobility services company.[1]

This vision would go on to shape the strategy of Ford Motor for the next decade and beyond, even as that vision continued to evolve and be refined. The vision has led to billions of dollars in new digital investments and acquisitions and has shaped the choice of the next three CEOs. It continues to shape the strategy of Ford today as it pushes ahead into the digital future.

Why a Shared Vision Matters

Change is easy . . . in a crisis. During the midst of the COVID-19 pandemic, Lucy Kueng, a scholar of the media industry, remarked that COVID provided a once-in-a-lifetime opportunity for legacy companies to transform. "Organizations are unfrozen. People are expecting change . . . There will never be a better time to tackle deeper changes that need to happen."[2] In the context of an immediate crisis, everyone in your business realizes that the status quo is untenable—and so everyone is primed for action and for setting aside old ways of working.

But in the vast majority of cases, you will not be in this kind of crisis. (Thank goodness!) The rest of the time, *transformation is very hard.* Change is resisted. The status quo is the default, and employees' bias is toward more of the same. The unspoken assumption of planning is that the future will look like the past. Success breeds complacency—why change what has been working? As one senior executive told me, "Our biggest obstacle for the future is that we have been so successful for the first 79 years of the company."

To generate urgency for change during a digital transformation (DX), consultants will commonly urge you to "find your burning platform." The expression comes from Nokia, from a memo that CEO Stephen Elop wrote to rally the company as its mobile phone business was being disrupted by Apple's iPhone and cheaper Android smartphones.[3] But did Elop's burning platform memo succeed? No. Nokia fell from its leadership position and eventually exited mobile phones completely. The real lesson from Nokia is that a burning platform is not enough.

Negative urgency alone—proclaiming the sky is falling and digital disruptors are just around the corner—is not a motivating story for employees or shareholders. One major Latin American retailer I advised was extremely focused on the threat posed by Amazon and told employees they needed to change to survive. But the message ignored the retailer's history—decades of growth driven by customer-centricity and business innovation—and how that might point the way forward in their digital future. Negative urgency is helpful only when it is paired with positive urgency: a vision of how digital transformation can create new value, unlock new growth, and solve new problems.

As you craft a positive story of value creation, be mindful that shareholder value is not enough. Explaining how your digital transformation will drive new efficiencies and raise earnings per share may inspire investors. But quarterly profits alone will not inspire employees to take on the uncertainty and hard work of transforming your organization. To inspire employees, leaders must show the impact and meaning of their work.

To drive change, leaders must appeal to *extrinsic* motivation (ROI; profits; cost savings; and earnings before interest, taxes, depreciation, and amortization [EBITDA]), which motivates shareholders. But leaders must also appeal to *intrinsic* motivation (value created for customers, employees, partners, and society), which motivates employees.[4] When Bill Ford laid out his case for the digital future of Ford Motor, he gave it intrinsic motivation by linking it to the company's founding: "My great grandfather, Henry Ford, really believed that the mission of the Ford Motor Company was to make people's lives better and make cars affordable so that everyone could have them. Because he believed that with mobility comes freedom and progress."[5] Bill Ford framed his vision of a connected transportation future as a way to safeguard core values of freedom and mobility for the next generation.

The first step of the Digital Transformation (DX) Roadmap is to define a shared vision of the future of your business, one that will inspire, align, and make the case for change. This vision must be *shared*; that is, it must be known by everyone in the organization. And it must be *unique* to your business. A generic commitment to "become digital-first," to "be recognized as a digital leader," or to "future-proof our business" will not suffice. Every business needs a vision that is specific—that describes where your world is going, what role your organization will play, and why.

The importance of a shared vision is well-established. Daniel Goleman's classic research on leadership found that the most powerful of six leadership styles is when leaders "mobilize people toward a vision."[6] More recently, McKinsey's research has found that the biggest single factor for DX success is having a "clear change story."[7]

It is, therefore, shocking how many companies lack this kind of shared vision. In my workshops with large organizations, participants have consistently chosen this as one of their top barriers: "[we have] no shared vision of our company's digital future." The incoming CEO of an insurance firm recently shared with me, "Honestly, if you ask three people what's our vision for digital transformation in this business, you'd get three different answers." In a discussion with fifty executives from a large biopharmaceutical firm, I was told that their CEO had announced that they would become a "digital-first" company and had hired a chief digital officer (CDO), just like their peers. But when I pressed these divisional leaders on what digital meant for their business, they confessed they were mystified and had hoped I would explain it.

Defining a shared vision of the future is not easy. But without a clear and compelling answer to the question, "Why must we change?," any DX will stumble. Table 3.1 shows some of the key symptoms of success versus failure in the first step of the DX Roadmap.

Table 3.1.
What's at Stake—Step 1: Vision

Symptoms of Failure: Vision	Symptoms of Success: Vision
• Employees fear change and lack a clear sense of where the firm is going.	• Employees at every level understand the digital agenda and push it forward.
• Backing for digital investments is weak from investors, CFOs, and P&L heads.	• Support for digital investments is strong from investors, CFOs, and P&L heads.
• Digital initiatives are generic, following the examples of peers.	• Only digital initiatives with a competitive advantage receive investment.
• Generic digital maturity metrics are used to guide efforts.	• The business impact of digital is clearly defined, with metrics to measure and track results.
• The firm follows the market, reacts to others, and is surprised by new entrants.	• The firm leads the market, alert to critical trends while there is time to choose a course.

What's Ahead

In this chapter, we will see how any leader can define a shared vision for the DX efforts of their organization, business unit, function, or team. We will examine four essential elements of a strong shared vision. Each element seeks to answer a different question:

- *Future landscape*—where do you see your world and your business context going?
- *Right to win*—what are the unique strengths and limits of your organization that will define the role you play?
- *North Star impact*—what impact do you seek to achieve in the long term, and why?
- *Business theory*—how do you expect to capture value and recover the investments you make for the future?

After examining each of these four elements and a range of case studies, we will introduce a strategic planning tool, the Shared Vision Map. This tool will help you to define each element of your shared vision for the DX you are leading. Finally, we will learn why defining a shared vision is so critical to making the shift from a top-down to a bottom-up organization.

Future Landscape

The first element of a shared vision for your business is what I call your *future landscape*, which is a description of where your world is going and how the context of your business is changing. As Microsoft CEO Satya Nadella describes it, a leader's job is to "see the external opportunities, and the internal capability and culture, and all of the connections among them." He goes on to explain, "It's an art form, not a science. And a leader will not always get it right. But the batting average for how well a leader does this is going to define his or her longevity in business."[8]

Your future landscape should capture the most significant shifts in the world of your customers, partners, and competition—and the threats and opportunities that these pose for your business. Are you a legacy business in a highly regulated industry (e.g., finance or health care) where regulations are shifting, and new entrants are appearing with digital-first business models that seek to "unbundle" your business by offering a subset of the services you provide but without the level of regulatory burden you face? Are you an industrial business that has sunk huge investments into fixed assets (e.g., oil wells, shipping fleets, or telecom networks) that used to provide barriers to entry by competitors, but new start-ups are appearing that are happy to sit atop your assets and build new business models based on data, predictive analytics, and systems integration? You might be a professional services firm (e.g., in advertising, auditing, or human resources) whose business has been built on deep relationships with your business clients. But the problems you used to solve for them are increasingly handled by algorithms and AI—forcing you to keep reinventing your business around new client needs, redefining the services you sell, and transforming the talent of your workforce to keep up.

Understanding your future landscape—where your particular world is going—will be critical to defining where and how you aim to compete in the digital future, what markets you will serve, and where you will hunt for growth.

Scanning the Future

As Sami Hassanyeh, CDO of AARP, one of the largest nonprofit organizations in the United States, said to me, "The job of a CDO is to ensure that culturally, technologically and strategically, your organization is living up to the ever-changing demands of the customer." To keep up with change, leaders of every organization must constantly be engaged in a process of scanning the environment, both inside and outside their immediate industry. Any business must learn from looking far beyond its traditional peers, competitors, and customers if it hopes to understand its digital future.

In developing your future landscape, I advocate focusing on four broad areas:

- *Customers*—Focus on understanding the changing behaviors, expectations, and needs of your customers. As you do so, be aware of influences outside your industry. Even if you sell machinery to purchasing departments of large companies, the individuals in those departments are using Amazon, Google, and Netflix every day, and their expectations (for customization, speed, self-service experiences, and more) are shifting rapidly. You will need to keep up! As you study the future of your customers, focus both on your existing legacy customers (who built your business and may still deliver the majority of current revenue) and on new emerging customers (who will provide your growth and future revenue). Very often, their behaviors and expectations are markedly different and will require tailored strategies to manage a split market.

- *Technology*—Identify and learn all you can about new technologies that are shaping the experience of your customers, especially technologies they use to discover, purchase, and use services like yours. But focus also on technologies impacting your internal business operations and the operations of your partners, supply chain, and adjacent industries. As you study the technology landscape, be sure to take a broad view of time and tech maturity. Start with technologies that are *actively being used now*: How is your manufacturing partner upgrading its factories? What social media are your customers using? Then look to technologies that are *just starting to be used* by a handful of early adopters. Tracking start-ups in your industry is a great way to see new applications of the latest technology. Last, keep an eye on research labs and venture capital investing in technology *not yet on the market* to spot the long-term trends that could reshape your industry.
- *Competition*—Take a broad view of competitors and partners as you seek to understand the business ecosystem that will define your future. Who are the new entrants in your industry? What new products and new business models are being tested? What is the pace of change and the level of competitive threat you face in different parts of your business? As you analyze your future competition, be sure to consider both symmetric competitors (your traditional peers, with the same business model as you) and asymmetric competitors (companies with a competing value proposition but a different business model). In many cases, asymmetric competitors will include your own closest business partners (see figure 3.1).
- *Structural trends*—Be sure to study major trends in the external environment beyond business that may shape your future context. Look at demographic trends—including population growth, generational differences, urbanization, and the aging of populations. Examine macroeconomic trends—including economic development, globalization, and resource availability—and government trends—including laws, regulations, tariffs, and investments. Finally, look at any other trends—social, environmental, health, climate, geopolitical—that you think may have an impact on your business. If your business operates

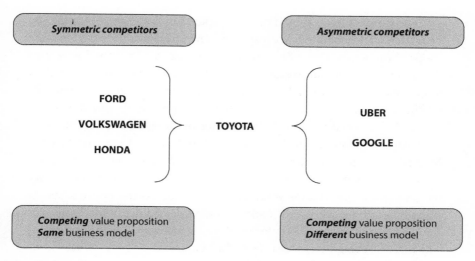

Figure 3.1.
Symmetric versus asymmetric competitors for an automotive manufacturer

in multiple markets, be sure to look for differences between them and identify which trends have the biggest potential impact in each.

Your insights into all four of these areas should come from sources inside and outside your firm—conversations with customers, meetings with new start-ups and your existing partners, research reports, and regular updates on the perspectives of frontline employees.

Tools for Scanning the Future

Four tools from my last book, *The Digital Transformation Playbook*, will be helpful as you work to develop your future landscape.

The Value Proposition Roadmap (in chapter 6 of the *Playbook*) is an indispensable tool for distilling knowledge about your customers' evolving needs. First, this tool helps you segment your customers based on their needs and the value they currently receive from your business. Next, you examine each value element you deliver (are any being replaced or disrupted?), and survey new technologies and trends to identify new possible value elements. Finally, the tool guides you to define a new value proposition to meet the future needs of each customer segment.

The Competitive Value Train (in chapter 3 of the *Playbook*) helps you understand your competitive ecosystem—the interplay of competition and cooperation between your firm and the businesses around you. I have used this tool with numerous executives to analyze new digital entrants to their industries (insurance, retail, consumer goods, etc.) and to understand the mix of competitive threat versus collaborative opportunity that they pose.

In chapter 8 of the *Playbook*, you will find two tools for assessing the threat of digital disruption to your business. The first tool, the Disruptive Business Model Map, helps you determine whether a new business model truly poses a disruptive threat by examining two sides of each business model (the value proposition and the value network). The second tool, the Disruptive Response Planner, helps you assess your options in the face of a disruptive challenger. The tool examines your disruptor on three dimensions to help you identify which of six strategic responses is your best choice.

All these tools define digital disruption as a call to innovate and lead toward your future. As Chris Reid, now an executive vice president (EVP) at Mastercard, told me, "I think disruption oftentimes is a good thing, as long as you're agile, as long as you can predict it. You should be able to figure out how do you either navigate around it, or how do you take advantage of it."

A clear view of your future landscape comes from continually educating yourself about what is happening in the lives of your customers, in the evolving landscape of digital technology, and among other businesses that you must compete and cooperate with to succeed.

What a Future Landscape Looks Like

So what should a future landscape look like? The output from the work above may be highly detailed or extremely succinct. What is important is that it provides actionable guidance for you to move forward as you think about the direction your business unit or company will take and the opportunities it will pursue. The next sections describe three examples: Merck Animal Health, BSH Home Appliances, and Acuity Insurance.

MERCK ANIMAL HEALTH

At Merck Animal Health (known as MSD Animal Health outside the United States and Canada), global CMO Fernando Riaza is focused on understanding the future of a business that serves both pet owners and agriculture companies raising livestock (beef, dairy, poultry, swine, and fish). He sees dramatic changes in the consumer side of the business as pets become integrated into our digital lives and equally big changes in the agricultural side as well. The customers' "path to purchase" for animal medications is changing dramatically, relying less on buying through veterinarians and more on direct digital sales. Rather than the vet making the decision, customers are seeking their own digital content and tools for decision making. Future opportunities are also being shaped by technology trends in the agriculture industry, where digital sensors are providing more and more real-time data for dairy and meat businesses.

BSH HOME APPLIANCES

BSH Home Appliances is one of the world's leading providers of home appliances for cooking, dishwashing, laundry, and refrigeration; it sells under the brand names Bosch, Siemens, Gaggenau, Thermador, Neff, and others. The company's future landscape starts with understanding the changing lives of digitally connected consumers and how they use apps, data, and smartphone-enabled services to meet their basic needs around food and clothing. As a result, BSH is not only tracking the digitally enabled products developed by competitor appliance manufacturers (i.e., the latest digital fridge). It is also watching new entrants like Uber Eats (for food delivery), recipe apps, online influencers, and laundry service start-ups. This view of the future is informing BSH's expansion from appliances to new digital solutions, to the cooking and cleaning needs of tomorrow's customers.

ACUITY INSURANCE

I had the chance to work in depth with Ben Salzmann, CEO of Acuity Insurance, as his leadership team developed a future landscape for their property and casualty insurance business. Acuity operates in the B2C market (personal lines) selling home and vehicle insurance to individuals. But they also operate in the B2B market (commercial lines), selling more complex insurance policies for small and midsize businesses in sectors like construction, trucking, and manufacturing. On the B2C side, Acuity sees a generational divide, with younger customers seeking more convenience, customization, and self-service options through their phones. On the B2B side, new customers include growing sectors like eldercare and gig economy workers, and long-standing customers are increasingly looking to Acuity for insights and advice on their industry.

Technology trends are moving fast as well. Customers today expect service across mobile, web, chat, and social media, and to be able to file and track a claim with a swipe and a click on a smartphone app. Popular home sensors like Nest and Ring are providing new sources of data for property insurance. Robotics and automation are being adopted by many of Acuity's business customers—which has an impact on which assets they need insured, as well as the worker's compensation insurance required for an increasingly skilled workforce. Meanwhile, Acuity is tracking the development of autonomous vehicles. In the future, if full autonomy becomes widespread, it will dramatically change the insurance needs for vehicles—whether they are owned by families, trucking companies, or other businesses.

The competitive landscape is shifting for Acuity as well. The firm is working with many new partners, from digital ad platforms to online marketplaces, to providers of data for underwriting and risk assessment. Its industry has attracted VC investment in a host of new start-ups with widely varying business models. We used the Competitive Value Train to analyze over 100 new digital entrants into a few categories—including aggregators, virtual agencies, value-added partners, and digital direct writers—and to define the competitive threat and opportunity for each. We also identified potential future threats, such as the "manufacturer as insurer" business model.

Although the excitement of investors in the insurtech sector is intense, it became clear that not all of these firms had a viable path to profitability. Acuity found that its B2C business faces more risk than its B2B business (where the complexity of insurance policies poses a barrier to new entrants). And few insurtech firms are attempting to disrupt insurers like Acuity (with most looking to partner with them instead). The most immediate digital threat is to insurance agencies that Acuity has historically partnered with. But in the long term, the biggest threat to Acuity is if it fails to adapt fast enough to changing customer needs.

Parmenides' Fallacy

Perhaps the most important reason to describe your future landscape is to be able to answer the question, What will happen if we do nothing?

This question is critical to avoiding what Philip Bobbitt calls Parmenides' fallacy: the mistake of comparing a new course of action against your present state rather than what the future will look like if you do nothing. (Parmenides' fallacy is named after the Greek philosopher who argued that all change was an illusion.)[9] Too often, decisions in large organizations are shaped by an unstated assumption that the future will look like a continuation of the present. (One of the more perverse arguments I have heard against DX is based on current financial success: "We can't afford to change; our EBITDA is too high!")

Parmenides' fallacy is so strong because of a series of well-known cognitive biases: status quo bias, endowment effect, and omission bias. Their net effect is that we tend to fear the risks of action while staying blissfully blind to the risks of inaction. But in a time of rapid change, this is a grave mistake. As John F. Kennedy is reported to have said, "There are risks and costs to a program of action. But they are far less than the long-range risks and costs of comfortable inaction."[10]

Right to Win

The second element of any shared vision is your *right to win* in the future you see ahead. Why you? What gives your business a reason to succeed in your future landscape? When Jim Hackett stepped into the role of CEO for Ford Motor, he said that the biggest challenge facing Ford's employees was "to have everybody see the future . . . and secondly, that it's our right to win there. That we don't have to cede that to anybody. Tesla, or any of them. It's our right to win."[11]

To find your right to win, you will need to understand your unique strengths as an organization, the qualities that set you apart from others. You will also need to identify the most important limits or constraints on your strategic choices. Where your future landscape arises from external knowledge (via continuous learning about customers, competitors, and forces outside your business), your right to win will stem from deep internal knowledge about your own organization.

Unique Advantages

Finding your right to win begins with knowing the distinct strengths of your business to compete in the marketplace. What is your organization uniquely good at? What assets or skills distinguish your business, add value to your products or services, and give you a competitive edge? I call these your unique advantages.

When Netflix filed for its initial public offering (IPO) in 2002, its paperwork identified three unique advantages that distinguished the firm: its subscriber base, its massive data sets on customers' media preferences, and its proven ability to deliver personalized experiences.[12] In the years since then, Netflix has leveraged these very advantages as it tested a variety of business models to drive its dramatic growth.

For Mastercard, its vast network of consumers and business partners (both banks and merchants) is one key strength as it looks toward the digital future. Another is its access to massive amounts of economic data tied to individual commercial transactions.

As Walmart focuses on growth in the digital era, it starts by looking at its unique advantages. First among these is its store network. As COO Jeff Shotts told me, "The biggest asset we have is 4,700 stores in the US that are within 10 miles of 90 percent of the population in America." Although built for the company's core retail business, Walmart's stores are now being leveraged for its online business too—thanks to the 150,000 products, on average, in each store, ready to be delivered to nearby customers. Another powerful asset is Walmart's vast data set of customer buying patterns, from 150 million shoppers in its stores each week.

The Canadian Automobile Association (CAA) faces daunting challenges to reinvent its business model given that many of the traditional services provided to its members can now be found for free via smartphone apps like Waze, Google Maps, and Uber. However, as their President Tim Shearman explained to me, CAA still retains some powerful strategic assets: a membership of 36 million; a treasure trove of data from transactions those members make using CAA's loyalty program with a range of other businesses; and the CAA brand, which was rated as the most trusted brand in Canada across every industry. These are precisely the kinds of advantages that can be leveraged in digital business model innovation.

Table 3.2 lists the unique advantages of all four companies: Netflix, Mastercard, Walmart, and CAA.

Every organization has its own unique strengths and advantages; otherwise, it would no longer be in business. These can range from physical assets to patents, technology, data, customer relationships, brand reputation, strategic partnerships, employee skills, and more. As you identify your unique advantages, it is essential that you take a critical and skeptical eye. Whenever an advantage is proposed for your list, ask yourself, how unique

Table 3.2.
Unique Advantages of Select Firms

Company	Unique Advantages
Netflix	• Subscriber base
	• Data on customer media preferences
	• Ability to deliver personalized experiences
Mastercard	• Network of business partners (banks and merchants)
	• Network of consumers (card users)
	• Unparalleled amount of actionable economic data from transactions
Walmart	• Retail stores
	• Proximity to customers
	• Data on buying patterns of 150 million shoppers
Canadian Automobile Association (CAA)	• Membership base
	• Data on transactions via CAA's loyalty programs
	• Most trusted brand in the country, across any industry

is this really? (Are we truly unparalleled in this dimension? Or are we in the top 20 percent of our peers? Or in the top 50 percent?) Next, ask, What is the competitive benefit that this affords to our business? (Does this advantage reduce our costs? Does it make our customers more loyal? Does it help us draw the best talent from others?) Without an honest assessment of these two questions, I have seen the discussion of unique advantage turn into a laundry list of things that an organization is quite good at but that are simply "table stakes" to operate a modern firm in their industry. These kinds of qualities are certainly necessary, but they will never differentiate you from the competition.

Putting Unique Advantages to Work

Knowing your unique advantages is critical because effective strategy is not about spotting opportunities that could work for *any* business. It is about finding opportunities that play to your strengths, where you will have an "unfair" advantage over other firms who might attempt the same thing. These opportunities are not just generically good ideas that any business should pursue. They are opportunities where you have a true right to win.

To leverage your unique advantages, look for how they may help you excel in creating value for customers. Just as important, find where they will help you capture value—achieving more profits than a competitor would from the same business model.

As part of its ambition to become a fintech company with services beyond credit card payments, Mastercard has pursued a variety of digital strategies. Each is designed to take advantage of Mastercard's unique strengths as a global hub for commercial transactions. One growth area has been in retail data analytics and insights. Mastercard has launched a service that allows businesses to tap into geographically mapped data on retail purchase patterns at the level of a city block. (Users have included banks, real estate developers, and even public policymakers looking to identify "food deserts" for intervention.) Another new strategy for Mastercard has been cybersecurity and digital identity authentication—using a range of new technologies (geolocation, biometrics, and more) to verify identity and thereby enable secure digital payments. Both its retail analytics and digital identity efforts are advantaged by Mastercard's existing strengths—its unparalleled network of business partners and its access to transactional data.

Another example comes from Intuit. When Rania Succar was recruited to work at the firm, it was already a market leader providing accounting, payroll, and payment tools to small and midsize enterprises under the QuickBooks brand. Succar was tasked with pursuing a new strategic opportunity for Intuit: providing credit for small businesses. The venture, she explained to me, was rooted in a unique advantage: "We believed at Intuit that we could solve small business lending in a way that no one else has. We have access to more data about small businesses—through what they put in QuickBooks—than anyone. And the hypothesis was that we could leverage that data on behalf of small businesses, to build best-in-class underwriting models and be able to serve small businesses profitably, and dramatically increase the access-to-capital rate." After experimentation and validation, the product launched as QuickBooks Capital, leveraging 26 billion data points to train an algorithm that could offer loans of up to $100,000 to small businesses in forty-nine states. Customers were delighted, with 90 percent saying it had a direct impact on the growth of their business.

RECIPROCAL ADVANTAGE

The most powerful strategies don't just leverage the existing advantages of the business to pursue new strategies. They pursue what I call a strategy

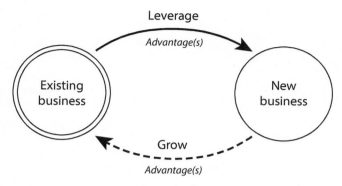

Figure 3.2.
Reciprocal advantage

of *reciprocal advantage*—as one business model succeeds, it both leverages and grows the core assets of the others, in a virtuous cycle (see figure 3.2). This is much more than a simple conglomerate that combines unconnected businesses (e.g., Samsung Group operating in electronics, financial services, and shipbuilding) or is vertically integrated within a single supply chain (e.g., an automaker buying a tire company). Instead, a reciprocal advantage organization combines business models that support each other's growth by sharing and improving the strategic assets that link each business (e.g., data, algorithms, and customers).

We can see this dynamic at work in the most successful businesses of the digital era—Google, Apple, Amazon, and others. Google Maps, for example, is an amazing product that the company is constantly evolving and innovating to be more useful for customers. Yet Google has done little to monetize Google Maps directly over the years. How can the company afford to keep investing in the product? The answer is that Google Maps not only *leverages* but also *grows* the unique advantages of Google's other business models—by capturing tremendous amounts of location data and greatly expanding the time that users spend logged into a Google service. Those other business models (search, display advertising, YouTube, and more) are where the company monetizes its advantages with high margins and tremendous revenue (see figure 3.3).

Reciprocal advantage is an opportunity in the DX of legacy firms as well. Walmart is pursuing this path as it looks at new digital strategies (see figure 3.4). Its e-commerce business, Walmart.com, can leverage the

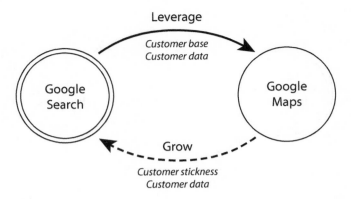

Figure 3.3.
Google's reciprocal advantage

proximity of stores for delivery to customers as well as the stores' sales data to predict product demand. But the website also expands Walmart's customer purchase data, with insights into browsing behavior. And by designing for online purchases to be returned in-store, the website also drives more traffic to the retail business. After establishing its e-commerce business, Walmart expanded into an online marketplace for third-party sellers. This strategy leveraged the company's existing online traffic. It also expanded the product selection on Walmart.com while generating more data on customers' search and product interests. More recently, Walmart has expanded into two promising new sectors—health care and finance—by launching services inside their stores (Walmart Health clinics and Walmart MoneyCenters, respectively). These new business models benefit from the

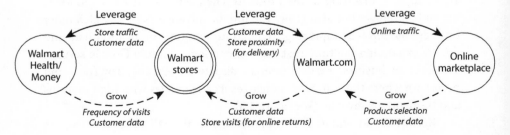

Figure 3.4.
Walmart's reciprocal advantage

stores' customer traffic as well as its data (e.g., in assessing a customer's creditworthiness). At the same time, these new businesses benefit the stores by growing their value to the customer, increasing the frequency of store visits, and generating even more data. As Shotts explained, "We think about what is the ecosystem that we're building . . . It's not only where do people spend their money, it's where do they spend their time, and how do you increase your value and relevance in both?"

Strategic Constraints

Just as important as understanding your unique advantages is understanding your strategic constraints. As you formulate new digital strategies, it is critical to identify any guard rails you won't touch, limits that your business will have to work within, or places you won't go (that other firms might).

We are not speaking here about the challenges of process, culture, talent, and technology, which the DX Roadmap is meant to address and improve with time and iteration. Rather, we are looking at constraints—like government regulation or legal agreements—that your business will need to work within, even as it digitally matures, and that anyone working in your organization needs to be cognizant of. Common types of strategic constraints include the following:

- *Ownership or legal structure*—Are you a publicly traded company? A private family business? State-owned? A franchise business? The CAA is part of a global organization, the Fédération Internationale de l'Automobile (FIA), which includes 246 automobile clubs in 146 countries, each facing very similar sources of digital disruption. But FIA is incorporated as a very small global organization, with budget and power residing in its affiliated national chapters. This structure means that FIA itself cannot dictate or even centrally manage a global digital strategy. Instead, it must focus on shaping the thinking of its national chapters, sharing their best practices, and coordinating their efforts to collaborate.
- *Partner agreements*—This often takes the form of channel conflict— when one company's ambitions conflict with those of its sales partners. Many firms I have advised have had to contend with such conflicts as they consider new digital business models. Others have been constrained by legal contracts with critical suppliers that prohibit them

from competing in certain product areas or certain markets. Recall that CNN was unable to bundle its most prized content (its daily cable news shows) into its CNN+ digital streaming service because this was prohibited by contracts with its cable distribution partners.

- *Legal regulation*—This is a major strategic constraint for many companies, especially in industries like health care and financial services. Banks like Citibank and Chase must contend with a wide range of regulations—around data privacy, know your customer (KYC) compliance, security and more—as they consider new digital strategies. Acuity's strategy for growth by geographic expansion is constrained by the different licensing requirements for insurers in all fifty U.S. states. In many cases, industry regulations are applied differently for new digital start-ups than for legacy businesses, leading to an uneven playing field.

- *Local infrastructure*—Infrastructure, such as the availability of broadband, strong transportation networks, or credit-scoring institutions, may pose significant constraints on your new strategies and business models. The availability of essential raw materials or a lack of technical standards within an industry can also pose significant constraints. When Amazon launched in India, its strategic constraints included government regulation but also logistics hurdles in a nation that lacked the shipping partners, highways, and street address system of more developed markets. When Alibaba first moved into mobile payments (launching Alipay), it was because the Chinese market lacked a well-developed system for consumer billing, like the credit cards seen in other countries.

- *Other factors*—Various other factors, such as a company's social mission, may pose strategic constraints. The New York Times Company's digital strategy is shaped by its commitment to its journalistic mission (not just to a goal of creating content that draws the most eyeballs). When Saudi Arabia's National Commercial Bank (NCB) began its DX, one major constraint was its low employee turnover and commitment not to let go of staff hired and trained to run a brick-and-mortar bank.

As you identify your constraints, recognize that they may have a variety of implications for decision making. Sometimes, a constraint will not rule out a strategy completely. Instead, that constraint can be treated as a risk factor to manage. New strategies that touch on the constraint will require thoughtful consideration of your risk appetite and of why you might be willing to push against it.

In other cases, your business will want to establish clear strategic red-lines that you will not cross. For example, Acuity's leadership has declared that they will not pursue growth by acquiring other risk-bearing entities (e.g., another insurer) because that would jeopardize Acuity's unique advantage of having exceptionally well-managed underwriting in its "book" of policies.

North Star Impact

The third element of a shared vision for a business is what I call your *North Star impact*, which is a statement of what you seek to achieve over time. Steve Jobs famously referred to Apple and its employees as seeking to "make a dent in the universe."[13] What impact do you seek to make through your DX? Your answer, like the North Star, can give guidance and direction to your efforts over time. As you consider your own North Star impact, try to answer these questions:

- What impact do you seek to have on the world?
- What problems are you uniquely able to solve?
- Why would the world miss you if you disappeared?

Your North Star impact should stem from your external knowledge of the world (future landscape) and internal knowledge of your organization (right to win), as well as an understanding of its history and founding. Your North Star impact should not simply be an inspiring string of words. It should be a statement that shapes business decisions for years to come—the investments you make, the people you recruit to leadership positions, and the strategies you choose to pursue.

Digital-native businesses are often known for defining a clear statement of the impact they seek to make. Google has a long-stated mission to "organize the world's information." Microsoft, with its long history of building technology tools for others, has a mission "to empower every person and every organization on the planet to achieve more." But we can also see examples from non-digital-native businesses. Every business I have seen with a cohesive agenda for DX has been guided by a very clear sense of the impact they want to make. Table 3.3 shows four examples.

Table 3.3.
North Star Impact at a Company Level

Company	North Star Impact for the Company's DX
Ford Motor	Meet the environmental and mobility needs of a growing, urbanizing planet with connected vehicles and transport systems.
Mastercard	Power and protect secure commerce in the digital world, across every device, partner, and platform.
BSH Home Appliances	Improve the experience of the digitally connected home consumer in their cooking and cleaning needs.
Domino's Pizza	Offer the ultimate pizza delivery experience for today's digitally connected consumers.

Two things stand out from the North Star impact statements given in table 3.3. First, they are extremely ambitious. None are goals that will be easily achieved and completed in the near term. Second, they encompass both the evolving core and the newest parts of the business. The goal speaks to everyone in every part of the organization. This means that everyone has a stake in the company's future.

While these four examples look at the impact of DX for an entire company, a North Star impact can be defined at any level of the organization. For Merck Animal Health, one team may define the impact of its DX for dairy farmers, while another defines the impact of DX for pet owners. For Acuity Insurance, its Personal Lines division would define the impact of DX for individuals and families with insurance, while the Commercial Lines division would define the impact for small businesses.

Why Versus What

The most important point to stress about any North Star impact is that it seeks to answer the question Why? rather than the question What? It should be a statement of what you hope to *achieve*, not what you hope to *do*. It is about outcomes not activities. This distinction is often missed by executives crafting what they believe to be mission statements or corporate strategies. Adam Bryant, who has interviewed hundreds of CEOs, has observed, "I've looked at a lot of strategy documents that go to a high altitude and just describe what the company does, not what they're trying to achieve."[14]

This is especially critical for DX. The focus of your North Star impact should be to answer "why" you must transform before you get into the eventual questions of "what" you will do. As I have written before, *digital transformation is not about technology*. I see many companies who cannot write a sentence about their DX efforts without leaping to terms like "artificial intelligence," "blockchain," and "metaverse." But before you start thinking about specific technologies that you will deploy, you must first identify the purpose for which you will be using them.

Domino's Pizza, for example, is not using digital technology for its own sake. This is why there has been no effort to 3D print its pepperoni, create a blockchain for its mozzarella, or sell non-fungible tokens (NFTs) for its garlic knots. While Domino's considers itself "a technology company as much as a pizza company," all of its digital efforts have been ruthlessly focused on the goal of delivering the ultimate experience for pizza ordering and delivery—simple, seamless, everywhere, fast, and stunningly convenient.

The most impressive Web3 start-ups I have seen are focused on the customer problem they aim to solve. For example, Qikfox's mission is "to make the internet more trustworthy, safe and reliable for consumers." It says nothing on whether the start-up will use blockchain or Javascript or some other technology to get there.

The goal of digital transformation should never be defined in terms of the technology you will use. Nor should it be defined in terms of the capabilities you will build (data analytics, machine learning, cloud infrastructure, etc.) or the processes you will use (customer journeys, agile squads, etc.). Instead, use your North Star impact to ensure that your DX efforts are focused on their impact. When Olivier Delabroy, vice president of marketing, describes the DX at industrial giant Air Liquide, he says that they are "obsessed" with defining digital as an enabler of value creation. "My goal for any transformation is that it is for the business, by the business . . . Not digital for the sake of digital, but to create value for customers, shareholders, and employees."

As you think about the impact you want to have, remember the power of intrinsic motivation and root your change efforts in the value that your DX will create for others—be they customers, partners, or society at large.

ZOOMING OUT

As you define your own North Star impact, it may be helpful to step back and redefine the category that you are in. I call this zooming out because it typically involves stepping back from a narrow product definition of your business to a broader definition based on the needs that you serve.

In thinking about its digital future, Ford zoomed out from the products it had previously made and focused on the challenges of environmental sustainability and mobility for a growing, urbanizing planet. Ford redefined itself from a car manufacturer to a mobility services company—with connected automobiles (networked, electric, autonomous) as a key component.

Longtime CEO Ajay Banga began Mastercard's digital journey by declaring that it was no longer a credit card company but a fintech using technology to enable commerce via payments and beyond payments. Mastercard zoomed out from the product category of "credit cards" or even "payments" to focus on the commercial needs of consumers and merchants in an always-on, mobile-connected world.

Of course, there are limits to zooming out. As one executive asked me, "If Ford is a mobility company, does that mean they should manufacture airplanes and compete with Boeing?" The key is to look to your right to win as you rethink the parameters of your business. Only a definition that matches your unique advantages and constraints will be sustainable in the highly competitive digital environment.

Try zooming out by asking, "What business are we really in?" Answering this question honestly can help any business to escape Ted Levitt's trap of strategic myopia and keep the focus on the problems it aims to solve.

Definition of Success

A statement of your North Star impact should be ambitious and qualitative in nature ("offer the ultimate pizza delivery experience," "power and protect digital commerce," etc.). But it can be very helpful to pair this kind of qualitative statement with one or more concrete metrics, what I call a definition of success. The point here is not to precisely measure everything you will do but to answer the simple question, How will we know if we're making major progress toward our North Star impact?

Mastercard's overarching goal is to transform from a legacy credit card company to a fintech that powers secure commerce in the digital world— and it has launched new business units focused on cybersecurity and other services for the financial sector. To measure progress toward its goal, the company has set two ambitious targets: to grow its services business at twice the rate of its core credit card business and to grow it to 40 percent of the firm's total revenue. Together, these two targets provide a powerful measure of success for Mastercard's DX.

Similarly, the New York Times has defined measurable targets for the transformation of its business model from advertising- and analog-first, to subscriber- and digital-first. The company's first target was to grow digital revenue to $800 million annually (a figure that would sustain the Times's journalism if the print edition went away completely). The second was to reach 10 million subscriptions across its news and non-news products.

Table 3.4 shows both these cases, the New York Times and Mastercard. In the table, I refer to the qualitative statement of each company's North Star impact as its "objective" and the measurable definition of success as its "key result(s)." These terms are borrowed from the management method known as objectives and key results (OKRs). Originating in Intel under CEO Andy Grove, the OKR method was refined by John Doerr (who began his career at Intel); evangelized by Doerr in his work as a VC investor and mentor; and eventually embraced by countless organizations, from Google and Intuit to Under Armour and the Gates Foundation. The key to the OKR method is to distinguish between your objectives (the goals you seek to achieve) and your key results (the measurable steps you believe will advance each objective).[15]

Your North Star impact (objective) offers a qualitative description of what you seek to achieve. It drives alignment by motivating everyone to think about how they can contribute to that ambitious goal. By contrast, your definition of success (key results) is quantified. It will never capture everything you want to achieve, but it drives alignment precisely because everyone can see the progress you are making objectively.

Table 3.4.
Definition of Success for a North Star Impact

Company	North Star Impact (Objective)	Definition of Success (Key Results)
Mastercard	Power and protect secure commerce in the digital world	• Grow new services businesses to 40 percent of the firm's revenue • Grow services twice as fast as core business in credit cards
New York Times Company	Secure our journalistic efforts in the digital economy	• Double digital revenue to $800 million, in five years (enough to sustain news reporting) • Reach 10 million subscriptions by 2025

There is tremendous power in aligning teams and individuals across an organization with clear, ambitious, and measurable goals like this. One example I have seen came from Google in the early days of its YouTube business. In 2012, YouTube's leadership set an audacious goal to grow the number of hours of video watched on its platform by a factor of ten, to reach 1 billion hours per day. This number seemed astronomical at the start, but it became a rallying cry across the business. Diverse teams each contributed to the goal by driving innovations in everything from YouTube's search and recommendation algorithm to improving its data centers for better bandwidth, to adding virtual reality and gaming videos for the first time, to improving the living room experience of "casting" YouTube onto your television. As YouTube CEO Susan Wojcicki explained, the point was for leaders to say to everyone in the company, "This is the direction we want to go, now tell us how you're going to get there."[16]

Another reason to craft a definition of success is to engage everyone in the process of choosing metrics. One of the key principles of the OKR method is that it is practiced at all levels of the organization, from the CEO to the bottom of the organizational chart. Every team is involved, constantly asking themselves, "what is our objective?" and "how will we know if we are achieving it?"

I have long held that the most important part of measurement is engaging in a thoughtful debate about what your metrics should be. Done right, this process brings about strategic alignment and employee empowerment. You will have already reaped 90 percent of the benefit of your metrics— before you even track anything!

Business Theory

To quote social psychologist Kurt Lewin, "There is nothing so practical as a good theory."[17] The fourth and last element of a shared vision is thus a *business theory*: your hypothesis about how you expect to recover the investments you will make for the future.[18] Your hypothesis should explain how you will not only create value for customers but capture value in turn. Let me be clear: a business theory is a causal theory that doing X will lead to Y, but it is *not a business case*, with financial projections of specific outcomes at specific times. It is not a quantitative model spelling out things like unit economics, gross margins, or your precise point of profitability. Instead, a business theory addresses broader, directional questions. Will your financial return come from selling more, reducing costs, generating new sources of revenue, or from some mix of these? Will your growth stem from internal innovations, acquisitions, or a mix of both?

Some of the most famous business theories have been captured in visual form. Walt Disney's diagram (easily found on the internet but guarded from reproduction here by Disney's licensing strictures) mapped out the business theory that would lead his company to decades of profitable growth. Sketched in 1957 (two years after the launch of Disneyland), the diagram visualized how each expansion beyond Disney's core business leverages, creates additional revenue from, and reinvigorates the core. The sketch places Disney's theatrical films business—with its unique advantage of creative talent—in the center of a web of crisscrossing, labeled arrows. The arrows link the core to all other categories—theme parks, television, music, books, magazines, comics, merchandise, and character licensing— and interlink these ventures, showing how the core and beyond-the-core categories cross-pollinate one another. For example, films "feed tunes and talent" to music; music "helps 'kick off' new [and reissued] films" and "keeps films in mind," while the theme park generates "ideas for albums" and "plugs movies."[19]

Great digital-era businesses have also been built on simple business theories. Amazon's e-commerce was guided from the beginning on a very specific theory. Jeff Bezos proclaimed it an "article of faith" that keeping Amazon's prices low would earn customer trust and that customer trust would drive free cash flow over the long term.[20] This theory was expanded when Amazon included third-party sellers on its site for the first time. In some ways, this move appeared risky—introducing competitors directly to Amazon's customers. But Bezos had a new business theory, which he called Amazon's "virtuous cycle" (or "flywheel"). The theory—which he sketched on a napkin (see figure 3.5)—explained how third-party sellers would grow Amazon's e-commerce business through cycles of mutual benefit. Amazon's low prices and large selection had created an experience that attracted customers. That customer traffic would attract third-party sellers to sell on Amazon. Third-party sellers would not only pay a commission; they would further expand the product selection on the site. They would also lower Amazon's cost structure—by increasing the use of fixed assets like servers and warehouses—which would enable Amazon to lower its prices even further. Lower prices and bigger product selection would attract even more customers, driving growth in a virtuous cycle.[21]

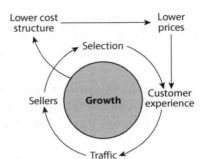

Figure 3.5.
Amazon's virtuous cycle business theory, circa 2001

A good business theory is essential for companies looking to invest significant resources in DX. When Saudi Arabia's NCB began its digital transformation, CDO Omar Hashem knew that it would not be easy or cheap.[22] In order to justify the large investments NCB would be making (in back-end technology, consumer-facing digital experiences, and retraining its retail workforce), the bank needed a theory for how digital investment would create value for the firm. Hashem and his CEO started with two major insights about their business. First, NCB was suffering from legacy IT systems whose bugs were causing a low straight-through processing rate. This meant that far too many transactions required manual intervention by bank staff each day. Second, NCB had a large untapped opportunity to serve unbanked customers beyond the urban areas of Saudi Arabia that the firm had historically served. The untapped market was well known, but NCB lacked the human resources to serve customers there.

Based on this, NCB's leaders developed a clear business theory for DX: reducing errors in the bank's straight-through processing would make it possible to design a best-in-class banking app and free employees to pursue new unbanked markets. At the same time, the improved digital app experience would help them win those new markets. The strategy took years to execute, but the results were clear: processing errors declined, customer use of NCB's apps rose, and the redeployed workforce drove a major geographic expansion. Without a clear theory for how DX would pay off, NCB might never have sustained the investments it took to make all this happen.

Pick Your Value Drivers

How do you get started on your own business theory? One way is to pick a few key value drivers for your DX. These value drivers are broad categories where you expect digital to generate value for your organization. I have seen several companies use the following value drivers to think about their DX:

- *Customer experience (CX)*—This includes any financial benefit from digital innovations that touch the customer: new products, new services, improved experiences, or changes in marketing. Typically, value is measured from customer acquisition, customer retention, and average revenue per user.
- *Operational excellence (OpEx)*—This is any financial benefit from digital innovations that improve your operations or reduce risk to your business, including efficiencies in your workforce and supply chain (e.g., through data, AI, automation, or other measures). Typically, this is measured in cost reductions.
- *New business models (NBMs)*—The first two drivers describe value from improving your current business, but this driver encompasses value from any new business models that you bring to market.

These three value drivers work well. However, you may want to define different value drivers for your organization. One nonprofit organization that I have advised defined its value drivers as *impact* (societal value created in support of its mission), *relevance* (loyalty and affinity among its millions of members, who are critical to the organization's work and financial health), and *revenue* (financial measures linked to its different business models). Every digital initiative at the nonprofit must define its contribution to one or more of these drivers to be approved.

Once you have agreed on your value drivers for DX, the next question is, Where do you expect the most value? Try to define a pie chart with an expected mix of your value drivers. Do you expect digital efforts to generate 50 percent of their value from OpEx, 40 percent from CX, and 10 percent from NBMs? Or is the mix 20 percent, 30 percent, and 50 percent? This is not a budgeting process but a conversation on priorities. Agreeing on expected value drivers will bring clarity to everyone's digital efforts. When Mario Pieper joined BSH as its first CDO, the CEO made clear that his number-one focus was top-line growth—with a target to double revenues while growing at twice the rate of peers. "When I heard that, it was clear we were not talking about using digital mostly for efficiencies in our production line," Pieper told me. "We would be looking at customer growth, at selling more valuable products, yes. But we would also need new business models like [digital] services that could expand us into new sources of revenue."

Benefits of a Business Theory

A clear business theory has many benefits. The first is alignment on the results you are hoping for. Taking the time to reach agreement among your top stakeholders on a business theory for DX is incredibly important. It is much better to get all stakeholders aligned on the theory for a modest investment than to secure a big budget for your DX without everyone agreeing on what it is meant to deliver. Far too many digital transformations begin with no shared agreement on how or when investments are meant to pay for themselves.

Another benefit of a business theory is to guide resource allocation. United Technologies Corporation's (UTC) CDO Vince Campisi used his own set of value drivers to think through the resource allocation that made the most sense for his company's DX efforts. Campisi defined the value drivers for UTC's digital efforts as "rebooting productivity" (OpEx), redesigning the current customer experience (CX), and pursuing new business models based on data and analytics from the industrial equipment UTC sold (NBMs). When he assessed the company's existing efforts, he estimated that 95 percent of digital resources were being spent on OpEx, 5 percent on CX, and 0 percent on NBMs. After setting the business theory for UTC's digital agenda, he quickly rebalanced: OpEx was still the largest part, at 70 percent, but the other two value drivers finally received enough resources to make a difference.

The third benefit of a business theory is that it can point you toward the right metrics (or key results) to assess your unique digital efforts. For NCB, its business theory suggested early metrics as it reconfigured IT systems (measuring the straight-through processing rate and how much time employees spent fixing bugs). Later, the theory suggested metrics to track business impact (customer expansion into new markets and user adoption of NCB's banking app). Amazon's virtuous cycle theory implies several metrics for tracking the health of its e-commerce business:

product selection, overhead costs, product pricing, and customer traffic and retention.

BUSINESS THEORY AND SHAREHOLDER COMMUNICATIONS

For any publicly held company, a business theory has one more important benefit: communicating your vision to shareholders. Any CEO of a public company has a responsibility to communicate the company's shared vision to investors and explain how it will generate financial returns. Every year since its IPO, Amazon's CEO has published a letter to shareholders that spells out the business theory for the company and how it relates to that year's investments.

When Disney CEO Bob Iger decided to make a huge strategic bet on streaming media with the launch of Disney+, he knew he would have to explain his business theory to investors. At the time, Disney had been licensing its most prized content (classic movies from Disney, Pixar, Star Wars, and Marvel) to Netflix and other digital streamers. But those lucrative licensing agreements would have to end before Disney+ could launch with a library of exclusive content. So Iger laid out his vision to investors and explained the thinking behind it. Disney's unique content was its greatest asset. For years, he said, Disney had been "selling our nuclear weapons technology" to a competitor (Netflix). By ending those agreements, Disney would be hit by a "substantial decrease in our revenue" in the short term. But, as Iger explained, it would "thrust us into a [streaming] business that is the most compelling growth engine in the media today."[23] Shutting off a current, renewable revenue stream is a risky move for any publicly traded company. Iger was very clear that Disney+ would not turn a profit in its early years. But when it launched in 2019, shareholders responded by raising Disney's stock price by 9 percent in two days.[24]

The aim of a good business theory is not to persuade every investor of your vision for the company. It is to explain your vision so that investors who will back it are drawn to your stock, while those who are not in agreement can shift their holdings to other companies. Bezos credits Warren Buffett for explaining this to him: "[Buffett] says, 'You can hold a rock concert, and that's OK. You can hold a ballet, and that's OK. Just don't hold a rock concert and advertise it as a ballet.' The job of the public company is to be clear about whether you're holding a ballet or a rock concert, and then investors can opt into that."[25]

Tool: Shared Vision Map

We have now seen the key elements of a shared vision for the future and why it is essential to any organization seeking DX. Our first planning tool, the Shared Vision Map, is designed to help craft a shared vision that is unique to your organization and that can align employees, investors, and other stakeholders behind your DX (see figure 3.6) Let's briefly walk through each step of the tool to see how to apply the Map in your business.

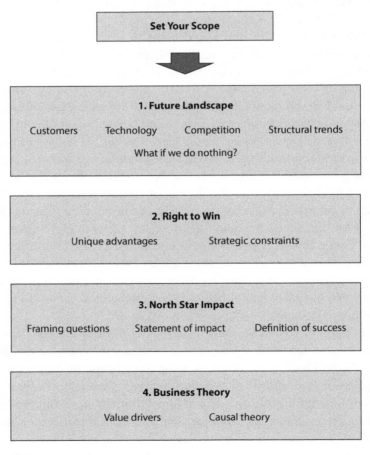

Figure 3.6.
The Shared Vision Map

Set Your Level

Before getting started, the most important step is to set the level at which you are trying to define a shared vision. Is this meant to be the shared vision for a company-wide digital transformation? Or are you tasked with leading DX efforts within a single business unit, or within a function (like marketing, HR, or supply chain)? The Shared Vision Map can be used at any of these levels or even at the level of an individual team to define where its world is going and the role it will seek to play in that future. Let's start by picking the level for which you are defining a shared vision.

1. Future Landscape

The first element of your shared vision will be your future landscape, which describes where your world is going and how the context of your business is changing. Be sure to involve as many perspectives as possible in crafting this; seek out customers, business partners, outside analysts, and diverse points of view from people at all levels within your organization. Your goal is to synthesize these different perspectives to define a rich landscape view of where your world is going. As you do this, focus on describing the four areas of customers, technology, competition, and structural trends.

CUSTOMERS

- *Changing needs and expectations*—How are your customers' needs changing in the digital era? What new expectations do they have from businesses like yours?
- *Legacy versus growth customers*—How do your long-standing customers differ from the customers driving your current growth?
- *Emerging customer segments*—Are there any customer segments you hope to target for the first time? What have you learned about their preferences and needs?

TECHNOLOGY

- *Commercialized technology*—Look to digital technologies that have ample market adoption. Which of these is most relevant to your business? Which have been adopted by your customers? By your partners? What use cases from other industries could be applied to your own?

- *Viable technology*—Look at technologies that are technically proven but whose applications are not clear. Can any of them be applied to solve specific customer or business problems in your industry? Can you learn from another sector that has found a viable use case?
- *Emerging technology*—Look at technology still in technical development. Where are VCs and large technology firms investing? Which technologies, if they were to become available in the future, might have the biggest impact on your industry?

COMPETITION

- *New products and services*—What new products and services are appearing in your industry? Which ones are coming soon but are already generating interest?
- *New entrants*—Who are the new digital-era entrants into your industry? Look at partners, disruptors, and substitutes.
- *Competitive Value Train analysis*—Apply the Competitive Value Train to analyze new entrants: how they intersect your current business model, and the mix of threat and opportunity they pose.
- *Pace of change*—How fast is change coming to different parts of your business? Who is moving faster and slower in your industry?
- *Threat levels*—How severe is the threat of digital change to different parts of your business? Look at different business units, customer segments, and product lines.

STRUCTURAL TRENDS

Look at broader structural trends that may have an impact on your operating environment, including demographics, talent, regulations, supply chains, macroeconomics, and more. Which ones are or may become key drivers of change for your industry? If you operate in different markets globally, look at commonalities and differences in these trends. Consider volatility: Are these trends likely to remain steady, or do you need to prepare for possible dramatic shifts?

WHAT IF WE DO NOTHING?

Your future landscape provides a clear viewpoint on the most important ways that your world is changing and the threats and opportunities to your unique business. Your future landscape should also answer the critical question, What happens if we do nothing?

Discuss the likely impact of trends on your business if you were to simply "stay the course." Consider posing the following question to colleagues: *If we change nothing—at what time in the future might we no longer be in business?* (There is no correct answer. The only wrong answer is never.) If some of your team members think the threat of total disruption is five years away, but others say thirty years, engage in a robust discussion and come to a shared point of view.

2. Right to Win

The second element of any shared vision is your right to win in the future you see. Where and how does your business have a unique reason to succeed in the future?

UNIQUE ADVANTAGES

Start by generating a list of your organization's advantages as it competes against similar organizations. Think of your strengths and advantages in any of the following areas:

- *Assets*—tangible assets and intangible assets
- *Capabilities*—skills, insights, training, or talent
- *Relationships*—brand reputation, customer relationships, or business partnerships
- *Positioning*—differentiation from peers in where you compete and how you go to market
- *Culture and process*—employee culture, effective management, speed to market
- *Other*—any strengths that don't fit the above categories

For each advantage you have listed, define how it benefits your organization. For example, you might define a unique advantage as your "brand reputation as an innovator." But how specifically does that *benefit* your company? (Does it lead to higher customer retention? Help you market new offerings? Attract top talent for your team?) If you cannot identify a clear business benefit, strike that item from your list. Score each of your remaining advantages on two dimensions:

- How unique they are
- How beneficial they are to your business

Now create a matrix of your advantages on the two dimensions. Your important advantages will score at the top on uniqueness or benefit. The most important will score at the top on both.

STRATEGIC CONSTRAINTS

Next, identify the constraints that will affect which strategic choices are available to you. Consider each of these areas:

- *Ownership or legal structure*
- *Partner relationships*
- *Social mission*
- *Regulation*
- *Local infrastructure*
- *Other industry constraints*

For each constraint you have identified, ask: What limit will this impose on your strategy? For example, do differences in regulations mean that you will need to pilot digital strategies in certain markets first, before attempting them in others?

Looking at all your constraints, create a list of your biggest strategic risks. What is your risk appetite for each? (Are you willing to take on a high amount of risk, a moderate amount, or no risk at all in this area for the right opportunity?) Then ask what trade-offs would make you consider assuming such a risk. (For example, are you willing to risk greater regulatory scrutiny to expand your business into a new product category or region?) Lastly, look at any constraints that seem inviolable: strategic redlines that you would never cross. Spell out any specific strategies that are completely off limits, and why. This will indicate when this redline might be reconsidered should conditions change.

3. North Star Impact

The third element of your shared vision is your North Star impact—what you seek to achieve over time and why.

FRAMING QUESTIONS

As you consider your North Star impact, try to answer these questions:

- What impact do we seek to have on the world?
- What problems are we uniquely able to solve?
- Why would the world miss us if we disappeared?

Try to reframe your business by *zooming out*, expanding your definition of your business. Ask yourself these questions:

- What products or services do we deliver?
- What fundamental customer needs do these products serve?
- What business are we *really* in?

STATEMENT OF IMPACT

You are now ready to write a statement of the impact you seek to have. As you write a North Star impact statement, make sure you focus on why you do things and not on what you do as a business. Your statement should describe outcomes and impact—not actions taken, tools used, or products delivered.

What is the most important goal that you would seek to rally your team, business unit, or company to achieve in its DX? Look to the future: What new problems could digital technologies enable you to solve that you couldn't solve before? How might DX enable you to serve a new type of customer? What problems have emerged in the digital era that you may be able to address?

Once you have a draft statement of impact, try applying the following tests:

- Is it ambitious (for example, not something you could complete in three years)?

- Does it encompass all your work (both long-standing work and new ventures)?
- Does it provide intrinsic motivation to employees (describing the value they will create for customers, partners, or society)?

DEFINITION OF SUCCESS

Next, pair this impact statement with a few concrete metrics—your "definition of success." These metrics do not need to capture everything that you will do in your DX, but they should be strong indicators that you are making progress toward your North Star impact. Choose one to three metrics that are clearly measurable and assign ambitious targets that will take you years to achieve. These metrics should align your DX work and provide evidence of its long-term value creation.

4. Business Theory

The last element of your shared vision is your business theory. Think of the kinds of digital investments you anticipate making. How do you think those investments will pay for themselves over time?

VALUE DRIVERS

Try to choose three to five broad value drivers that capture the different types of value your DX efforts will bring. Consider these common value drivers: customer experience, operational excellence, and new business models. Also consider your own formulation of the value drivers that apply to your business. If you are a mission-driven organization (e.g., a nonprofit, public sector, or nongovernment organization), choose value drivers that define the impact you are seeking from your DX. Create a pie chart with the expected mix of your value drivers. What percentage of the value from digital do you expect from each driver?

CAUSAL THEORY

Try to go beyond your value drivers and sketch a working theory of how your investments will drive value within your firm. Look to examples like the business theories of Disney, Amazon, and NCB.

What current barriers do you see to growth or profitability? What new actions will you be taking? What do you believe will be the results of those actions? Do you see a virtuous cycle where one positive change will lead to another?

As you sketch a business theory for your DX, ask yourself if it will pass the investor test. If you explained your theory to your CFO or in a letter to shareholders, do you think they would be persuaded to give you the resources to pursue your vision?

Vision from the Bottom Up

A shared vision is often thought of as coming from the top, but a shared vision is not a tool meant for command-and-control leadership. In a classic top-down organization, there is no need for a shared vision. Employees do not need to understand the long-range thinking behind their tasks. They don't need to understand what mission or purpose guides the organization (although that may improve morale). They just need to be told what to do and what numbers to hit for their next performance review.

But a shared vision is essential to leading any organization in a truly bottom-up fashion. Only when everyone is aligned around a vision of where the business is going and why can individuals and teams be given real ownership and accountability for decisions. This is what unleashes the speed and adaptability at every level that are the hallmarks of a bottom-up organization. As Bill Ford said, "A clear view of the future—once you have that, you make decisions very rapidly."[26]

A Vision at Every Level

We often think of a shared vision as something that sits at the level of the entire organization, and that central shared vision is certainly essential. But for real transformation to happen, every part of the organization should define a shared vision at its own level. That means a vision for each business unit, each function, and each team.

If you are leading DX for the marketing function of your business, for example, it is imperative to define a future landscape for marketing: Where do you see the future of your work as you look to new marketing technologies, new customer expectations, and new marketing partners and competitors? What new structural trends, such as data privacy regulations, will affect you?

The marketing team should define the remaining elements of a shared vision as well. What is the North Star impact that you seek to achieve through DX of your marketing? What are the unique advantages and strategic limits that shape your right to win? What is your business theory for how DX in marketing will deliver financial returns? What are the value drivers for digital in your part of the business?

Cascading Up, Not Down

Whatever level you start from in defining your vision, what you do next is critical. Typically, when I talk about a shared vision, executives will say "I've got it! The leaders come up with this, and then we cascade it down to the rest of the organization." "Cascading down" means that a plan is set at the top by leaders who tell their next reports, who tell theirs, and so on, down the organizational chart. But that is not the way transformation happens in cases of great DX success. I encourage leaders to think instead about what I call cascading up.

The difference between cascading down and cascading up is in the conversation that happens at each juncture. In a top-down conversation, the leader says, "This is my goal," and *tells* their direct reports, "Here is what I need you to do to support this." In a bottom-up conversation, the leader says, "This is my goal," and *asks* their direct reports, "What do you think you should do to support this?" Ideas then come from those who will do the work. Discussion ensues. The leader must still sign off on the plan, but it is each person's responsibility to propose what role they should take and what goals they should achieve. Once an agreement is reached, each of those direct reports can have the same bottom-up conversation with those who report to them.

Recall YouTube's audacious goal to grow its total daily watch time by a factor of ten. Leaders did not tell every team what they needed to do to support the goal. They told them the goal and asked, "How are you going to help us to achieve this? What metric and target do you propose for your own work?"

As you share your vision for DX with others, keep in mind that your role as a leader is not what it would be in a traditional top-down organization. Leadership in the digital era consists of three jobs: define a vision of where you are going and why, communicate and align everyone to that vision, and enable others to act in support of that vision.

~

No effective digital transformation can start without first aligning everyone with a shared vision of the future. A shared vision provides alignment of purpose and direction. It provides a shared understanding of where your world is going and the role your business will play in the digital future. A shared vision also provides the motivation for change. For investors and executives managing P&Ls, your business theory provides extrinsic motivation—an answer to how digital will generate financial rewards. This will be essential to securing the long-term resources for your transformation. For employees, your North Star impact will provide intrinsic motivation—through a promise of value created for customers, society, and others. This will be essential to muster the sustained effort, will, and creativity for ongoing change. Both your business theory and your North Star impact require that you have a clear and compelling view of your future landscape and your unique right to win.

A shared vision can shape the actions of a business for years. Nearly a decade after Bill Ford's TED speech, the company's Chief Transformation Officer Marcy Klevorn told me that "the themes in that speech were a lot of my and my team's inspiration for how we prioritized work." But a shared vision is also a work in progress. In the DX Roadmap, you do not "finish" your shared vision and put it on the shelf as you proceed to the next step. You continue to work at it, deepen it, and renew it, even as you begin to use that vision as the foundation for the next steps of the DX Roadmap. With the first draft in hand, you are not finished with your shared vision, but you are ready to begin your next step.

When starting a DX, many organizations are quickly overwhelmed with ideas for digital projects and innovations, with no criteria to judge them. A compelling shared vision—with a commitment to empowering teams—will quickly inspire ideas from every level of an organization. How do you choose among these ideas and avoid moving in 100 directions at once? In the next chapter, we will see how any leader can define strategic priorities to pursue the goals of a shared vision. You may think of these priorities as critical problems to be solved or as opportunities for growth. Together, they will give focus to your digital efforts—defining the scope of where you will compete and seek to create value with your DX.

4

Step 2: Pick the Problems
That Matter Most

PRIORITIES

When Imran Haque stepped into a new role leading digital strategy for Pfizer Animal Health, he was an ideal candidate. Haque had started his career at a digital agency and founded a health-care start-up before moving into the corporate world of pharmaceuticals. At Pfizer, he had led a variety of technology projects: applying big data to the clinical trials processes, revamping the analytics tool for safety and risk management, and overseeing technology investments for worldwide operations. Now Haque was tasked with a different role: defining a digital growth strategy for the animal health business unit, which would soon be spun out as a separate business named Zoetis.

Haque began by studying major trends that would define the digital future of animal health. In the broader technology landscape, he tracked the rise of the mobile web and social media, the growth of online education, and trends in cloud computing, big data, and the Internet of Things (IoT). The animal health industry had not been a pioneer in digital innovation, but Haque was focused less on his peer businesses than on the rapidly changing needs of his customers. These included pet owners; agricultural businesses raising cattle, swine, poultry, and fish; and the veterinarians who, up until now, were both the sales channel and the key influencer of every purchase decision. Among these customers, Haque observed a growing appetite for animal health content, a nascent interest in e-commerce, and evolving needs in animal husbandry, such as the growing importance of diagnostics as farmers sought to spot disease earlier in their animals.

With a clear vision of the future, Haque's next challenge was turning this into a strategy for growth. He did this by looking for specific customer problems to solve and business opportunities to leverage. He developed a short list of strategic priorities for his business, including (1) improve the customer's digital path to purchase—from online discovery to e-commerce, to loyalty programs; (2) provide online learning and content for animal health professionals; (3) enter the growing diagnostics market to detect and prevent illness in animals; and (4) empower livestock management with digital tracking and analytics. Where others in his industry were still focused on optimizing their legacy operations and sales channels, Haque now had a clear set of priorities for growth.

These strategic priorities led Haque and his team to launch a wide range of digital innovations over the next several years. Some fell under the umbrella of digital marketing—revamping the mobile, web, and social media presence of a diverse family of product brands; growing a digital loyalty program for the cattle industry; and launching the industry's first e-commerce channel. Others were opportunities for new revenue streams, including e-learning training and certifications for veterinarians, and paid content publishing in the form of wellness reports targeting different customer segments. Still others involved new business models. Zoetis launched a digitally powered services business for animal husbandry, helping farmers with everything from digital billing to verifying which pigs were impregnated. The firm moved quickly into the diagnostics business through internal innovations and several start-up acquisitions. And with new IoT ventures like Smart Bow, Zoetis gave cattle owners the ability to track their herd using small sensors on each animal that could measure and analyze its movements, water and food consumption, and vital signs to detect sickness, health, and the ideal timing for impregnation.

Zoetis's digital innovations were widely adopted by customers and built support for digital transformation (DX) over time throughout the organization. During its first four years as a public company, and while

Haque served as head of digital business, Zoetis grew from a $13 billion market cap at launch to $60 billion. Throughout that time, Haque led and supported a diverse range of digital initiatives. These initiatives did not arise haphazardly but from a clear and evolving list of strategic priorities for digital growth.

Why Priorities Matter

As we consider the role of strategy in DX, it is helpful to start with a simple question—why does any organization *need* a strategy? Management theory tells us that the purpose of strategy is to guide decision making by defining priorities amid limited resources. Every business must make critical trade-offs between options. Thus, strategy is fundamentally about choices—defining the opportunities you will focus on and, just as important, those you will not. As Michael Porter observes, "The essence of strategy is choosing what *not* to do."[1]

Defining strategic priorities might seem like an obvious early step in DX. We can see how well it worked for Zoetis. But strategy is often overlooked. As one seasoned CDO confided to me, "This is what makes it so difficult to find peers to talk to [at other firms]. They haven't done that exercise. They went a different route: doing digital projects, but without a strategic focus."

In too many organizations, DX operates in a strategic vacuum, as little more than a collection of individual projects. Without clear priorities for growth, it is extremely common for a business to find itself overwhelmed with ideas for new digital projects. Lacking any clear criteria for decision making, digital becomes hijacked by the latest shiny new things from the technology world. Often, DX becomes limited to cost cutting and optimization of legacy processes. At worst, digital may be handed off to a dedicated team, separate from the day-to-day challenges of the business. This small group focuses on blue-sky digital ideas while the rest of the firm continues their work unchanged.

In the first step of the Digital Transformation (DX) Roadmap, your task was to define a shared vision of the digital future for your firm. In the second step of the Roadmap, you must build on that vision by defining specific priorities for investment of your limited resources and time. What are your biggest digital priorities for the future? Think of these as *problems* to be solved for your customers and your business, and as *opportunities* for your firm to create and capture new value.

Table 4.1.
What's at Stake—Step 2: Priorities

Symptoms of Failure: Priorities	Symptoms of Success: Priorities
• Digital transformation is a series of scattered projects with no clear direction.	• Clear priorities provide direction to digital transformation across the organization.
• Digital efforts are defined by the technologies they use.	• Digital efforts are defined by the problems they solve and opportunities they pursue.
• Digital is focused solely on operations, cost cutting, and optimizing the current business.	• Digital is focused on future growth as well as improving the current business.
• A few people in the organization drive digital while the rest stick to old ways of working.	• Every department is pursuing its own digital ventures, with a backlog of ideas to try next.
• Transformation is disconnected from business needs and loses support over time.	• Transformation is linked to the needs of the business and gains support over time.

Your conversation here should not be about technology ("we need to leverage machine learning") or digital skills ("we need people who understand crypto"). It should be about priorities for growth and value creation. You are not yet looking for a list of digital projects or innovation ideas. Instead, you are defining, at the start, *where* you will look for innovations— that is, the *scope* of ideas you will explore. Instead of new digital products or solutions, think first about where you will innovate and compete.

Picking the priorities that matter most to the future of your business is not easy. But without a defined set of strategic priorities, any DX will fail to achieve a lasting impact. Table 4.1 shows some of the key symptoms of success versus failure in Step 2 of the DX Roadmap.

What's Ahead

In this chapter, I will take you through Step 2 of the Roadmap. We will see how any organization and any leader can define a focused set of strategic priorities for their DX efforts. We will look through two lenses—*problems* and *opportunities*—and see the power of each to help define your strategic priorities. We will see how popular methods—such as customer journey maps and customer interviews—can help to identify valuable problems and opportunities. We will introduce two new tools: problem/opportunity statements (to crystalize your strategic priorities and spark ideas for new innovation) and the Problem/Opportunity Matrix (to define strategic priorities at any level of the organization). We will also learn why engaging everyone in the strategy process is critical to making the shift from a top-down to a bottom-up organization.

The Problem Lens

The first lens through which we must define our strategic priorities is the *problem* lens. This entails thinking about strategy in terms of a set of problems that we aim to solve rather than in terms of known solutions that we can build. For example, rather than simply focusing on ways to sell more cattle antibiotics, Zoetis chose to focus on a major problem for farmers— how to track vital signs in a large herd in order to detect illness and treat it earlier. Other problems that Zoetis chose include veterinarians' need for professional training and certification, and pet owners' need to shop more easily for products like medicated shampoos.

In this chapter, I'll guide you on using the problem lens effectively for your DX. At the start, it's important to note that much of modern innovation practice is rooted in this perspective. In both agile and product management, every cross-functional team is defined in terms of a persistent problem that it is working to solve iteratively over time, whether as part of launching a new product or optimizing a long-standing business process. In design thinking, the problem lens matches a key goal study and solve problems that are complex, human-centered, and systems-based. Many of the most popular tools in design thinking are focused on problem definition. Thomas Wedell-Wedellsborg's book *What's Your Problem?* encapsulates much of the best of this thinking.[2]

You may recognize the problem lens under many other names; an innovation "problem" may be called a "pain point," a customer's "job to be done," or an "unmet need." As Microsoft CEO Satya Nadella has stressed, "The more we can invoke our ability to meet unmet, unarticulated needs, that's the source of innovation."[3]

Whatever you call it, the problem lens requires a major shift for traditional organizations. Product managers often refer to this shift as "product thinking" or a "product mindset." Never mind that these names are a bit misleading; the point is that you should focus on the *problem* you aim to solve rather than on the *product* you think you might build.[4] This shift is aptly described in one of Amazon's innovation principles as "working backwards from customer needs."[5]

Fall in Love with the Problem, Not the Solution

Focusing on customer problems is not easy. In most companies, people love to start with the solution in mind: "Tell me what to build, and I will tell you how we deliver it!" The natural tendency in an established business is to focus on your own core competencies and the products and services you deliver. Instead, you must frame everything from the customer's point of view rather than your own. It all begins with asking, What is our customer's need? How will we fill it? In a famous analogy of Ted Levitt's, if you are running a hardware store, you may think you are *selling* a quarter-inch drill bit, but the customer is *buying* a quarter-inch hole. Jeff Bezos applied the same reverse thinking to Amazon's e-commerce business, observing, "We don't make money when we sell things. We make money when we help customers make purchase decisions."[6]

This mental reversal requires humility and a willingness to temper our enthusiasm for our initial ideas. The lean start-up method recognizes that most entrepreneurs begin with a solution in mind—some brilliant invention they want to bring into the world. Hence, the method starts with talking to customers in order to validate what problem your innovation would really solve.

Very often, the problem lens requires some coaxing. At United Technologies Corporation's (UTC) digital accelerator, managers from different business units regularly bring in requests for a new digital solution they would like built. The first job of the digital accelerator team is to engage the manager in a workshop to define a clear problem statement, including the customer experience or outcome the business is trying to create. The business unit's initial request is really "a problem disguised as a solution," says CDO Vince Campisi. "Ten out of ten times, when an opportunity walks in our door—by the time it leaves, the solution we will actually build looks a lot different."[7]

Perhaps the biggest benefit of focusing on the problem is that it helps you look more broadly at possible solutions to explore. Mario Pieper explained how it helped his team at BSH Home Appliances to look beyond incremental innovations—such as adding recipe screens to its refrigerators—to envision wholly new ways to help customers meet their kitchen needs. "If the pain point of somebody in the kitchen is that he wants to eat, then of course you can cook, but you also can order something," Pieper observed. "The question is, should we also discover innovations where we deliver food and do not use the kitchen? This is exactly what we wanted to do—asking ourselves 'what is the best solution for the problem?' and not 'what product do we have and what can we do with it?'"

As you pursue any effort at DX, it is critical to understand that technology itself can become a distraction from strategy. Too often, business managers become fixated on a specific new technology and how they are going to use it rather than focusing on the problems they are trying to solve (see the box "The Distraction of New Technology"). For years, I have been telling executives that AI is not a strategy. The same is true of blockchain, NFTs, Web3, or any other technology. But what do you do if your organization has already allocated resources to a dedicated team focused on a technology like AI or blockchain? A common workaround I have seen is to ask that team to focus on a few early use cases. In other words, pick a few problems you think could be solved using this new capability and test to see if you can deliver results. In this parlance, "use case" becomes a synonym for a business problem—a substitute that seems palatable to those who think technology first.

The Distraction of New Technology

New technology can exert a powerful gravitational pull, drawing business leaders' attention away from strategic thinking and the focus on problems. When any new technology reaches the peak of its hype cycle (think IoT in 2016, blockchain in 2019, metaverse in 2022), less passionate observers will describe it as "a solution in search of a problem." This description rings true, but it describes a particular stage—before the attention shifts to solving real-world problems.

Let me give an example. During the period 2012–2014, a series of breakthroughs in artificial neural networks (using what is called deep learning for pattern matching) sparked tremendous excitement about the potential for AI. In a series of demonstrations, technologists at Google demonstrated for the first time that AI systems trained on vast amounts of data could detect pictures of cats among images pulled from the Web. Other companies made similar dazzling demonstrations of how deep learning could understand speech. This generated tremendous excitement about the little-known field of AI. Suddenly, every executive with a digital pedigree was expected to explain their "AI strategy."

Despite a rush of venture capital, the new generation of AI struggled at first to produce value. Early efforts to sell deep learning as a raw capability to other companies failed in the market. Yes, AI could spot a cat among a thousand images, but . . . so what? Within a few years, however, things began to change. The real value of deep learning emerged as new start-ups began to define common business problems that it could address. Deep learning became "productized" into numerous niche services: an algorithm trained to detect fraudulent transactions for banks, an algorithm to spot defects in concrete construction using photos from drones, an algorithm that could hear when callers on your customer service line were frustrated with your staff. By this time, the buzz had moved on to the next new tech. But that too was a signal that deep learning had finally started to create real value.

I have seen more than one company move its DX efforts out of its IT function to ensure that DX is focused on customer problems—which the business units know best. An executive leading digital strategy at the oil and gas services business Schlumberger stressed to me the importance of their moving digital out of IT, where it had started. "We needed to take digital out of our software vertical and bring it into a horizontal that cuts across [the organization... because] one of our key tenets is for digital to solve customer problems."

As you focus on digital innovation in your own business, remember this enduring mantra of Silicon Valley entrepreneurs: "Fall in love with the problem, not the solution."

Whose Problem Is it?

Every problem has a stakeholder—the person or group of people who are directly affected by it and will benefit from a solution. Commonly, we think of problems where the stakeholder is a customer—whether an end consumer (for a B2C business) or an enterprise customer (for a B2B business). Zoetis's digital strategy has focused on solving problems for pet owners as well as commercial livestock businesses and veterinarians. But it is also important to recognize that the problem you are solving may belong to a stakeholder within your own company—what we might think of as a "business problem."

We can see examples of both customer problems and business problems in the DX work at Air Liquide, global supplier of gases and technologies to health-care and manufacturing companies. An important *customer problem* that Air Liquide is focused on is helping hospitals and manufacturers know when their tanks of gas (oxygen, hydrogen, etc.) are running low so that they can be replaced before running out. Solving this problem requires innovations in the tanks' digital sensors, predictive analytics based on consumption, user alerts and notifications, and seamless reordering. Every aspect of the solution must be designed and tested to ensure that it works for Air Liquide's customers in the context of their daily work.

Air Liquide is also working on a *business problem* in the same division: how to predict customer churn. Solving this means predicting which customers are at greatest risk of unsubscribing from its service in the next thirty days. Solutions involve predictive models based on usage patterns across the entire customer base, being careful to avoid statistical false positives (such as when a small business lowers its usage during a vacation or seasonal slowdown). In this case, the problem's stakeholder is internal— Air Liquide's marketing team in charge of current accounts and customer retention. Any solution to the problem must be designed for that team, be adopted by that team, and deliver results in the context of their daily workflow.

Of course, it is important to recognize that trying to understand one stakeholder's problem will sometimes lead you to uncover a problem that touches a different stakeholder. For example, I know a software-as-a-service (SaaS) company that was very successful at selling a new software solution but struggled with a *business problem* of high customer churn. By examining not just who was unsubscribing but also why, they discovered an unaddressed *customer problem*: users found the software exceedingly difficult to use. After a few months of paying for it without reaping its benefits, customers unsubscribed. By addressing the external customers' problem (with a better training program to accompany new sales), the SaaS business solved its own business problem of customer churn.

The Limits of the Problem Lens

The problem lens is powerful for defining strategic priorities in any business, but it is not without its limits. Too much dependence on defining problems can lead you to focus exclusively on your current customers and fine-tuned improvements to the business you know best—your current core. In practice, I have seen how many design thinking tools are more likely to uncover problems within your current business than to point you toward new opportunities outside your comfort zone.

How can we overcome this inherent bias of the problem lens? We can start by pressing more deeply into our customer insight work. The popular five whys method uses repetition to seek the deeper underlying motivations or needs behind a customer's actions. And we can return to Levitt's "strategic myopia" question that pushes you to reconsider the boundaries of your enterprise—*what business are we really in?* In addition, we can expand our search for strategic priorities by deploying a second lens to give us another perspective on the search for growth: the opportunity lens.

The Opportunity Lens

The second lens through which we can define our strategic priorities is the *opportunity* lens. This entails thinking about strategy in terms of new ways to create value, both for customers and the business. The power of the opportunity lens is that it can push you to look beyond your current business and think about strategy more expansively.

One of Zoetis's strategic priorities for its DX was to enter the growing diagnostics category in animal health. Zoetis had no role in diagnostics when the company was first spun off from Pfizer. Entering this market was not a solution to any current problem, yet it was a compelling opportunity to create value.

In the digital era, many of the biggest breakthrough products have come from pursuing a clearly defined opportunity to create new value. When Apple began work on the iPod, Steve Jobs's vision was to give the customer "1,000 songs in your pocket." When Amazon began work on what would become the Kindle, its ambition was to offer "every book ever printed, in any language, all available in less than 60 seconds."[8] These were each incredible strategic opportunities to pursue, but they were not exactly pressing problems where Apple's or Amazon's customers were crying out for a solution. When looking to create something truly new to market, boundary-pushing ideas are more likely to be discovered with an opportunity lens.

Another way of thinking about this comes from the world of venture capital (VC). When looking at start-ups to invest in, VC Kevin Fong would famously ask entrepreneurs, "Are you selling painkillers or vitamins?"[9] In other words, are you creating a product that will solve a pressing problem for the customer, or will it give them a better life in ways they may not yet know they want? The common investing wisdom is that "painkillers" have better odds of success. It is easier to market the product because customers understand its value immediately and see why they would want it. On the other hand, there may be a bigger upside if a start-up can succeed with a "vitamin," a breakthrough product no one was asking for because they had not yet imagined it.

The two lenses are also helpful when thinking about your value proposition for an established product or business. When defining the benefits you give to customers, try asking two questions: What current frustrations or pain points are we alleviating? What new delights are we providing? (I refer to both as value elements. Alex Osterwalder calls these two types "pain relievers" and "gain creators."[10])

As we make use of the opportunity lens, it is important to remember what a strategic opportunity is and what it is not. A strategic opportunity is not just a business metric ("grow top-line revenue 20 percent this year"). Nor is it a solution you have already decided on ("build a virtual reality [VR] headset with longer battery life"). Rather, it is a focused idea about the *value your business could create* and *where it could compete* ("create a VR meeting experience for designers that is better than being in the same conference room").

Whose Opportunity Is It?

Just as with problems, we can think of strategic opportunities from the point of view of the customer or the business.

Customer opportunities focus on ways to create new value for a specific customer. Think of the vision statements for the iPod and the Kindle. When Uber began business, it defined an opportunity to offer "transportation as reliable as running water, everywhere for everyone."[11] Whereas customer problems address an evident point of friction or pain, customer opportunities produce an unexpected benefit or delight. This quality of unexpected delight is critical to theories of customer satisfaction. The Kano model, for example, distinguishes product benefits that the customer values, demands, and expects versus benefits called "delighters," which are unexpected but create the greatest excitement among customers when delivered.[12]

Business opportunities, on the other hand, focus on new growth and expansion for the business. Zoetis, for example, identified an opportunity to expand into the growing diagnostics business. Recall YouTube's ambition to achieve 1 billion hours watched per day—another clearly defined opportunity. Amazon Web Services (AWS) began as an opportunity for the retailer to generate revenue from its new IT infrastructure by renting it to other companies as a service.

Defining an Opportunity

I have seen four powerful ways that companies define strategic priorities with the opportunity lens:

- *Customer delight statement*—Try describing an unexpected and delightful experience to create for the customer. Bezos's dream for the Kindle was "every book ever printed, in any language, all available in less than 60 seconds."
- *Attractive market with a right to win*—Find a large or growing market to enter, one where your business has a built-in advantage. For Zoetis the opportunity to "enter the diagnostics business" meant selling to an existing base of customers, one that it was already serving with treatments and vaccines.
- *New capabilities with clear application to your business*—Look for new skills or emerging technologies that are relevant to an important part of your business model. Amazon chose to invest in robotics because of a specific application: picking products off warehouse shelves. More recently, drugmakers have invested in machine learning because of its specific application to key steps in the drug discovery process.
- *10x stretch goal*—Try envisioning value creation at scale, not just incremental improvements. "Grow watch time to 1 billion hours a day" was a huge goal for YouTube and a compelling business opportunity. One of Google's core principles is to "think 10x, not 10 percent."[13] Similarly, the Gates Foundation defines ambitious goals for public health by interviewing doctors and pushing them to think big, asking, "What would you do if you had unlimited resources?"[14]

When defining opportunities, push yourself to think big about what matters most. Remember, strategy is about defining your top priorities for growth, which must rise above all others.

Two Complementary Lenses

It is important to realize that problems and opportunities are two powerful and complementary lenses for looking at strategy. In fact, a problem and an opportunity may just be two ways of describing the same idea. For Zoetis, entering the diagnostics market was a clear business opportunity. But it could also be described as a customer problem for farmers—how to detect their animals' disease sooner to treat it better.

What begins as a broad growth opportunity will often evolve into more specific problems to be solved. Zoetis's entry into diagnostics was a huge opportunity for the business to capitalize on its position in the marketplace. But pursuing that opportunity meant choosing which customers to serve first. Who among its customers had the biggest unmet need to detect animal disease? What precise problems could Zoetis help them solve first? This is a typical evolution: from defining an opportunity to identifying key stakeholders, to understanding their biggest unmet needs or problems to be solved.

I often advise companies to begin their strategy process with the problem lens and then to expand their thinking with the opportunity lens. The best opportunities, in time, will lead back to new problems to solve.

Tool: Problem/Opportunity (P/O) Statements

Now that we have a clear understanding of why strategic priorities are important and how they can be identified through the complementary lenses of problems and opportunities, let's get started with the first tool in Step 2 of the DX Roadmap: the problem/opportunity (P/O) statement.

Whether you are using the problem lens, the opportunity lens, or both, you want to end up with one list of strategic priorities. Each priority should be summarized in a concise statement that offers clear guidance and inspiration for a range of different possible solutions. I call these problem/opportunity statements, or P/Os, for short.

Table 4.2 lists examples of P/O statements that spell out strategic priorities for the DX Roadmaps for four companies. In each case, the statement describes a clear strategic opportunity or problem for the business or its customers.

Table 4.2.
Problem/Opportunity Statements for DX Strategy

Company	Problem/Opportunity Statements for DX Strategy
Zoetis	• Improve the customer's digital path to purchase—from online discovery to e-commerce, to loyalty. • Provide online learning and content for animal health professionals. • Enter the growing diagnostics market to detect and prevent illness in animals. • Empower livestock management with digital tracking and analytics.
Mastercard	• Provide financial inclusion to unbanked communities. • Solve enterprise needs for cybersecurity via digital identity authentication. • Harness our retail transaction data for analytics and insights. • Deliver innovation as a service for partners in the financial services sector.
Air Liquide	• Leverage the data in our physical assets—from manufacturing plants to gas cylinders—to improve operations and unlock new value. • Empower and connect with our customers across every channel of communication—from app to web, to phone call, to sales representative. • Collaborate with an expanding ecosystem—of employees, partners, and new start-ups—via new digital business models and tools for collaboration.
Acuity	• Offer new insurance policies to commercial customers for the business risks of the digital era. • Use new data sources in our underwriting and marketing models to offer the right customer the right coverage at the right price. • Provide seamless, omnichannel customer service and claims. • Sell insurance directly to buyers wishing to purchase online rather than through a traditional intermediary.

Notice that each P/O statement provides a clear description of where the company will seek to create and capture value, without deciding in advance the type of solutions it will build. When defining your own strategy, remember to focus on the "what" and not yet the "how." Define the opportunities or problems you will address but hold off on describing the solutions you may use to address them.

When Amazon began work on what would become its Kindle e-book platform, the company did not even attempt to specify what the solution would look like in terms of hardware and software. It defined the opportunity: "every book ever printed, in any language, all available in less than 60 seconds." As Kindle succeeded over several years, the solution changed significantly, evolving from an e-reader hardware device to a cloud-based library of books created by both traditional publishers and self-publishers and accessible on almost any smartphone, tablet, computer, or e-reader.

P/O Statements at Different Levels

Strategic priorities should be set not just for the entire enterprise but at other levels as well. P/Os can be used to define the strategy of a single function (e.g., marketing or human resources) or a specific business unit (like Pfizer's animal health unit). P/Os can be defined for an individual team to clarify strategy for whatever part of the business it manages. P/Os can even be defined for a specific decision or event—such as an acquisition of another business—to define the strategic opportunities that it poses.

For an example of P/Os at different levels of the same organization, let's look at the DX of Walmart in table 4.3. At an *enterprise level*, we can see three major P/Os for Walmart: define the e-commerce future of grocery purchases, leverage retail stores to win the last mile of online-to-offline commerce, and reinvent the interaction of humans and AI in the retail workplace. Further down in the table, at a *channel level* (stores versus e-commerce), P/Os can describe Walmart's strategic priorities for each

Table 4.3.
Walmart Problem/Opportunity Statements at Different Levels

Level of the Organization	Scope of Strategy	Problem/Opportunity Statements
Enterprise	Walmart, Inc.	• Define the e-commerce future of grocery purchases. • Leverage retail stores to win the last mile of online-to-offline commerce. • Reinvent the interaction of humans and AI in the retail workplace.
Channel	Walmart stores	• Ensure availability on the shelf when a customer walks in the door to find a specific product.
Channel	Walmart.com	• Improve our customer's purchase frequency online.
Channel	Omnichannel	• Leverage our store employees to enable faster delivery of online orders to customers nearby.
Team	Walmart mobile app	• Improve the customer's returns experience in-store.

channel. For Walmart stores, one P/O is to "ensure availability on the shelf when a customer walks in the door to find a specific product" (an area where Walmart has used robotics successfully). For Walmart.com, one P/O is to "improve our customer's purchase frequency online." For omnichannel efforts to link the two channels, an important P/O is to "leverage our store employees to enable faster delivery of online orders to customers nearby." Further down still, at a *team level*, we can see how specific P/Os guide Walmart's DX. The team working on the Walmart mobile app is focused on solving a number of customer problems, including "improv[ing] the customer's returns experience in-store." This P/O led to the addition of a Mobile Express Returns feature within the app that allows customers to scan their paper receipt with their phone, select which items they want to return, drop off those products in a fast-track lane at the store using a quick-response (QR) code, and receive a refund within a day. The final solution reduced customers' in-store return time by 74 percent.[15]

A highly diversified Latin American business that I have advised has applied the P/O approach to prioritize its DX at three levels. First, each operating unit focused on strategic opportunities for digital *within* its own business (these were in very different industries). Second, the corporate team focused on strategic opportunities *across* the businesses—by linking their data and capabilities to generate new insights and value. Third, the company's venture team identified opportunities *outside* its existing industry mix—to pursue by acquisitions, joint ventures, and investing in digital start-ups.

Statements That Spark Ideas

A great P/O statement is meant to spark new ideas for innovation. This is particularly clear in innovation challenges or hackathons, which can involve internal employees or outside partners, start-ups, and customers. At the start of any innovation challenge, the problem-to-be-solved is declared, and a reward—for example, a cash prize, start-up investment, or a chance to work at the business—is promised to whoever comes up with the best solution.

In order to generate useful ideas, it is essential to have a well-defined P/O statement. Stephen Liguori, the former head of global innovation at General Electric (GE), told me of their first innovation challenge: the company simply asked for participants to submit "innovative clean energy solutions." They were quickly overwhelmed. "We got 77,000 entries for five judges to review!" says Liguori. The submissions included ideas like "put a bunch of electric eels in a swimming pool with power cables." In subsequent challenges, GE offered much clearer problem statements, working with engineers to add technical detail. In a challenge to explore 3D printing for jet engine parts, Liguori said, "We received 155 entries, of which 125 blew away anything we had figured out by that point!"

Clarity, detail, and focus are essential to any good P/O statement. But grammar can matter too. One easy way to improve a P/O statement is simply to turn it into a question. The benefit of writing your P/O as a question is that it will force you to truly focus on the problem, not the solution. One of my favorite techniques is to begin each P/O with the words "how might we." For example, the first Zoetis P/O statement in table 4.2 would be rewritten as, "How might we improve the customer's digital path to purchase—from online discovery to e-commerce, to loyalty?" "How might we" is a popular phrase in innovation and design; it was coined by Min Basadur while he was working at Proctor & Gamble in the 1970s. Today it is widely used at firms like Google, Facebook, IDEO, and the Cooper-Hewitt National Design Museum.[16] By using "how might we," you quickly step back from any presumed or foreordained solutions (e.g., thinking only of the loyalty program for veterinarians that your marketing teams are already working on), and open your thinking to more wide-ranging innovations. A great question is worth a thousand answers.

EIGHT QUALITIES OF GREAT P/O STATEMENTS

From my own observations and coaching of leaders on strategy across diverse settings, I have identified eight key principles of an effective P/O statement:

1. It is posed as the question "How might we. . . ?" ("How might we provide financial inclusion to unbanked communities?")
2. It focuses on an important problem or opportunity to create value. ("Improve the customer's digital path to purchase—from online discovery to e-commerce, to loyalty.")
3. It takes the point of view of the customer or the business. If the P/O statement is for a customer, use language the customer would use ("works well on my current phone"); if it is for the business, phrase it in business terms ("upsell customers on our latest data plans").

4. It focuses on the desired outcome ("improve tracking in our supply chain") and avoids suggesting a solution (not "create a blockchain ledger to track our supply chain").

5. It is open enough to inspire different choices. ("Enter the market for diagnostics," not "acquire diagnostics company X.")

6. It is narrow enough to give helpful guidance. ("Improve the in-store product returns experience," not "create a better user experience.")

7. It avoids compounds. (Instead of "reduce shipping errors and increase speed," write one P/O to "reduce shipping errors" and another to "increase shipping speed.")

8. It includes a measurable definition of success. ("Reduce employee onboarding time by 75 percent.")

The real test of a P/O statement is the inspiration it sparks in those who read it. Remember that a good P/O will help you to fall in love with the problem, not the solution.

From One P/O to Many Ventures

As you begin to develop a short list of strategic priorities for your own team, business unit, or enterprise, it is important to understand the link here between strategy and innovation. Put simply: each P/O statement should generate many different innovation ideas. If every P/O poses a question ("How might we?"), that single question should generate numerous possible answers. Those answers—new products, services, processes, business models—each suggest a different possible solution to that same problem or opportunity.

We can see this illustrated in the case of the NextGen Cup Challenge, a moon-shot innovation project launched jointly by Starbucks and McDonald's with the support of design firm IDEO. The two sponsor businesses alone produce billions of paper cups each year, and in order to hold a customer's hot coffee durably, these paper cups are coated with a plastic lining that prevents recycling. Both companies are looking for innovative ideas to reduce the environmental impact of all those cups. Rather than submitting a request for proposal (RFP) for cup manufacturers to build a specific solution, they announced an open innovation challenge, with a clear P/O statement to solve the problem of coffee cup waste.

The NextGen Cup Challenge has attracted submissions from hundreds of teams proposing a wide range of solutions to the same P/O statement. CupClub adapted ideas from bike sharing, with an innovative plan for reusable cups that could be dropped off in specially marked recycling bins. Muuse proposed putting QR codes on reusable cups to enable tracking, collection, cleaning, and reuse. Colombier Group focused on the dimension of recycling instead of reuse, aiming to replace the plastic layer with a water-based coating that is recyclable or compostable. The success of these ideas will require iterative tests and prototypes in the real world to validate technological feasibility, human behavior and adoption, and economics at scale. To begin that process of validation, winning teams were each given $1 million to test and attempt to commercialize their ideas.[17]

The NextGen Cup Challenge demonstrates the goal of any good P/O statement: to generate a variety of possible innovations, or what I call growth ventures. A growth venture can take many forms. It could be a process innovation, a new product or service, or even a new business model. I use the term "growth ventures" to underline that these initiatives should always be defined in terms of growth. Any digital innovation at this step should be defined as *creating value* and *capturing value* for the firm. Be careful that your own growth ventures are not defined in terms of technology ("invest in cloud computing"), or skill building ("upskill our marketers on social media"). That kind of capability building is critical, but it will come in Step 5 of the DX Roadmap, when you have already begun to explore and test a variety of possible innovations sparked by your P/Os.

Table 4.4 shows how a single P/O can lead to many possible venture ideas for a company. At Walmart, teams innovating on the P/O of "How might we provide convenient online grocery ordering for customers?" have pursued ideas that range from an annual membership fee for grocery delivery to a free buy-online-pickup-at-store (BOPS) experience, to partnering with the delivery app DoorDash, to having Walmart employees drop off packages on their drive home.

A major opportunity for DX at the New York Times Company has been to use digital audio to engage new audiences. Its different ventures have included news podcasts with Times reporters talking about the biggest stories of the day, opinion podcasts from the writers at its Opinion desk, acquiring a successful podcast producer, and buying a start-up that produces audio versions of articles from leading magazines.

At Citibank, one key P/O for digital has been "How might we increase economic vitality for underserved individuals and communities?" This has

Table 4.4.
Each Problem/Opportunity (P/O) Leads to Multiple Possible Ventures

Company	P/O	Different Possible Growth Ventures for That P/O
Walmart	How might we provide convenient online grocery ordering for customers?	• Unlimited grocery delivery with annual membership. • Buy-online-pickup-at-store (BOPS) experience, with no charges. • Partner with the delivery app DoorDash. • Walmart employees drop off packages on their drive home.
New York Times Company	How might we reach audiences seeking an audio experience of journalism?	• Launch a daily news podcast that interviews our reporters on top stories they are covering. • Launch a mix of opinion podcasts on different themes, as part of our Opinion department. • Acquire Serial—a producer of popular investigative nonfiction podcasts. • Acquire Audm—a start-up that hires voice actors to read long-form journalism from leading magazines.
Citibank	How might we increase economic vitality for underserved individuals and communities?	• Online platform to connect investors with opportunity zones investment. • Digital tool for job seekers, using market data to evaluate career paths and develop skills. • Invest in fintech start-ups offering peer-to-peer lending or microcredit.
Starbucks and McDonald's	How might we reduce the impact of coffee cup waste?	• Create a sharing system for reusable cups dropped off in recycling bins. • Put QR codes on reusable cups to enable tracking, collection, cleaning, and reuse. • Replace the cups' plastic lining with a water-based coating that is recyclable or compostable.

led to multiple innovations, including an online platform connecting investors to opportunity zone investments, and a data-driven tool to help job
seekers evaluate career paths and develop new skills. At the same time,
Citibank's venture investing arm can contribute to this same P/O by investing in start-ups that offer their own solutions to economic empowerment.

Our goal, then, for the strategy process is that a few P/Os will generate
a *venture backlog*—a prioritized list of new growth venture ideas that are
aligned with your strategic priorities and your shared vision. The appropriate team, unit, or division can then begin validating and testing those
venture ideas and investing in those that work best. (I am borrowing the
term "backlog" from its use and meaning in agile software development.)
We will see more about the use of a venture backlog in Step 4 of the DX
Roadmap, the topic of chapter 6.

Effective Tools to Identify P/Os

Where do great P/O statements come from? First, they should emerge from
the shared vision that you defined in Step 1 of the DX Roadmap. There are
also some helpful tools commonly used in customer insight research. And
I particularly recommend using four of the strategy tools I developed in
The Digital Transformation Playbook. Let's look briefly at how you can bring
these tools together to identify valuable P/O statements for any business.

Shared Vision

The first place we can look to identify valuable P/Os is in the shared vision
that we defined in Step 1 of the DX Roadmap. This includes our future
landscape, right to win, North Star impact, and business theory. Each of
these four elements should assist us in identifying P/Os.

FUTURE LANDSCAPE

Your future landscape is a shared view of how your business context is
evolving based on insights about your customers, new technology, the competitive ecosystem, and broader structural trends in the economy. These
are precisely the kinds of insights that should point you to new problems
and opportunities for your business. Let's look at some examples:

- Zoetis's P/O to "Empower livestock management with digital tracking and analytics" arose from trends in big data and IoT, as well as understanding how midsize farms were still struggling to adopt these technologies successfully.
- Walmart's P/O to "Define the e-commerce future of grocery purchase" arose from seeing a customer need in grocery delivery that competitors had still not solved, leaving more space for innovation than other categories of e-commerce.
- Acuity's P/O of "Offer new insurance policies to commercial customers for the business risks of the digital era" was spurred by trends toward robotics and automation within manufacturing firms, the growing gig economy, and customers' vulnerability to cybersecurity risk.

RIGHT TO WIN

P/Os should also arise from your right to win—your definition of the unique advantages and limits of your own organization. As Michael Porter says, "Strategy is about being different. It means deliberately choosing a different set of activities to deliver a unique mix of value."[18] By linking your strategy to your right to win, you can pursue opportunities where you have a unique advantage.

- Intuit used the unique advantage of its data—payroll and tax data shared by customers using its existing products—to identify an opportunity to provide credit for small businesses unserved by other lenders.
- Walmart used its own unique advantages—its retail store network and its shopper data—to identify opportunities to enter consumer health care and financial services.

NORTH STAR IMPACT

Your North Star impact—the long-term impact you seek to achieve—should also be a source of guidance in identifying P/Os.

- Mastercard's North Star impact, to "power and protect secure commerce in the digital world" helped point it toward the P/O of solving enterprise needs for digital identity authentication.

- Ford Motor's North Star impact, defined by Bill Ford, is to "meet the environmental and mobility needs of a growing, urbanizing planet." Several P/Os emerged from this, including those for autonomous vehicles and fleet management, electric vehicles and charging networks, ride-sharing and urban mobility solutions, and in-vehicle transactions and payments.

BUSINESS THEORY

Your business theory—explaining how you expect to capture value from your investments in the future—can point you to specific P/Os for your business.

- Walt Disney's business theory map from 1957 clearly identified P/Os in theme parks, merchandise, television and music, character licensing, and books, magazines, and comics.
- Amazon's theory of the virtuous cycle of product selection and customer growth pointed the company to the P/O of working with third-party sellers.

Customer Insights Tools

In addition to your shared vision, I have found that many popular methods for customer insights research can be useful in identifying P/Os. Three tools used in lean start-up, agile, design thinking, and product management can be particularly helpful in uncovering customer problems to solve and opportunities for customer delight. Let's look at each.

GET OUT OF THE BUILDING

The spirit of lean start-up is perhaps best captured by Steve Blank's imperative to "get out of the building"[19]—to stop creating business plans in your office and engage directly with the customer to learn from them. In fact, the first stage of the lean start-up process of "customer development" starts with simple customer interviews—no prototypes, no MVPs, no slide decks—just talking with the customer on their own turf.

UTC's digital team spends regular time in the field—from Las Vegas to Shanghai, to Turin—talking to industrial customers to gauge their interest in the digital innovations it is considering. At Zoetis, the digital team goes on regular customer ride-alongs, such as spending a day with a veterinarian to learn what is happening in their business and how industry needs are changing. Observing a day in the life of a customer will yield far more insights than a survey or focus group.

PR/FAQ

Another powerful tool for identifying and defining P/Os is what Amazon calls a press release/frequently asked questions (PR/FAQ). This tool was developed as a way of instilling the philosophy of "working backward from customer needs." In other words, don't start with the product you intend to sell; start with the impact you want to create for your customer. The PR/FAQ comes in two parts: a press release that announces the imagined product as if it were ready to launch, and an FAQ section that answers additional questions. The press release is less than a page long. It should name the product in a way that the customer will understand. It then describes the benefits the customer will gain and the problems that it will solve. It concludes with quotes from the company and a hypothetical customer describing the value they are receiving from the new product. The FAQ follows, and it can be up to five pages long. It answers a list of expected questions from the customer (How will the product work? What will it cost?) and also from the business (What about market size, economics, technical feasibility, business partners?).[20]

CUSTOMER JOURNEY MAPPING

Customer journey mapping is a popular research method widely used in both design thinking and agile. The customer's current experience of your business is defined as a journey, broken into a sequence of stages (e.g., from prepurchase to postpurchase). Research is conducted at each stage to understand the customer's behavior (actions taken, touch points used), and experiences (their goals, motivations, questions, feelings, pain points). These findings are used to identify strategic opportunities for improvement.

Customer journey mapping can be a powerful tool to identify P/Os for your current business, especially customer problems to solve. But take note: this tool has become so popular that I have met companies who believed the purpose of their DX was to "map customer journeys." Don't mistake the process for the goal! The purpose of DX is, and remains, value creation, which begins with a great P/O statement.

Digital Strategy Tools

Several strategy tools in my last book, *The Digital Transformation Playbook*, are designed to help any business identify strategic opportunities, that is, P/O statements. Four tools in particular can be helpful to you:

- *Customer network behaviors*—In the chapter on customer strategy, I describe five customer behaviors—the desires to *access, engage, customize, connect,* and *collaborate*—that influence us in the digital age. The tool explains how to uncover opportunities to create value (in products, services, and customer experiences) by designing around these core behaviors of customers.
- *Data value templates*—In the chapter on data strategy, I describe four templates for value creation from data—*insights, targeting, personalization,* and *context.* The accompanying tool shows how any business can identify opportunities for value creation by applying these templates to its existing data assets and taking steps to grow those assets over time.
- *Competitive Value Train*—In the chapter on competitive strategy, I introduce the Competitive Value Train (also described in chapter 3 of this book). By applying this tool to any part of your current business, you can identify the upstream and downstream partners that help you deliver value to your ultimate customer, and the value exchange and leverage that exists at each point of interaction. With those insights, the Competitive Value Train can help identify new business opportunities that give you more leverage in your ecosystem—such as increasing the uniqueness of your role, extending your business further upstream, or extending it downstream to a direct customer relationship.
- *Value Proposition Roadmap*—In the chapter on value proposition strategy, I introduce the Value Proposition Roadmap (also described in chapter 3 of this book). By analyzing your current value proposition and its declining and growing elements of value, this tool will help you identify strategic P/Os that will increase your future value for each of your customer segments.

Tool: The Problem/Opportunity (P/O) Matrix

We are now ready to introduce another new tool, the Problem/Opportunity (P/O) Matrix. The purpose of this tool is not to generate a single new P/O. Rather, it is to organize and clarify a short list of the most important P/Os for any business, division, unit, function, or team. As such, it is best used after initial work with some of the tools described in the prior section.

The Problem/Opportunity Matrix in figure 4.1 has two dimensions: problem versus opportunity (our two lenses for defining strategy), and customer versus business (the points-of-view of external versus internal stakeholders). The resulting matrix is composed of four quadrants—customer problems, business problems, customer opportunities, and business opportunities. Each of these four quadrants offers a different means of identifying a strategic priority for your business. But remember that the same P/O can be written in different ways (e.g., as a customer problem or a business opportunity) and that P/Os evolve over time. The point of the P/O Matrix is not to select the "correct" quadrant for any given strategy. Rather, use the four quadrants to help you spot different priorities for growth that you might otherwise miss.

I developed the Problem/Opportunity Matrix while working with numerous organizations to define the most important strategic priorities in their DXs. Let's briefly walk through each step of the tool to see how to apply the Matrix in your own organization.

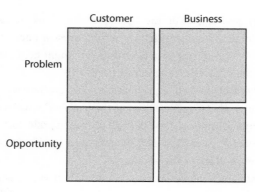

Figure 4.1.
The Problem/Opportunity (P/O) Matrix

1. Pick Your Level and Your Customers

First, start by deciding which level of your business you are defining strategic priorities for. Is it for a product team? A particular sales channel? A business unit or geography? A function like marketing, finance, or HR? The entire organization? The P/O Matrix can be applied at any level of your enterprise. So, before you begin, you need to choose the organizational unit you will focus on.

Next, identify your most important customers. These are your key stakeholders outside your chosen unit. You will typically have multiple customer types. Recall that Zoetis's customers include pet owners; farmers raising cattle, swine, and other animals; and the veterinarians who serve each of them. If you are using the Matrix to set strategy for an internal function (like HR or finance), your customers may include stakeholders in other parts of your company. For an HR division, "customers" could include company employees as well as colleges where you recruit talent. For a supply chain division, "customers" could include teams or business lines whose products you deliver.

2. Write P/Os for Each Quadrant

Now that you know your organizational unit and the customers you are serving, it is time to start writing down P/Os for each of the four quadrants of the Matrix.

- *Customer problems*—For the first quadrant, look at each of your customers that you identified in step 1. For each one, what are their biggest, most enduring problems that you might help them to solve? What is their most pressing unmet need?
- *Business problems*—In this quadrant, ask: What are the most pressing pain points currently facing your part of the business? (Again, think of the organizational unit you chose in step 1.) For each problem, who is the key stakeholder (for example, a marketing manager or HR director) that will need to use and adopt any solution?
- *Customer opportunities*—Look again at each of your customers identified in step 1. What unexpected value, gain, or benefit could you create for them? Try writing a "customer delight statement" for each

customer—much like the Kindle's promise to offer "every book ever printed, in any language, all available in less than 60 seconds."

- *Business opportunities*—In this quadrant, ask, Where could my unit expand to create and capture new value for the business? Try to identify an attractive growth market where you have a clear right to win. Look for a new capability with a specific application to your business. (For example, instead of "use machine learning," write "use machine learning for drug discovery.") Try writing a 10x stretch goal—for something you normally try to improve 10 percent but where there might be an opportunity to improve by 10x.

Within each quadrant, identify as many interesting P/Os as possible. Aim for at least three or four per quadrant.

As you write each P/O statement, think back to the eight qualities of great P/Os identified earlier in this chapter, and follow these guidelines:

- *Make it a question*—using Min Basadur's words: "how might we."
- *Avoid compound sentences*—if your P/O has the word "and" in it, split it into two ideas!
- *Never give the "how"*—specify the outcome you want, not the means. A good P/O is not a solution masquerading as a problem.
- *Write with a clear point of view*—if you are writing a customer problem, don't use business jargon; use the language the customer would use.

Remember that a given P/O could be written differently to fit in more than one quadrant. If one of your P/Os doesn't seem crisp or compelling enough, try rewriting a problem as an opportunity (or vice versa), or flipping the perspective from the business to the customer (or vice versa).

3. Pick Your Keepers and Combine

In the next step, you should review all the P/Os you have written and choose only the most important P/Os to keep. Each one should be focused on solving a real problem or creating significant value. Each should clearly matter to a specific customer (external) or the business (internal). The P/Os should be interesting as well, sparking new thoughts about how you might create and capture value. Then, take your chosen P/Os out of the four quadrants and combine them into a single list. You should now have one list of P/O statements written as questions ("how might we...?").

4. Refine Each P/O

Take some time to discuss and refine each of the P/Os on your list. For each P/O, spell out again who the key stakeholder is that must use and benefit from any eventual solution.

Be sure each P/O is *narrow* enough to give focus to a team. For example, do not write "How might we attract more customers?" Instead, write "How might we engage audiences who prefer audio journalism?"

Be sure each P/O is *broad* enough so that it can be answered in multiple ways: not "How might we create a daily news podcast that interviews reporters on the morning's top story?" but "How might we use audio to engage readers with our news coverage?"

5. Brainstorm Test

Now it is time to give your P/Os what I call the brainstorm test. Look at each of your refined P/O statements and try to brainstorm multiple ideas for solutions—that is, different answers to the same question. As you do, try to find ideas that are genuinely different from one another; that is, they take a different approach to solving the same problem or to capturing the same opportunity.

This step will reveal if a P/O will be genuinely helpful to future innovation efforts. If you can think of only one solution idea for a P/O, seek the input of others to broaden your thinking. If you still can see only one solution, your P/O is probably a "solution masquerading as a problem."

6. Success Metrics

In the last step, you will try to define success metrics for each of your P/Os. Ask yourself, How would we use data to choose the best solution among the ones we just brainstormed and others that may be proposed in the future? For each P/O still on your list, define a metric (or two or three) that would distinguish the best solution for that problem/opportunity.

If you have done your work right, you should now feel willing to assign a team of high-value employees to work on any one of your P/Os. And you should be willing to give that team wide latitude to explore new innovations, knowing they will test and validate them with your success metrics as their guide.

Strategy from the Bottom Up

The approach to strategy that we have seen in this chapter is a departure from how many established businesses operate. At many organizations, "strategy" is an annual agenda item for a select group. Senior executives take a few weeks each year to spend time in meetings or perhaps at a retreat to update the strategy for the firm. The resulting strategy is a document—a deliverable, like a budget, that must be handed in once a year—that is meant to trickle down to the rest of the organization.

But this model completely fails the challenges of the digital era, with its constant change and need for adaptation. For any business today, strategy must happen not just at the top but at every level of the organization. And strategy must become not just an annual product but an ongoing, continuous process.

Strategy at Every Level

As we have seen, strategic priorities (P/Os) are critically important at every level of the organization. Whether you're leading DX for the firm, division, function, or team—every organizational unit should be focused on identifying its most important problems to solve and opportunities to create new value. When an organization makes that shift, people at all levels of the business will be engaged in strategy.

At the energy services firm Schlumberger, every business unit head is expected to develop their own digital strategy, drawing on guidance and insights from the corporate level digital strategy team. In its 2020 Group report on digital innovation, the New York Times laid out a goal that every "desk" (a group of journalists covering an area of news) needs to have its own strategy statement—defining its customers (target audience), value proposition (what it will and will not cover), competition (and how it will distinguish itself from them), metrics (what success looks like), and operations (what skills it needs to develop and how it will interact with other desks or departments).[21]

Any company's overall enterprise strategy should shape the work of every other part of the organization. But again, this influence should happen by the process I call cascading up. A senior leader does not tell her reports, "My strategic priorities are X, so yours should be Y." Instead, she should say, "My strategic priorities are X," and then ask, "What do you think your team's strategic priorities should be to support this?" Through cascading up, company P/Os are linked to strategic priorities at every level and in every department.

Strategy as Ongoing Conversation

Defining your strategic priorities is a continuous, ongoing process. Every leader and team should regularly review its P/Os to consider and incorporate new learning. A strategic priority may wax or wane in importance for many reasons: customer interest may fade, new competitors may enter the same space and reduce the likelihood of profit, an unexpected event like the COVID pandemic may scramble your time frames or add new external constraints.

Strategy must be reimagined—not as a deliverable but as an ongoing process that everyone contributes to. Donald Sull describes strategy as a series of conversations that need to happen at every level of an organization, in an ongoing, iterative fashion.[22] This approach can be seen in the DX of UTC. Steve Serra, who leads UTC's digital accelerator, describes how its teams have regular meetings with the presidents of UTC's business units to understand what is top-of-mind in their business, to show them emerging trends and examples from other markets, and to identify strategic opportunities that are of the greatest importance to their business.

A powerful shift in mindset will happen as everyone gets involved in these strategy conversations. At every level of the organization, people will start to take a problem-defining mindset. Their every task, project, or workflow will begin with a step back to ask, "Why am I doing this? What am I solving for?" As everyone begins to make that shift—as they start to think of new ways to solve the problems that matter most to their own work—their creativity will be unleashed.

Teams and Leaders

The results of doing strategy continuously and from the bottom up will be clear. Every team will be guided by its own *shared vision* defined for its particular division or unit. Every team will have its own set of *strategic priorities*—perhaps three to seven P/Os—that guide its own work and are aligned with the priorities of the whole company. And every team should have its own *venture backlog*—a list of perhaps ten to thirty ideas for innovations to pursue—that changes regularly but is aligned to its strategic P/Os.

As strategy becomes more bottom up, leadership changes as well. The role of a leader is no longer to think of the right answers but rather to frame the right questions.

Recall the three jobs of a leader from chapter 3. These translate into three tasks that any leader should focus on in relation to strategy. First, leaders must define the most important problems and opportunities that will guide their team's efforts. Second, they must communicate these in clear P/Os and work to align everyone in their team. Finally, they must empower others as they test new ideas and pursue new solutions to these shared strategic goals.

~

For digital transformation to succeed, you must first define where it will compete and seek to create value. Without priorities, any DX will become a series of scattered projects that are disconnected from the needs of the business and easily hijacked by the hype of new technologies. In Step 2 of the DX Roadmap, you saw how any organization can define its strategic priorities and link DX to a clear agenda for growth. You saw the power of thinking in both problems and opportunities, and how various strategy tools can help define P/Os for your own business. And you saw the link between strategy and innovation—why you must first define the problems that matter most before seeking ideas for solutions.

Every strategy is a work in progress, but with a good first draft in place, you can now begin the next step of the DX Roadmap. With P/Os identified and ideas for new digital innovations sparked by them, you are ready to begin turning those ideas into real-world growth ventures.

As we embark on Step 3 of the DX Roadmap, we will grapple with the challenge of uncertainty identified in chapter 2. Humility and experimentation will be key. To turn your new venture ideas into engines of growth for your business, you don't need a crystal ball. You need a clear process to rapidly validate any idea, test its business assumptions, and discover if it will deliver results at scale in the real world. In chapter 5, we will see how to validate new ventures throughout your organization and start to create real value through DX.

5

Step 3: Validate New Ventures

EXPERIMENTATION

When I visited Walmart Labs in Silicon Valley to meet with COO Jeff Shotts, his company was engaged in a broad digital transformation (DX). Walmart was pursuing numerous innovations at the same time, ranging from operational improvements to new customer experiences, to new digital business models.

One recent innovation was Jetblack, an invitation-only service for conversational commerce. Jetblack allowed customers to text a shopping request—for example, "I need a birthday gift for a ten-year-old boy"—and, with a few exchanges back and forth, have the perfect product delivered within a day. In another innovation, robots that roamed the aisles of Walmart's retail stores cleaned the floors while using machine vision to scan shelves for products that needed restocking. Another robotics solution was being developed in Walmart's fulfillment centers to expedite pick-pack-ship for a selection of millions of products offered on its website. Meanwhile, Walmart's plans for online grocery ordering were gearing up for a broad national rollout.

With each digital innovation, Walmart's teams were careful not to "fall in love with the solution." Instead, in teams across the company, Walmart was engaged in a constant cycle of rapid experimentation—testing in the marketplace, often with quick and simple prototypes, to learn what would and would not work in the real world. Much of this learning was about customers. What were their biggest unmet needs? Which features mattered most to them? How could Walmart create the right customer experience? Other learning related to operations. What were the technology requirements for a given solution? What security or data privacy issues needed to be addressed? How scalable was this idea in practice? Still other experiments focused on economics: running tests on pricing, operating costs, and the value to the firm of benefits like additional customer data. As Shotts explained to me, with every innovation, Walmart must "try to figure out how can we scale an offer that's good for the customer, while still meeting some economic thresholds that we have." This means being open to learning as you test and validate new ideas in the market—and staying flexible on your next steps.

One example of such learning came from Walmart's robots, where market testing led to different decisions for different use cases. The robotic floor sweepers performed well at first, saving labor costs on restocking of store shelves. So they were rolled out from a few locations to a national test in 10 percent of Walmart stores. But ultimately, the program was shut down when the company found it could achieve comparable results by improving human performance.[1] In Walmart's fulfillment centers, however, robots have remained key to the online business model. In fact, they found a new role as Walmart began to build much smaller warehouses, each one adjacent to a traditional store. Robots in these small warehouses worked in tandem with human employees who walked the aisles of stores to pull the right products for same-day delivery. Testing at a store in New Hampshire showed this hybrid solution led to more product availability, faster order fulfillment, and greater utilization of Walmart's warehouse space. Those proven results led to a much bigger investment and rollout.[2]

Not every innovation moves forward after testing. Shotts pointed to the example of Jetblack, the service using text messages to provide concierge shopping. Customers loved it. "We're seeing that we have launched a value proposition that resonates with customers enough that they'll stop using the competition [Amazon]. But we can't stop there. We have to figure out, how would we scale this offering for 200 million people in the US—and can we do it profitably?" Jetblack's early trial was in select urban markets. It relied on a human-powered back end that would never scale but allowed Walmart to test what user experience would shift customer behavior. But delighting the customer was not enough. The goal had been to run Jetblack on machine-learning algorithms, but the technology was not ready to take over from human agents. Scaling up Jetblack would be impossible. So Walmart took what it had learned and chose to wind down the project.

At the same time, Walmart's experiments in online grocery ordering proved there was real customer demand and multiple paths to meet it at scale. One key unknown was the customer's willingness to pay for grocery delivery. "It's hard to make money on a $25 basket if you are delivering it for free," Shotts explained. "I'm not opposed to testing that. But scaling it is a real challenge." Walmart ran numerous experiments, testing different price points for paid delivery, free delivery with a minimum basket size, and an annual membership model like Amazon Prime. With Walmart's low prices and razor-thin margins, finding the right formula was essential to drive customer adoption while being financially sustainable. Ultimately, the firm launched a nationwide service called Walmart+, where membership gave you free one- or two-day delivery of online products, plus same-day delivery of groceries from a store. Grocery delivery was also offered without a membership, priced at $7.95 per delivery.

Testing and learning does not end when a product or service launches, though. As Walmart's online grocery service grew in market, the company continued to learn and adapt to customers' changing behaviors. Widespread lockdowns during the COVID-19 pandemic led to a huge surge in demand for what Walmart called "click and collect"—ordering groceries online, then driving to the store where an employee would bring out your bags and put them in the trunk of your car.[3] As lockdowns eased, Walmart discovered a surprising new customer wish—to have a delivery person not only bring groceries to their home but come inside and put them away. The service, dubbed Walmart InHome, comes with greater personalization, additional security measures, and a premium price for customers.[4]

Why Experimentation Matters

In describing the New York Times Company's remarkable DX during his tenure, executive editor Dean Baquet confessed, "We have no idea what the future of journalism is going to look like. When we started podcasts, we had no idea. We take risks, we screw up, we try stuff . . . we don't know what's going to stick."[5]

Transformative leaders share Baquet's humility. They recognize from the start that any digital idea they have is just a set of untested hypotheses—about customers, competition, operations, profits, technology, and more. They approach every idea ready to learn because they know what they don't know. This is why the Four Religions—lean start-up, design thinking, agile, and product management—are each built around rapid cycles of testing and experimentation. Each one starts by recognizing the uncertainty of any new venture.

Many businesses leaders mistakenly think that the key to innovation is coming up with good ideas. But *ideas are rarely a source of competitive advantage*. The real challenge of innovation is to become great at validation: learning as early and cheaply as possible which of your ideas could work and how. The mistaken focus on ideation comes in part from traditional innovation theory that put all its attention on where ideas come from. But modern innovation theories give far less attention to ideation; instead, they focus on the best methods for validating and improving on ideas (by identifying their assumptions, talking to customers, designing MVPs, gathering data, and adapting based on learning). Great ideas are made, not born.

In the first two steps of the Digital Transformation (DX) Roadmap, you worked to define a shared vision of the future, chose strategic priorities (your P/Os), and began to generate ideas for new ventures based on those P/Os. In the third step of the DX Roadmap, your goal is to rapidly test these new ventures to validate which ones may work and how.

The best digital businesses succeed because they learn rapidly from customers and the market, and use that learning to revise, pivot, and adjust an idea until it reaches the right combination of factors for liftoff. The challenge for Walmart and any business pursuing DX is to become good at doing this for different ideas across the company. Growth ventures may take many shapes: new products, new customer experiences, new marketing strategies, or entirely new business models. To build even one venture that has an impact on your business, you will need to test many ideas, shut some down, and change others, repeatedly, in response to testing and feedback. Doing this requires important shifts in how companies think about and manage innovation:

- *Think like a scientist*—Avoid debates based solely on opinion. Instead, ground every strategic decision in data. Use data from your own experiments, not preexisting third-party data. Every experiment should begin with a theory and aim to validate something specific—about your customer, your technology, the problem you think you are solving, and so on. Think in hypotheses. And don't design tests to prove you are right; instead, think like a scientist and design tests that could prove your hypothesis is *wrong*. If your venture keeps passing those tests, you know you are on to something!

- *Get to market sooner to learn faster*—Push to get your ideas into customers' hands in the real world as soon as possible. Only six months after beginning work on Intuit's small-business credit product, Rania Succar's team launched a streamlined version in a limited release in the state of Georgia. It felt incredibly early, but it proved incredibly valuable. "We learned that everything we expected to happen in the product . . . it was 100 percent different," she explained to me. Her team had to pivot immediately and change the scope of the product to respond to the features that mattered most to drive customer demand. "What I learned from that experience is that you have to get to market super fast, to know what you don't know. Because your roadmap is probably all wrong, based on assumptions you're thinking about in your head. So you've got to push teams to get to market quickly." As Steve Blank puts it: no business model survives contact with the customer.[6] Remember that all true learning comes from the customer—not from benchmarks or experts. So the only way forward is to go to customers directly, as early and often as possible.

- *Accelerate your learning*—Once you have started to document your assumptions and test your ideas with MVPs, the next step is to accelerate the whole process. "Test in minutes, not months" is an axiom of design thinking. Agile methods like Scrum set their cadence around a unit of work called a sprint, which includes a cycle of ideation, design, writing code, publishing it, and measuring response. Sprints are short, from one to four weeks. When Jonathan Becher was building SAP Digital, he found the most important metric for his start-up within an enterprise was not return on investment (ROI) but speed measured as time-to-market for each new innovation, feature, or experiment.[7] Experimentation is a constant cycle of learning and adaptation. Each test will shed new light on the opportunities and weaknesses of your idea, which in turn will lead to new ideation and new questions to test. Speed up this learning cycle.

Innovating through rapid experimentation may sound simple in theory, but it is hard in practice. I have seen many established organizations

Table 5.1.
What's at Stake—Step 3: Experimentation

Symptoms of Failure: Experimentation	Symptoms of Success: Experimentation
• Innovation is focused on coming up with a few great ideas.	• Innovation is focused on testing many ideas to learn which work best.
• Decisions are made based on business cases, third-party data, and expert opinion.	• Decisions are made based on experimentation and learning from the customer.
• Once they start a project, teams are committed to building the solution in full.	• Teams stay focused on the problem but flexible on the solution.
• Failures are costly, so the fear of risk is high.	• Failures are cheap, so there is a bias toward risk taking.
• Good ideas move slowly and don't seem to move the needle on the business.	• Good ideas grow fast and deliver business value at scale.

hire agile coaches or conduct design thinking workshops but then struggle to change the way they operate. Leadership remains focused on choosing a few big ideas. Detailed analysis and business cases are expected before any decisions are made. Once a solution is chosen, everyone is locked into delivering it according to plan. Some genuinely good ideas may emerge, but they advance slowly compared to digital-native competitors. In these organizations, DX produces a stream of projects that make good press releases but never deliver a sustained impact on business fundamentals.

Becoming a truly experiment-driven company requires deep change in the practices, habits, and mindset of most organizations. But it is the only path to effective DX. Table 5.1 shows some of the key symptoms of success versus failure in Step 3 of the DX Roadmap.

What's Ahead

In this chapter, we will see how any team in any organization can rapidly validate new ventures and drive new digital growth. I will provide a new model, the Four Stages of Validation, to organize the process of continuous learning for any new venture. You will learn how to use MVPs to test your ideas in the market, and you will learn the difference between illustrative and functional MVPs. I will also provide a new tool, the Rogers Growth Navigator, to guide any new venture through the Four Stages of Validation, and from the earliest napkin sketch to global delivery at scale. Finally, you will learn why experimentation at every level and in every function and department of your business is critical to becoming a bottom-up organization.

Before we get to the Four Stages of Validation, let's look at two elements that are often misused or misunderstood: MVPs and metrics. Each is essential to the Four Stages of Validation.

MVPs That Accelerate Learning

One of the most important but most misunderstood ideas in innovation theory is the MVP, or minimum viable product. Let me offer my own definition: an MVP is *a minimal artifact designed to test a business assumption.* An MVP can be as simple as a napkin sketch that you show to a prospective client across a table or as complex as a beta version of a video game released to early customers for feedback. The term "MVP" was coined in the 1980s by Frank Robinson and popularized by Steve Blank, Eric Ries, and others as a central element of the lean start-up method.[8] The main confusion around MVPs comes from the word "product" in the name. As Blank and Ries have stressed, an MVP need not be a product at all—in fact, it is often much less than a working prototype.

The key to a great MVP is two things: *minimal cost* (in time as well as money) and *maximum learning.* The "lean" in lean start-up is because your goal is not just to learn what does or doesn't work in your business venture but to spend the absolute minimum time and resources to learn it.[9] Stop spending months building a complex prototype just to validate if customers are interested in your product—you could likely learn that in days with a simple online test! In fact, a rougher MVP is often better for generating insightful customer feedback. As IDEO's Joe Brown told me, "If you show the customer a polished looking prototype, they will see only its flaws. If you show them a very rough one, they'll see its potential."

One famously rough MVP was used by Marc Lore and Vinit Bharara to test their vision of an online store focused on baby products, Diapers. com. For an initial MVP, the two entrepreneurs announced an offer— overnight diaper delivery—on their and their wives' personal Facebook pages. By morning they had received 240 orders, which they scrambled to fulfill by driving their family minivans to nearby stores and sending packages from their local UPS Store. This bare-bones experiment was no test of the operations, costs, or profit margins of a scalable business, but the founders got their first real-world data on customer demand, product preference, and price point, all in just twenty-four hours. Five years later, after phenomenal growth, they sold their start-up for over $500 million.[10]

Illustrative Versus Functional MVPs

In many organizations, terms like "MVP," "prototype," and "proof of concept" are used without a clear definition or purpose. The result is innovation where MVPs are too few and not at all minimal—they consume far too much time and resources and yield inconclusive data. By contrast, effective innovators have a clear understanding of the different types of MVPs they are using and why.

I have found it useful to think of two broad types of MVPs: illustrative MVPs and functional MVPs. Each type has its place, helping you learn different things at different stages of validating a new venture.

ILLUSTRATIVE MVPS

Illustrative MVPs *illustrate* the benefits, features, and design of your proposed solution, *but they do not yet deliver* those benefits to the customer. An illustrative MVP could be a napkin sketch that you show a prospective customer to gauge their reaction. It may be a static wire frame showing screenshots of a planned digital experience or an interactive wire frame that includes scrolling, buttons to click, and simulated feedback with fake data. An illustrative MVP for a service could be a video that shows what that service will look like in the life of the customer. For a physical product, it could be a prototype made of clay that a customer can hold in their hands and imagine putting to use. You may hear other names for an illustrative MVP, such as a low-fidelity MVP (per Steve Blank and Bob Dorf), a pretotype (per Alberto Savoia), or a proof of concept (POC) in product management.

The point of an illustrative MVP is to give the customer something tangible to react to rather than just listening to you describe your planned innovation. As customers interact with the illustrative MVP, be sure to watch and listen carefully for what they notice or miss, what they don't understand, and what questions they ask.

FUNCTIONAL MVPs

A functional MVP is a version of your innovation that is limited in scope but *delivers your essential value proposition* to the customer *within their real work or life context*. A functional MVP really does work. Any data it uses is real (not placeholder data). It delivers value and solves a problem for the customer. And, critically, it must be used by the customer in the real-world context that the innovation is meant for (whether their work setting or personal life). A functional MVP is sometimes called a high-fidelity MVP (per Blank and Dorf) or a prototype (although to engineers, that term often implies a one-off product built with the complete set of features, which is *not* what we want here).

Note that a functional MVP is *not* a complete version of your product or service. It should be limited in scope, with only the minimum features for use (reflecting the goal to "get to market sooner"). It is provided only to limited customers at first—whether by invitation only, in a limited location, or for a limited time. It will often rely on manual operations that are not scalable for a final release.

Rania Succar uses the metaphor of hamster wheels to describe how Intuit employees manually processed data for the first test of Intuit's loans product for small businesses. She knew that the process would need to be automated before the product could be launched widely. The first MVP for Diapers.com followed the same approach. Spending all night driving to stores, repackaging diapers, and mailing them by hand was not meant to be a scalable operation. But it gave customers the experience of overnight diaper delivery, and it generated invaluable insights about how customers would use the service in real life.

Not One MVP but Many

Remember that a successful venture team does not produce one MVP but many of them! A single innovation should go through several illustrative MVPs (from napkin sketches to robust wire frames) to clarify and validate what you are planning to build. When you get to functional MVPs, this iteration continues. Succar told me, "We launched seven versions of our product over three months during the test flight, while we were inviting customers to use it and comment on the interface, features, and more." There is no standard number of MVPs to be made. But the more you make, the faster you can accelerate your pace of learning.

Testing multiple MVPs promotes flexibility in your team. Lean start-up guru Bob Dorf says, "Your early MVPs should be cast in Jell-O"—that is, infinitely malleable. You want your team to have an unwavering commitment to the problem you are solving, matched by an open-minded flexibility on what the best final solution will be. Eric Ries describes this as a willingness to pivot. Every entrepreneur starts with a solution in mind, but those who succeed do so by constantly modifying their ideas as they get new feedback from customers. Always be ready to listen to the customer and to respond.

Every good MVP is designed to answer specific questions that matter most to its venture at that moment in time. One of my favorite examples is from the early days of Netflix, when the company was planning to launch a DVD-by-mail rental service. Cofounders Marc Randolph and Reed Hastings mailed a single disc to themselves (a recording of Patsy Cline's greatest hits), using a pink greeting card envelope and the local post office in Santa Cruz, California. This simple test was critical. Although no customers were involved, it allowed them to validate three things: Could they use the U.S. Postal Service for delivery? How fast would delivery be? Could DVDs be mailed in paper envelopes without breaking? The success of that test led them to press ahead with an idea that turned out to be revolutionary.[11]

Always remember: every MVP is a creative leap. It must be designed around the needs of that particular moment in your innovation journey. To design your next MVP, ask yourself these three questions:

1. What is the one thing I need to *learn next* about my venture?
2. What *data* would be most helpful to my learning that?
3. What is the quickest, cheapest, simplest *test* that I can run to get that data?

Remember: minimum cost, minimum time, and maximum learning. Let your creativity do the rest.

Metrics that Matter

As you take an iterative approach to MVPs, you will want to do the same with metrics. Keep in mind these guiding principles:

- *Measure what matters now*—At any moment in the life of your venture, the most important metric you should focus on will vary. The thing you need to learn one week may be which type of customer is most interested in your solution. But a week later, it may be which features will convince your free-trial users to become paying customers. Focus on what you need to validate next and choose the metrics that match. Your metrics will change rapidly as you move ahead.

- *Be skeptical*—Beware of vanity metrics—data that is easy to collect and makes your idea look good but doesn't yield critical meaning for your business. Also, don't believe everything a customer tells you they like, value, or would do. Customer feedback is most meaningful when they have "skin in the game"; that is, they are investing money or time, which proves their interest is genuine.

- *Balance behavioral and psychological data*—It is a common maxim in experimentation to prioritize behavioral data—measuring what customers do rather than what they say. But psychological data is essential as well: what does the customer care about, remember, attend to, think about? This type of data will help you understand their needs and point you to the design changes that will drive your next change in customer behavior. Look to balance both qualitative and quantitative methods.

- *Match lagging and leading metrics*—Lagging metrics measure current business results, including revenue, traffic to your site or store, and other key performance indicators (KPIs). Leading metrics are data that are predictive of future results. You may find that how often a customer uses your service (twice a month, or twice an hour) is predictive of whether they quit in the next thirty days. Customer complaints or word of mouth may be leading metrics too. Seeing the future by knowing the causes of growth versus decline is powerful! So always look for leading metrics that predict your future KPIs.

- *Focus on a few metrics at a time*—Keep your list short. Give laser-focus to three to six key variables that matter most to your venture at that moment. To find them, remember the design principles of MVPs: start with what you most need to learn next and then find metrics to match. There will always be other metrics that seem important too, but you can focus on them in your next test.

The Four Stages of Validation

With any new growth venture, the path from exciting idea to success at scale is incredibly daunting. So many things could go wrong. As Succar told me, "Whenever we start a new venture, the amount of uncertainty is crippling." Any new venture faces a range of questions, such as:

- Who is my customer?
- How big is the market opportunity?
- Who is my competition?
- What's my competitive advantage?
- What price should I charge?
- Should I charge a flat price, charge on usage, or charge a membership fee?
- What features should I build first?
- Can I deliver the experience I'm promising?
- Do I have the necessary skills or intellectual property (IP)?
- Will the technology work?
- Will partners agree to work with me?
- Where do I find my first customers?
- What channels should I use to market to them?
- What are my costs of doing business?
- Am I solving the right problem?
- Does anyone really care?

The possible experiments you could run and the MVPs that you could build will be just as numerous. For the leaders I meet, the most perplexing challenge is where to start. We know we must take an experiment-driven approach. But where do we begin? How can we organize all this testing and learning? What I have seen across scores of companies is that teams desperately need a guide to navigate from their very first market tests to driving growth at scale.

Based on my own years of advising teams and studying successful new ventures, I have developed a framework to define the sequence of effective innovation. I call this framework the Four Stages of Validation (see figure 5.1).

Each of these stages seeks to *validate* (i.e., prove or disprove) a different aspect of your innovation. The Four Stages of Validation test four things—the *problem* (you think you are solving), the *solution* (you think will

Problem ▶ Solution ▶ Product ▶ Business

Figure 5.1.
The Four Stages of Validation

Table 5.2.
The Four Stages of Validation and Key Questions to Answer

Validation Stage	Key Question to Answer
1. Problem validation	Are we focused on a genuine problem for an actual customer?
2. Solution validation	Does the customer see value in our proposed solution?
3. Product validation	Can we deliver a solution that customers use?
4. Business validation	Can we capture sufficient value from this innovation?

address it), the *product* (you think the customer will use), and the *business* (you think you can build from this innovation). Each of these stages is focused on answering a single, essential question (see table 5.2). Every test, MVP, and customer interview should be designed to yield data that helps to answer one of these four fundamental questions. Only by answering all four questions can you validate whether a new venture will create value in the real world.

Sequenced and Overlapping Stages

You must understand two critical aspects of the Four Stages of Validation before you can put them to work.

The first critical aspect of the four stages is their *sequence* (shown in Figure 5.1). This is where corporate innovation frequently runs into trouble. In most large organizations, teams rush to start on the later stages—focusing on the product, its features, or the business case—before they validate the problem being solved and who (if anyone) has that problem. For example:

- In finance-driven firms, we see a rush to start with stage 4: business validation: "Show me the business case first. Then we can approve a budget to spend on market testing or validation."
- In engineering-driven firms, we see the urge to start with stage 3: product validation: "We know the solution we need. Let's build a prototype as a proof of concept to see if it can be done. You can show it to customers just as soon as we build a complete product for them to try."
- In marketing-driven firms, we see a greater focus on the customer and an inclination to start with stage 2: solution validation: "We have a great idea that came out of our strategic brainstorm. Let's mock up some wire frames to quickly get customer feedback!"

All these approaches are mistaken! Each starts the process of validation in the wrong place. By contrast, every effective innovation process I have ever seen begins with stage 1—validating the problem you hope to solve with the customer you think it will matter to—and then moves sequentially through the stages.

The second critical aspect of the Four Stages of Validation is that they are *overlapping*. The sequence in figure 5.2 (problem > solution > product > business) marks only the beginning of each stage. That is, you begin to validate your problem before you start to validate your solution; you begin to validate the solution before you start to validate a working product; you begin to validate your product before you start to validate your business. The arrows circling back in the figure show that each stage continues even as others begin.

The Four Stages of Validation is not a waterfall or stage-gate process where success means that you conclude one stage then move on to the next. In fact, each stage is never finished. Even as you test the finances of your business (stage 4) and move to a public launch of your product, you will continue to learn and revise your understanding of the problem you are solving (stage 1), the features you need next for your solution (stage 2), and how you can deliver them for the right customer use cases (stage 3). Eventually, you will be validating all four stages simultaneously. By the time Intuit had a test flight of its loans product in the hands of early customers, Succar's team was dealing with issues and questions on every level—how to underwrite loans accurately (product), stimulate customer

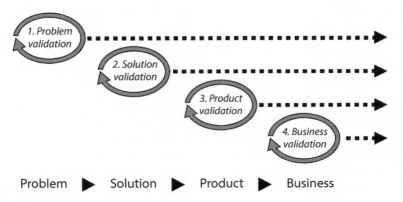

Figure 5.2.
The overlap of the Four Stages of Validation

demand with the right features (solution), revise revenue projections (business), and more.

For any innovation to deliver value to your business, you must validate all four stages. Real innovation means more than just proving that customers want your solution (product-market fit). It means validating the entire business model. This is why the Four Stages of Validation does not stop with your first functional MVP in the hands of early customers; it takes you all the way through usage, delivery, costs, revenue, and path to profit. As Chris Reid told me, "That's the Product Manager's job. In my view, you're accountable for the value chain of your solution: a cost base that's competitive, developing a value prop, how do I operate it competitively, and how do I sell it competitively. I just think that last piece, in a digital environment, is where some people pause and don't give enough thought."

To see how all this works in the real world of growing a new venture, let's look at each of the Four Stages of Validation in detail. For each stage, we will identify the best use of MVPs, the key metrics to track, and the biggest threats to your innovation's success.

Stage 1: Problem Validation

The first stage of validation for any new venture is problem validation. In this stage, the critical question to answer is, *Are we focused on a genuine problem for an actual customer?* Answering this question begins with defining the problem you think you are solving and then talking to real customers to find out *if* and *how* that problem truly matters to their life or work.

I cannot stress enough how important it is to begin your innovation journey here, validating your problem and your customer first. It is tempting to rush to work on designing your solution but, as Bob Dorf regularly reminds me, "Most new businesses die from lack of customers!" This is why Citibank's Discovery 10X process always begins with problem validation. As Chief Innovation Officer Vanessa Colella explained to me, every Citibank venture begins with an in-depth effort "to try and get at what is it that clients want to do differently. We use a variety of techniques to validate this very early on, before anything has been built."

Problem validation focuses on understanding and confirming the *problem* you are solving, the unmet needs of the customer, the context in which they experience that problem, and its urgency for them. This stage also focuses on learning as much as you can about who the *customer* is, where you might find them, and which customers care the most about your problem. Your goal should be to find a highly motivated segment of customers, called early adopters, who will be willing to try your earliest solution before anyone else. (*Hint:* If no customer cares passionately about what you are solving, you should move on to solving another problem!)

If you do identify an urgent problem, you also need to learn what customers are currently doing to address it. This can range from makeshift solutions to simple resignation (i.e., "We just live with it"). We can think of these as *existing alternatives* to any solution you may seek to develop. It is important to learn what these alternatives are, how satisfactory they are to the customer, and where they fall short.

Know Who the Customer Is

Problem validation starts and ends with listening to the customer. To find your first customer, ask: Whose problem do we think we are solving with this growth venture? Who would actually use any solution we develop? Be careful that you don't mistakenly label the *company* you are selling to as your customer. The customer is always a *person*—whether a consumer archetype ("tech-savvy new parents") or a business job role ("plant supervisor").

If you are developing an internal innovation, your customer will work at your own company. Think of Air Liquide's problem of predicting customer churn for its gas canister business. In order to validate this business problem in stage 1, Air Liquide's team must talk to the marketing employee who will use the solution in their day-to-day work.

Any innovation that uses a platform business model will serve multiple customers, each with their own needs. Think of Uber's platform, which connects drivers and riders, or Amazon Marketplace, which connects third-party sellers with customers. Uber needs an app that is successful with drivers just as much as it needs an app that succeeds with riders. If you have a multisided business model, you must validate your innovation with each type of customer it touches.

B2B innovations typically serve multiple customers as well. If you are creating an enterprise SaaS solution, your customers will include every stakeholder in the client's company whose needs must be met in order for your innovation to succeed. These could include the users of your new

SaaS service, the IT supervisor who must approve it for their intranet, the procurement manager who must agree to your subscription terms, and the finance officer who must approve the budgetary expense.

In problem validation, every customer matters! Make sure you know who your customers are and that you listen to each to validate their unmet needs.

Stage 1: No MVPs

Each of the Four Stages of Validation uses MVPs differently. In this first stage of problem validation, it is actually best to avoid using any MVPs at all. The reason: at this stage, you want to keep the focus entirely on understanding the customer's problem and not on your proposed solution.

Instead of an MVP, use in-depth observational interviews to learn from customers. Often called problem interviews, these are the starting point for customer discovery in lean start-up. In design thinking, this is the ethnographic and qualitative research done early on to capture the experience and voice of the customer. Whatever you call it, the goal is to uncover the customer's own stories, language, and experience in order to understand their needs and motivations.

The most important thing to remember in problem interviews is that these are conversations and not sales pitches. You should refrain entirely from talking about your own proposed solution. Instead, focus on listening and observing. Here are a few key tips for problem interviews:

- *Use open-ended questions*—Your goal is to get the customer talking. Never ask a yes or no question.
- *Shut up and listen!*—Say as little as possible. Be patient and give your customer time to elaborate.
- *Interview and observe in context*—If possible, talk to the customer in their own home or workplace to see where and how the problem takes place.
- *Look for emotion*—Your goal is to focus on the most extreme pain points and needs of the customer. Always listen for whatever triggers an emotional reaction.
- *Probe for specifics*—Follow up with when, where, how, and why questions. Ask the customer what they are currently doing about the problem and how well that is or isn't working.

- *Don't talk about your solution*—This is not a sales conversation! Don't pitch your idea. Instead, postpone saying anything about your proposed solution until future conversations.

Stage 1: Metrics and Learning

Your metrics for problem validation will be the simplest among the four stages because your validation here is mostly qualitative, not quantitative. It is critical, however, to set goals for your team members and push them on some important numbers. Your most important metric is the sheer number of customers that you speak with. As you identify different customer segments, make sure to track the number of interviews you conduct with each segment. Track measures of depth, such as number of site visits to a customer's home or workplace, pages of interviewer notes, verbatim text from customers, and interview videos. You should also track the number of high-interest customers you speak to in interviews—those who express great interest in your problem and might become early adopters.

GOLD STANDARD

In problem validation, the gold standard of learning (i.e., the best possible outcome) is to find a few lead users who are not only obsessed with your problem but will show you the hacks or prototypes they have built as workarounds and then ask you to make something similar for them to purchase. The term "lead users" comes from Eric von Hippel, who first observed that many of the best innovations come from watching the industrious efforts of hypermotivated customers.[12]

TYPICAL LEARNING

It is more common in the problem validation stage that you will learn that your customer or problem definition is not quite right. Your intended customer may face a somewhat different problem than you imagined, or the problem you are focused on may matter but to a different customer. The faster you learn this, the faster you can iterate and refocus your innovation on its best opportunity for success.

Stage 1: Threats

As you begin work on problem validation by engaging customers in problem interviews, look for the following red flags—common indicators that your planned venture is not off to a good start:

- *No problem found*—You can't identify a pressing customer problem you are solving (which means you have a "solution in search of a problem").
- *Low priority problem*—Customers nod their heads when you mention the problem, but no one shows great urgency to solve it. (Dorf says that, unless it is among a customer's "top five problems," there is no business to be built solving it.)
- *Status quo is good enough*—The customer is satisfied with the existing alternatives for addressing the problem. They may not be perfect, but they are good enough for the customer.

In the problem validation stage, your key competitive threat is *customer inertia*. Does your customer care enough about the problem you identified to change their behavior? In many cases, the answer is no. That is why it is critical to examine existing alternatives. If the customer is satisfied enough with their current workaround (i.e., muddling along with their current state of affairs), then even the most ingenious new product will fail.

Stage 2: Solution Validation

Once you have started to validate the problem you are solving with a group of real-world customers for whom it is truly urgent, you are ready to begin work on the second stage of validation: solution validation. In stage 2, the critical question to answer is, *Does the customer see value in our proposed solution?* This means testing whether the customer understands your innovation idea, cares about the features and benefits you plan to deliver, and is motivated and ready to change their behavior to adopt it.

This stage requires defining and validating your *value proposition*: What are the pains you will relieve and the gains you will provide to your customer? What is the job you will help them get done? You need to list each value element that you are planning, and for each one, validate if the customer really cares.

You will also be validating the design of your *solution*—that is, how you intend to deliver your benefits to the customer (Face-to-face or self-service? immersive experience or clean-and-simple? Twelve-month training program or a library of online resources?). This also means drafting and validating a feature roadmap: What features do you need to launch with, and which ones are the next highest priority for the customer?

At this stage, you will also seek to measure and quantify *customer demand*. How many customers really want your product? How badly do they want it, and what features are they willing to pay for? Successful proof of customer demand for a new innovation is commonly referred to as "product-market fit."[13]

Stage 2: MVPs

In stage 2: solution validation, we will make extensive use of illustrative MVPs. As explained earlier in this chapter, these are MVPs that *illustrate* the features, benefits, and design of the proposed solution without yet *delivering* those benefits to the customer. An illustrative MVP can be extremely rudimentary (a hand-drawn sketch), or relatively elaborate (a wire frame of a planned digital service showing different interactive screens with simulated data).

Air Liquide's Olivier Delabroy stresses the simplicity of an illustrative MVP (or proof of concept, as Air Liquide calls it) and how it is used at his industrial firm: "It can be super simple—a mockup or a simple screen. You just want to check that the end user will understand its value and use it." He also stresses using minimal time and resources: "Build something super cheap that you can put in the trash the next day. The only expectation is to validate that it creates value." This kind of validating of design and user experience can be done virtually, but it often benefits from in-person testing—where you can observe how the customer interacts with the MVP, hear what questions they ask, and see what features they request or ignore.

Customer demand is best validated with behavioral data. Don't ask if the customer will buy. Instead, give them a buy button and see who puts their money where their mouth is. Advertise your planned innovation to different audiences with ads describing different benefits or features, and measure who clicks and which descriptions they respond to. This kind of test can be done quickly with low-cost advertising in search engines and social media. For a paid product, your goal should be to see if someone will provide their credit card number to preorder. (The crowdfunding service Kickstarter is built entirely around this idea—collecting customer's paid deposits in advance for an unmade new product—as a way of learning if the market really wants it.) In other cases where you don't plan to charge the user (e.g., an advertising-based product or an internal innovation for employees), you can measure how many customers are willing to create an account or enter their email address to be notified when the innovation goes live.

Building such simple MVPs rapidly and in constant interaction with the customer is a big change for companies with a traditional engineering culture. "This is not in the DNA of our industry," Delabroy explains. "We were used to only going to see the customers when we were 200 percent confident the product was working. Our mindset is now progressing fast." Unlearning these kinds of habits is essential if you want to accelerate learning at the early stages of your innovation process.

Stage 2: Metrics and Learning

Metrics are critical to effective solution validation. At this stage, you should be measuring the priority of the benefits you are promising and the features you intend to build. Which benefits matter most to which customers? What features do they want you to prioritize in your product roadmap? In addition, stage 2 metrics should focus on measures of customer demand. Depending on your innovation, these measures could include online registrations, app downloads, product trials, customer purchase orders, or even cash deposits. Remember, you are not yet delivering an actual working solution to any customers (that comes in stage 3). But if you can illustrate the expected solution well enough, you should see measurable demand from customers who are ready to start paying or using your innovation.

Lastly, don't just believe the customer when they tell you what they want! The best test of how much credence to give a customer's response is to look at how much "skin in the game" they have (one of Alberto Savoia's favorite points).[14] The more time, effort, or money your customer commits, the more you can trust what they are telling you. This is why a cash deposit is a much better signal of customer demand than an email registration.

GOLD STANDARD

The gold standard of solution validation is for customers to give you a cash deposit for your forthcoming product—like Tesla collecting $1,000 deposits for its Model 3 more than a year before the first car was built.[15] For a B2B innovation, the equivalent is a customer providing a signed purchase order, with the required delivery specifications and an agreed price if you deliver on time.

TYPICAL LEARNING

It is more common at this stage that you will learn that many of your planned features or benefits don't really matter to your customer, while other features that you hadn't prioritized will be essential for them to even consider your innovation. The key is that you want to learn this *now*, before you build your first working product! This avoids the huge waste of time and resources that can be spent engineering a working prototype without first validating what your customers truly want and why.

Stage 2: Threats

As you use illustrative MVPs and validate customer interest in your proposed solution, look for the following red flags—common indicators that you have not achieved product-market fit:

- *No urgent demand*—You receive polite interest in your solution ("That's very interesting. Please keep in touch and let us know when you launch"). But there are no requests to register, use, or buy ("How soon can you have something ready?" or "We'd love to be part of your first pilot").
- *No killer feature*—When you test your value proposition, no single feature or benefit pops out as driving customer demand. Many of your benefits seem nice to the customer, but none are enough to motivate behavior change.
- *No advantage over existing solutions*—Once you describe your planned solution, customers identify a comparable solution in the market, and they don't see a compelling reason why they must choose yours instead.

At the solution validation stage, your key competitive threat is *existing solutions*. As soon as you propose a specific solution to your customer, they will view it in comparison to an existing solution already in the marketplace (whether you agree with that comparison or not). Be sure to validate. What existing solutions do customers compare yours to? Does your solution have any point of differentiation or advantage in the customer's mind? If not, you are setting yourself up for a costly, losing battle.

Stage 3: Product Validation

In start-up culture, there is a huge focus on achieving product-market fit (the goal of stage 2). And in many enterprises, innovation teams think that, once they discover a value proposition that customers are clamoring for, they can hand off their venture to marketing, sales, and supply chain to build the product and scale it in the market. But the innovation team's job is only half done! Once you have validated that a promising segment of customers sees value in your planned solution and is eager to try it, you are ready to begin the third stage of validation: product validation.

In this stage, the critical question to be answered is, *Can we deliver a solution that customers use?* This means testing two things at the same time. The first is how the customer uses your innovation in the real world—that is, in their day-to-day work or life context (not sequestered in a test lab at your offices). The second is what your business must do to deliver the essential value of your innovation to the customer (what tasks must be done, what resources are needed, what partners will be critical, etc.).

Use and Delivery

Much of stage 3 is focused on validating *usage* by the customer—what are the different use cases (or contexts) in which customers use your solution? For each use case, what is the customer's journey from start to finish? You will never know how customers will use your product until you put it in their hands.

Susie Lonie was working for telco Vodafone and its Kenyan subsidiary Safaricom when her team developed a new mobile phone app called M-Pesa. The app allowed small payments to be made and received by anyone with a mobile account on their network. The company's plan was that M-Pesa would be a tool to support the microfinance sector of Kenya's economy, facilitating small loan repayments by entrepreneurs who lacked a bank account. But once M-Pesa was in the hands of its earliest customers, they started to find many more uses for it. Business owners used it for security while traveling, depositing their cash into the digital wallet before departing on a trip and withdrawing it when they reached their destination. City workers used M-Pesa to send remittances to their families in distant villages. One customer used it to text money to her stranded husband to catch a bus home. As customers found more and more uses for M-Pesa, the world's first mobile wallet took off, quickly dominating the economy of Kenya. In other countries, it has been used to fight corruption (one government switched to paying its police force digitally to ensure everyone got their full salary) and to bring gray-market transactions into the formal economy.[16] With any truly novel innovation, the early adopters will teach you the real use of your product. So get an early functional MVP into their hands as soon as you can and find out the real potential of your innovation and what features it truly needs.

The other major area of validation in stage 3 is how your business will *deliver* your solution to the customer. This includes validating what assets and skills you will need, what activities your business will need to do well, and what should be handled by external partners. It also means validating the feasibility of your technology and your ability to meet any requirements related to risk, regulation, or security. These kinds of operational questions can only be answered by delivering your value proposition to at least a few customers in the real world.

When restaurant chain Panera first developed a suite of new digital services for ordering (including in-store kiosks, a mobile app, and delivery drivers), it didn't launch them across all its hundreds of stores. Instead, it tested the new digital-ordering experience for months in a single store in Braintree, Massachusetts. The results showed that customers loved the new digital features, but they caused operational issues, including food preparation errors and new bottlenecks of customer traffic. Only after these issues were resolved was the new customer experience launched at scale and to great success.[17]

Customer usage and product delivery are often critically intertwined. Before heading down a particular path for delivery, be sure to validate your customer's willingness to use it. Chris Reid of Mastercard explained how customer willingness matters when designing digital solutions for finance. "Even before you pick up a pen on your product's design, or hand it over to a Scrum team, you may say, 'This has to fit into someone's app.' So, will we deliver this by a simple API [application programming interface]? Or is it an SDK [software development kit] integration, which is a heavier lift?" Your business may have a clear preference between these two technical routes, but if the customer is unwilling to use your preferred model, there is no point in going forward with it. As Reid said, "If you haven't thought that through, there is a significant risk that even a great product won't be successful."

Lastly, for any innovation to succeed in the long-term, you will need some kind of *competitive moat* to prevent others from doing the same thing just as well. As part of product validation, you need to verify that you have some unique advantage over other firms that will help you deliver this innovation.

Stage 3: MVPs

In the product validation stage, illustrative MVPs have only limited use, such as showing a customer different possible use cases for your product to learn which ones are most relevant to test.

Instead, almost all your learning in stage 3 will come from functional MVPs, which deliver your essential value proposition to the customer within their real work or life context. Your earliest functional MVP should be a bare-bones product with the absolute minimal features. (Remember the purpose of a functional MVP is not to deliver a finished product but to deliver learning!) First, use this MVP to learn if your innovation really does create value in the life of your customer. Second, learn how the customer uses it. (When and where do they use it? Which features gets used versus ignored? Is the user interface confusing or obvious?) Third, use the MVP to learn what you must do to deliver this innovation. (What issues must be addressed in terms of supply chain, compliance, customer service, etc.?)

For the sake of speed and rapid learning, your first functional MVP may work in only a single limited use case. It may take technical shortcuts and rely on work being done manually in the background. (I've heard this called a "Wizard of Oz" MVP, or, by Eric Ries, a "concierge" MVP.[18]) It will likely have only a limited release for a few users to try in the real world (perhaps just to selected employees). Remember that speed of learning is your top priority. As LinkedIn founder Reid Hoffman said, "If you are not embarrassed by the first version of your product, you've launched too late."[19]

As product validation continues, you should evolve from a makeshift, often jerry-rigged functional MVP to a much more scalable product or service. Each iterative MVP should add more features based on what users request. It should work in a wider range of use cases. The back end should become more robust—more automated, more secure, using more data, and able to serve more customers. This iterative process will guide your product validation from a limited release (invitation only or a local test market) to a true public launch.

Stage: 3 Metrics and Learning

During product validation, many of your most important metrics will revolve around customer adoption and usage. You want to measure not just how many customers try your innovation once but what happens next. Do they keep using it? How frequently? In what locations and at what times of day? What features are most popular? Do they recommend your innovation to others?

One critical metric to track will be growth in total number of users over time. Just as important, however, is to track specific customer cohorts (small groups who start at the same time with the same feature set) so you can measure their repeat usage (stickiness), their satisfaction, and their referral rates or advocacy (such as Net Promoter Score). It is also critical to measure different customer segments, keeping an eye out for differences between them. Do businesses in one industry make more frequent use of your product than those from another sector? That kind of insight will be critical to scaling your product.

In addition to customer usage, you should be tracking metrics related to your own delivery and operations. How many errors do you see in your product or service? How reliably can you deliver it on time and to the right customer? How fast and well are you delivering to different customers and in different use cases? What growth rate are you able to sustain in rolling out your product? All these points will be critical to improving operations and validating that you can scale your current product.

GOLD STANDARD

The gold standard in product validation is for customers to adopt your product, keep using it, and attract others with word of mouth—leading to exponential growth in your number of customers. At the same time, customer data and feedback provide clarity about which use cases are most promising and which features are most important. Your operations prove to be robust and easily scalable.

TYPICAL LEARNING

It is more common at this stage that you will learn that the customer uses your innovation in very different ways than you planned. You may learn that the technical uncertainty around your innovation is greater or less than you expected, that your delivery time line will be longer or shorter than you thought, or that tasks you planned to do yourself are better off outsourced (or vice versa). All this learning will put you in a much better position to deliver your innovation at scale in the real world.

Stage 3: Threats

As you use functional MVPs to validate customer usage and delivery of your product or service, look for the following red flags:

- *Usage doesn't follow interest*—Customers may like your innovation in theory, but they don't use it when it is offered. Or you may see strong initial trial by customers but little repeat usage, or rapid churn.
- *Too hard to deliver*—You can't find a path to deliver a solution customers will use. The current technology may not be ready. You may lack essential skills, assets, or distribution partners, or you may be unable to overcome regulatory hurdles.
- *Too easy to deliver*—Your solution works well, but competitors can easily deliver the same thing as well or better than you can.

In the product validation stage, your key competitive threat is *copycat products* launched by other companies once your innovation proves popular. If other firms copy your product, will you have any unique advantage (exclusive partners, unique data or IP, network effects) that allows you to deliver it better or more cheaply than they do? Imitation may be the sincerest form of flattery (per Oscar Wilde), but it can crush many a first-mover in business.

Stage 4: Business Validation

Once you have started to validate how customers will use your solution and how you will deliver it, you are ready to begin work on the fourth stage of validation: business validation. In this final stage, the critical question to be answered is, *Can we capture sufficient value from this innovation?* For any venture to succeed, it must deliver not just value to customers but also value for your business. That means proving not just product-market fit and use by the customer but ROI for your firm.

A historical example may illuminate this point. Perhaps no individual is more associated with innovation than Thomas Edison, and the invention he is most known for is the electric light bulb. But the incandescent bulb itself was invented by English chemist Humphry Davy and others. What Edison contributed on top of that technical breakthrough was a dogged search for an economic model that could make electricity the dominant technology for lighting the home. Only by making the economics and pricing work could Edison persuade average consumers to switch from kerosene lamps to an electric future. Without the right economic innovation, the technical innovation would mean nothing to people's lives.

One of the economic hurdles that Edison recognized was the high cost of copper, which was used to transmit electricity from power stations to the home. Through experimentation, Edison discovered that you could reduce the amount of copper needed if the electric current were run at a higher voltage. But this voltage would burn out every light bulb unless filaments were designed with a much higher resistance. This ran counter to the thinking of the bulb's engineers (high-resistance filaments wasted energy), but it was critical in bringing down transmission costs and ultimately lowering prices enough to trigger customer adoption. In studying Edison's notebooks, historian Thomas Hughes found that they held as many notes on economic experiments as scientific ones.[20]

To succeed with any innovation, we must all learn, like Edison, to focus on testing and perfecting our economic models just as much as our products and value propositions. Our fourth stage, business validation, requires that for any new growth venture, we must test and learn the answers to several questions:

- *How will your business capture value from your innovation?*—Value may come from new revenue. It may come from reducing costs or operational risks. Some innovations generate nonmonetary value, for example, data or customer relationships that you monetize elsewhere. For a nonprofit, value may be measured in terms of impact on your core mission.

- *What is your customer lifetime value (CLV)?*—Innovations often create value by customer acquisition, by improving customer retention, or by expanding the average revenue you earn per user. Which of these will be affected by your innovation?
- *What is the cost structure of your innovation?*—Costs may include marketing, operations, and outside partners, as well as ongoing research and development (R&D) to maintain the competitiveness of your innovation. It is critical to understand which costs are variable versus fixed (e.g., the same cost whether you serve ten customers or 10,000) and what economies of scale you might achieve if you grow.
- *What is your path to profit?*—The goal of innovation should always be net value creation. Getting there requires a formula for when value capture will surpass costs. Even if your innovation is certain to be profitable, you need to know when and also the maximum upside. Based on margins and market size, is your innovation a $1 million opportunity or a $1 billion opportunity? The answer may be critical in deciding how far to pursue it.

As you validate the economics of any innovation, be careful not to leverage false economies to exaggerate its promise. For enterprise innovations, it may be possible to get your company's sales team to promote your product to existing customers or leverage other relationships to accelerate your venture's initial growth. But help like this, which can't be scaled indefinitely, can mask the true economics of what you are building. It is better to find out early on what it would cost to deliver all aspects of your new venture out of your own budget rather than be surprised later that a promising idea turns untenable when it has to run on its own steam.

One more warning on business validation: I often meet executives who are told to do stage 4 first. That is, to build a business case for the ROI of their new venture *before* they have validated the problem they are solving, the customer they will serve, the solution they are planning, or the product they will deliver. It is important to realize that any business case built before those three stages of validation have begun is pure fiction. Don't get boxed into delivering fake data at stage 4! If your current bureaucracy will not release any innovation funding without a business case, don't ask for it. Instead, ask for a small budget for "market research." (No one expects an ROI from market research.) Use this money to start your early stages of validation, and then come back to business validation (and the bigger budget request) once you have some validation of what you are even trying to build.

Stage 4: MVPs

At the business validation stage, illustrative MVPs will be of limited use for gathering data. You could show customers different offers and ask their willingness to pay. You may be able to estimate your customer acquisition costs by "dry testing" different marketing channels (i.e., promoting a product you don't yet have with ads placed in different media).

Almost all your learning in stage 4, however, will come from functional MVPs—versions of your innovation that deliver your essential value proposition to customers in their real-life contexts. A functional MVP is the only way to start learning about your true operating costs and path to profitability. You may think you can predict your revenue by surveying customers on the price they would pay, but you will never know your true price point until you start to deliver value to customers. After they try your product, they may demand a price cut. Believe it or not, they may ask to pay you more! (I have seen this with entrepreneurs whose first customers desperately wanted them to stay in business.) With a functional MVP, you will learn how many customers return your product or ask for a refund and whether you can grow your revenue by offering a volume discount.

In practice, business validation will require tests on a wide range of financial drivers. For example, just validating your marketing costs may require several tests—of advertising channels, conversion rates, customer churn, and word of mouth. Your earliest MVPs will give only partial information on these drivers. Diapers.com's first MVP measured how much an average customer might spend in one week on diapers by mail but that was just one factor in estimating revenue. The Netflix post office test measured the cost of shipping one disc to one customer, but shipping costs would also be shaped by how frequently customers mailed back their DVDs each month.

As you continue down the path of business validation, you should progress from tests of specific financial drivers (weekly revenue, shipping costs, etc.), to broader tests of total profitability. In the case of Panera's digital redesign of the customer's order experience, this meant validating the total impact on store profit based on numerous changes in costs, revenue, and customer behavior from its digital innovations. As your own functional MVPs become more complete, the economic data they validate will become richer as well.

Stage 4: Metrics and Learning

In business validation, all the metrics you focus on will be financial metrics. These will include measures relating to revenue (price point, total revenue, top-line growth, etc.), as well as costs (variable and fixed) and net profit. Your key financial metrics will depend on your business model. Retailers focus on metrics like sales per square foot. Subscription businesses focus on average revenue per user (ARPU) and CLV. In ventures where your value comes from risk reduction, financial metrics should focus on underwriting and the cost of reinsurance. For innovations that serve internal customers in your enterprise, the simplest financial metric is often to determine what you would pay an outside vendor for this same outcome or what are you currently paying.

Nonprofits are often less skilled in developing financial models, but it is no less critical for them to validate investment in new innovations. The Gates Foundation uses disability-adjusted life years (DALYs) as a metric to compare the impact of wide-ranging investments in global health. Nonprofits should ask of any innovation, What does it cost us to achieve a comparable outcome (e.g., lives saved or children educated) through our current means? Does this innovation deliver the same impact with fewer resources? For every innovation, the organization must ask whether this is the most effective use of its resources.

GOLD STANDARD

The gold standard in business validation is to capture value, or turn a profit, from your very first users—that is, to have a self-funding project from the beginning. In the start-up world, this path is known as bootstrapping— when you are able to grow a new business without the help of venture capital.

TYPICAL LEARNING

It is more common at this stage of validation that you will learn that costs, revenue, and profitability are all different than what you imagined. You may find that the customers you were focused on are not the most profitable ones to build a business on (but others may be). You may find that what you thought was a new revenue project is actually better run as a customer retention project or a cost-savings project. A great solution to a real problem can usually capture value for your business somewhere, but it might not be in the place you were originally looking! The sooner you learn any of this, the sooner you can find out what the path to profitability might be for your innovation and whether the opportunity is big enough that you want to continue down this path, or if you should shift your focus to another innovation idea.

Stage 4: Threats

As you use functional MVPs to validate the business value of your new venture, look for the following red flags:

- *No value capture*—Customers like your offering but they won't pay for it, and you can't find another value stream for your firm.
- *No path to profit*—You are capturing some value, but your costs are too high, and they won't go down enough to break even as you scale.
- *Too small a prize*—Even with a margin of profit, you may find the maximum upside of your innovation is not large enough to merit a continued focus by your organization. As an innovation manager at a large firm once told me, "The worst thing I can bring our leaders is a $10 million idea."

At the business validation stage, your key competitive threat is *other investment opportunities*. Every venture comes with an opportunity cost—you are pursuing it instead of something else. In many enterprises, the CFO will calculate an internal rate of return (IRR), to reflect the financial return the firm can get by spending money on safe investments (e.g., paying down debt or investing in infrastructure). The classic CFO rejoinder to any proposed innovation is, "Sounds great. But can your ROI beat my IRR?" At stage 4, you should ask the same thing. Even if your venture grows to scale, will there be better places to invest the firm's resources?

Recap: Metrics and Competition

To conclude our tour of the Four Stages of Validation, let's recap what we've learned by summarizing the metrics we use at each stage and the competitive threats that we face. Table 5.3 recaps the important quantitative metrics in each of the Four Stages of Validation. It is true that much of the learning

Table 5.3.
Quantitative Metrics by Stage of Validation

Stage of Validation	Types of Metrics	Sample Metrics
1. Problem validation	Customer interview metrics	• Number of interviews • Customers spoken to in each user segment • Number of site visits • Hours of conversation recorded • Verbatim transcripts • Early adopters identified
2. Solution validation	Customer demand metrics	• Adoption rate or conversion of leads • Number of online registrations • Requests to pilot the product • Product trial or downloads • Customer deposits or purchase orders
3. Product validation	Use and operations metrics	• Total number of users • Growth in the number of users • User satisfaction • Repeat use/stickiness • Customer referral rate • Net Promoter Score • Operational accuracy • Operational downtime • Speed of delivery
4. Business validation	Financial metrics	• Price point • Total revenue • Customer acquisition cost • Retention or churn rate • Cost to serve (marginal versus fixed) • Profit margin or ROI • ARPU • Customer lifetime value • Total profit versus loss

from customer interviews and MVPs will be qualitative (the questions customers ask, the problems they bring up, the emotion of their responses, etc.). But quantitative metrics will clarify many of your biggest insights, and they will help you to measure your team's progress in validating any venture.

Table 5.4 lists the key competitive threats you will address in each of the Four Stages of Validation. Each stage must address a different key

Table 5.4.
Competitive Analysis in the Four Stages of Validation

Stage of Validation	Key Competitor	Key Competitive Question
1. **Problem validation**	Customer inertia	Does the customer care enough about this problem to change their behavior?
2. **Solution validation**	Existing solutions	Does your solution have a compelling advantage versus comparable solutions?
3. **Product validation**	Copycat products	If other firms copy your product, will you have any unique advantages in delivering it?
4. **Business validation**	Other investment opportunities	If this innovation succeeds, will it deliver a better return than other known opportunities?

competitor, and each stage poses a different competitive question. Only if validation provides a clear yes answer to all four questions will your innovation be ready to implement at scale.

Tool: The Rogers Growth Navigator

We are now ready to introduce our next tool, the Rogers Growth Navigator. I developed the Navigator over years of work with innovation teams to address their most critical area of confusion: how to sequence and organize business experimentation. The Rogers Growth Navigator ends this confusion by enabling you to visually map your progress through the Four Stages of Validation (see figure 5.3).

The Navigator is designed to guide growth ventures of any kind—whether a disruptive new product, a redesigned customer experience, or a plan to optimize your business operations. It works for large enterprises and start-ups alike. And it works for the full life cycle of innovation—from whiteboard sketch to operation at a global scale.

The Rogers Growth Navigator captures three things: your current business assumptions, your experimental learning to date, and what you need to test and learn next. By combining all of this in one diagram, the Navigator provides a single, shared view of the venture, which you can use to align both your team and your sponsors. As you test and learn, your Navigator will go through many revisions. Keeping copies of each weekly iteration allows you to capture your thinking over time.

1. Problem Validation

Problem	Customer
Problem definition	Addressable segments
Existing alternatives	Total addressable market (TAM)
Unmet needs	Early adopters

2. Solution Validation

Value Proposition	Solution
Value elements	Delivery and design
Job to be done	Competitive differentiation
	Feature roadmap

Top-Line summary   For [Customer] Who [Problem], X is a [Solution] That [Value Proposition].

Metrics That Matter Now   Three to Six Key Metrics Right Now

3. Product Validation

Usage	Delivery
Customer use cases	Business activities
Customer journeys	Technical requirements
	Compliance and risk

Capabilities	Right to Win
Key assets	Unique advantages
Key skills	Competitive benefits
External partners	Deepen the moat

4. Business Validation

Value capture	Customer Lifetime Value (CLV)
Revenue model	CLV by segment
Paying customers	Acquisition
Cost/risk savings	Retention
Nonmonetary value	Expansion

Cost Structure	Path to Profit
Fixed costs	Profit formula
Marginal costs	Time frame
Scale economies	Maximum upside

Figure 5.3.
The Rogers Growth Navigator

Let's briefly walk through each block of the Rogers Growth Navigator to see how you can use it to capture learning across all Four Stages of Validation for your next growth venture.

1. Problem Validation

The first two blocks of the Rogers Growth Navigator will capture your hypotheses and learning from stage 1: problem validation.

PROBLEM

In this first block of the Navigator, you will capture everything about the problem that your innovation is meant to solve, including:

- *Problem definition*—What exactly is the problem that you are trying to solve? Why does this problem matter? How urgent is this problem? (Is it among anyone's "top five" problems?)
- *Existing alternatives*—What existing alternatives are being used to address this problem? Even if you think your solution will be the first of its kind, customers are clearly taking some approach to the problem currently (even just to mitigate it). What is that alternative approach?
- *Unmet needs*—What are the shortcomings of these alternatives? What needs do they leave unmet among the customers you are trying to serve?

CUSTOMER

In this block, you will capture your learning about the customer who faces the problem you are solving. Begin by breaking your customers into distinct segments who might use your innovation in different ways or for different reasons:

- *Addressable segments*—Who are the different segments of customers with this problem? Focus on distinct groups that you could reach or address separately. For consumers, describe each segment in terms of demographics, psychographics, and technographics. For business customers, describe the type of organization and the role of the person who will use or make decisions about your innovation.
- *Total addressable market (TAM)*—For each segment, what is the total addressable market? That is, how many people or companies are there that currently match your description? How might this change if you create a compelling enough offering?
- *Early adopters*—Every successful innovation is adopted first by a handful of customers who are exceptionally motivated. Who will your early adopters be? Why does the problem you are solving matter more to them than to other customers? Why will they be willing to try an early solution or MVP?

2. Solution Validation

The next two blocks of the Rogers Growth Navigator are where you will capture your hypotheses and learning from stage 2: solution validation.

VALUE PROPOSITION

In this block, define the value that you will provide the customer. It is critical to avoid talking about product features and instead to describe the benefits of your venture from the point of view of the customer:

- *Value elements*—List all the benefits you will provide to the customer. Include as many as possible, and always describe them from the customer's point of view. First, think of current pain points your innovation will solve for the customer, and then list ways it will delight the customer and enhance their experience. (The concept of value elements is explained in detail in *The Digital Transformation Playbook*.)
- *Job to be done*—This powerful concept comes from the writing of Clayton Christensen and Michael Raynor.[21] The idea is to describe the benefit of any innovation by asking what it enables the customer to do or to achieve. Describe this "job" as something that truly matters to the customer.

SOLUTION

In this block, define the product or service that you will use to deliver your value proposition to the customer. Now you should switch from describing the customer's experience to describing your product and its features:

- *Delivery and design*—How will you deliver the benefits of your value proposition to the customer? For a product, what will it look like and how will it work? For a service or process innovation, when, where, and how will it be delivered?
- *Competitive differentiation*—What existing solutions will the customer compare this innovation to? What difference will motivate customers to pick your solution over these competitors or to switch if they are already using these competitors? Are customers "locked

in" to using those competitors, or will it be easy to get them to switch?

- *Feature roadmap*—Which features have you built so far, if any? Which features do you need to add next, and in what order? Which existing features could you cut? Which planned features can be delayed?

Top-Line Summary

The aim of this block is to capture the essence of your venture in a single sentence. Think of this as the elevator pitch you would use to sell your idea to a potential sponsor or investor.

A good top-line summary uses a single sentence to capture the most essential points from the first four blocks of your Navigator. At the beginning of your journey, this will be a statement of your vision for the new venture. As you validate, you will revise the summary to capture the most essential things you learn from stages 1 and 2. I recommend using the following template for your top-line summary:

- *For* [Customer]
- *Who* [Problem],
- [your innovation's name]
- *Is a* [Solution]
- *That* [Value Proposition].

For example, a top-line summary for Walmart's InHome service might be: "For shoppers who want affordable groceries plus time-saving and convenience, Walmart InHome is an annual membership program that lets them order affordable, fresh groceries online and have them delivered right into their home's fridge and cabinets by a safe and trusted Walmart agent."

As you write your top-line summary, be sure to test it on people who are not fully familiar with your venture. Avoid jargon. Ask yourself if your top-line summary would be clear to an average customer. (Better yet, use it on a customer and see if it is clear.)

Metrics That Matter Now

In this block, identify three to six key metrics that matter most to your innovation at its current stage of development. In doing so, draw on every block of the Navigator, encompassing all Four Stages of Validation. Think of lagging and leading metrics. Focus on customer metrics with "skin in the game." And remember that the metrics that matter most should be constantly evolving. Identify what matters to your venture *right now*.

3. Product Validation

The next four blocks of the Rogers Growth Navigator will capture your hypotheses and learning in stage 3: product validation.

USAGE

In this block, you want to capture learning about the customer's usage of your innovation:

- *Customer use cases*—In what different situations do customers use this innovation? List as many use cases as possible, describing the context of each one and how it shapes the customer's usage.
- *Customer journeys*—In each use case, how does the customer actually use the innovation? Describe the sequential steps of a typical customer's experience, including when, where, and how they use the innovation. Which features do they use and why?

DELIVERY

In this block, you want to capture learning about the back-end operations required to support your venture:

- *Business activities*—What does the business need to do in order to deliver your innovation to the customer in all these use cases? Focus on your repeated activities and those that you must do exceptionally well for the venture to work.
- *Technical requirements*—What technology standards must your innovation meet to work reliably and effectively? What other technologies must it integrate with? What standards of interoperability must it meet? How will your solution meet these requirements?
- *Compliance and risk*—What legal requirements must your innovation adhere to? What company rules for compliance or risk management must you meet? How will you ensure your solutions meets all of them?

CAPABILITIES

Use this block to define the capabilities that will be needed to deliver this solution, the partners that will support you, and the roles they will play. Remember that few innovations will be delivered solely by your own organization.

- *Key assets*—What tangible assets are needed, such as infrastructure, real estate, or manufacturing materials? What intangible assets, including intellectual property, data, software code, and brand reputation, are needed?
- *Key skills*—What does your business need to be skilled at in order to deliver this innovation and to excel at it?
- *External partners*—Who do you need to partner with to help your business deliver this innovation? What essential activities will these partners perform on your behalf? What assets or skills will they provide so you don't need to?

RIGHT TO WIN

If your venture is to succeed in the long term, there will need to be some kind of barrier or competitive moat that prevents competitors from doing an equal or better job of delivering the same thing.

- *Unique advantages*—What unique skills, assets, relationships, or other advantages do you hold that will enable you to deliver this innovation? For ideas, look back at our discussion of unique advantages in chapter 3.
- *Competitive benefits*—How exactly do these advantages help you deliver this innovation better than others? For example, do they lower your costs, lock in an established customer base, or provide a uniquely better customer experience?
- *Deepen the moat*—Look to the future as you consider your competitive moat. How will you reinforce your unique advantages for the future? Or how can you invest to develop a competitive moat that you currently lack?

4. Business Validation

The final four blocks of the Rogers Growth Navigator are used to capture your hypotheses and learning in stage 4: business validation.

VALUE CAPTURE

Here, you need to define the value captured by your own organization from this innovation, including any revenue streams or other streams of value to your business:

- *Revenue model*—Will you charge customers for this innovation? If so, how? Options include sale, license, rental, or fee for performance. What price is the customer willing to pay, and how can you influence this? Are you charging a fixed price or a sliding scale, or using a free-mium model (with free versus paid versions)?
- *Paying customers*—Who pays you? Is it the user or someone else in their organization? For a multisided business model, which customer type pays? If your innovation grows, could you add revenue streams from another customer type, for example, from an advertiser seeking to reach your primary customer?
- *Cost/risk savings*—Will your innovation deliver cost savings to your business? Will it reduce a significant risk for your business? If so, can you quantify the financial value?
- *Nonmonetary value*—Will your business capture value in other ways, for example, data, or new relationships? How might you monetize these assets? What would you pay for them from a third party? If your innovation delivers value toward a nonprofit mission, how can you measure this? What would you need to spend elsewhere to achieve an equivalent impact?

CLV

Use this block to define the CLV for your innovation—a measure of the total profit you can expect to earn per customer. CLV is calculated based on average customer revenue, profit margin, and life span (i.e., time before they churn). To maximize your CLV, focus on four aspects of customer value:

- *CLV by segment*—How does CLV vary by customer segment? Which customers have the highest lifetime value and why? Which segments should you avoid due to their low value?
- *Acquisition*—What is your cost to acquire customers (CAC)? How can you reduce this cost? If CAC is less than CLV (your goal), how much and how fast can you spend to acquire more customers?

- *Retention*—What is your current customer churn rate? What triggers, influences, or predicts churn in an individual customer? How can you retain customers longer? What will that cost?
- *Expansion*—How can you expand revenue or profit margin—or both—per customer, for example, upgrade their plan, increase their purchase frequency, sell additional products, or encourage referrals to new customers?

COST STRUCTURE

Use this block to capture all your costs. These will include your costs to acquire and retain customers (look at the CLV block of your Navigator), the costs to deliver your solution (look at your delivery and capabilities blocks), and your ongoing costs of innovation (look at your value proposition, solution, and right-to-win blocks). To understand your cost structure, categorize all these costs into three types:

- *Fixed costs*—Which of your costs are roughly the same no matter how many customers you serve?
- *Marginal costs*—Which costs are variable and proportional to your number of customers? Think of these as the extra costs (from acquisition to delivery) for each new customer.
- *Scale economies*—Which of your costs are variable but will cost less per customer as you grow in scale?

PATH TO PROFIT

In this block, bring together costs and revenue to project the net value of your innovation and to judge whether it is worth pursuing:

- *Profit formula*—Combine your cost structure and your value capture to create a formula for the net loss or net profit as your venture scales in size. At what point will you break even? What should the profit margin of this venture be at full scale? (The interplay of costs, revenue, and scale are described as your business's unit economics.)
- *Time frame*—When do you aim to achieve a net financial return on this venture? Is it meant to be a near-term revenue boost or cost-cutting effort? Or is it a long-term investment in growth?

- *Maximum upside*—What share of your total addressable market can you realistically capture? What would that mean in total profit for your firm if you succeed? Is that opportunity large enough to continue to pursue this innovation?

Tips on Using the Navigator

At the start, each block of your Rogers Growth Navigator will contain only hypotheses and assumptions about your new venture. (Any third-party data you might have found is just another hypothesis that will need to be tested in the real world to see if it holds true for your venture.) Remember, all learning comes directly from the customer!

I advise teams to fill only the top six blocks of the Navigator when they begin. Once you have made progress on stage 1 and stage 2 validation—and learned something about your problem, customer, value proposition, and solution—you can start to write down your hypotheses for the bottom eight blocks of the Navigator.

As you test and learn with your team, you will gradually replace the untested hypotheses you wrote in the Navigator with validated facts you have learned in the real world. As you do, use color coding to distinguish hypotheses from facts (I recommend writing hypotheses in red and validated facts in green). Choose a third color (e.g., blue) for the hypotheses you need to validate next. This use of color will help your team visually track your progress.

Keep copies of your Navigator's weekly iterations to capture your thinking over time. You may choose to add supplemental documents digging into a block in more detail (e.g., a detailed map of your customer journey or your CLV calculation per segment). But the Navigator itself will remain your single-view summary—both of your current understanding of your business model and of what needs to be tested and learned next.

In some cases, your venture may use a platform business model (one that facilitates a value exchange between two or more distinct types of customers).[22] If so, you should complete a separate Growth Navigator for each customer type. For example, for Uber, you would create one Navigator for drivers and one for passengers. Each Navigator will define that customer's problems, your value proposition to them, their customer journey, and so on. A few blocks may repeat unchanged between your Navigators, but it is critical that you validate your business model for each distinct customer type. I also suggest using the Platform Business Model Map (a tool from *The Digital Transformation Playbook*) to analyze the exchange of value between customers and through your business.

Validation Never Ends

For any innovation, growth venture, or new business—the process of validation never ends. As Bob Dorf says of running a start-up, "Validation only stops when you sell your business for millions, or the furniture for pennies!" As we have seen, there is a sequence to the Four Stages of Validation, but each stage repeats iteratively. None of the stages—problem, solution, product, or business—is ever "done."

Any successful venture will make progress in validating at stage 1, 2, 3, and even 4. Yet we still need to keep going back to revisit, and revalidate, every stage. Why does this happen? Why, for example, would you need to continue problem or solution validation once you are already in the market with a product that customers are using and paying for? There are many reasons why an innovation will need to circle back and iterate on earlier stages. These are some of the most common:

- *Feature rollout*—Your current customers are actively using your product (stage 3). Now you are ready to build the next items on your feature roadmap (which you validated in stage 2). Before you build anything, be sure you go back to your customers to revalidate: do they want the same features next, now that they're actually using your solution every day?
- *Unexpected business problems*—Is growth stalling? Customer churn increasing? Profit margins starting to narrow? No matter the problem your growing venture may face, the best way to identify the root cause and address it will be to go back to the customer and validate from stage 1 onward, with continuous learning.
- *Scaling operations and delivery*—If your new venture is succeeding and is profitable (stage 4), you will want to scale up operations in order to expand into new markets and new use cases. This may require rebuilding the back end of your product in a number of ways: more

automation and less human oversight; more data from more sources; more robust IT architecture with greater scale, reliability, and speed; different sales and marketing channels that can scale to higher volumes; different partners (versus doing it all yourself); more security because bigger ventures attract more malicious actors; more compliance, especially if new markets bring new regulations. Each of these changes will require stage 3 validation to test and learn what works best to deliver a robust and scalable product.

- *Unexpected changes in the environment*—Whenever competitors enter the market or change their product or pricing, you will need to revalidate whether your offer is still differentiated in the eyes of the customer (stage 2). At other times, your customers' needs will change. A former student of mine was leading digital sales for Brazil's leading bank, Itaú Unibanco, when COVID struck. His customers' banking needs changed overnight due to quarantine, requiring a rapid redesign of the bank's mobile app. This meant going back to stages 1, 2, and 3— revalidating the customer's new problems, the features that would help, and the best product design to deliver them.

- *New market, new customer*—As any new venture grows, it will find itself shifting to serve different customers. As Geoffrey Moore explains in his book *Crossing the Chasm*, there is often a major shift when a venture expands from its early adopters to the broader customer population.[23] You may also change customers because you are expanding into a new market or geographical location. Successful teams focus on understanding each unique customer segment and continually repeating the Four Stages of Validation. For every customer segment, be sure you understand *that* customer's problem, *their* best solution, *their* use cases and delivery needs, and how to price and capture value from *them*.

- *Finding your ideal customer*—Once an innovation achieves product-market fit and adoption, it is no longer enough for you to sell to any customer that has your problem and will buy your product. Instead, you need to focus on validating and learning which of your customers will drive repeatable, scalable, profitable growth. Any business leader should be asking themselves, Are we focused on the right customers to scale this business? For a good example, see the box "Optimizely Revalidates for a New Customer."

Optimizely Revalidates for a New Customer

When Jay Larson arrived as the new CEO of Optimizely, the start-up was eight years old and ready to push for its next stage of growth. Optimizely was founded to give businesses the tools to run data-driven experiments—to test features, design, pricing, and personalization within websites and communications.

In its early days as a SaaS start-up, growth was all that mattered to Optimizely, and every customer was a good customer. By the time Larson arrived, they had over 5,000 business customers, ranging from small local businesses (whom Larson dubbed "Joe's House of Wicker") to global brands like Nike, Best Buy, and the *Wall Street Journal*. Larson quickly realized that not all customers were equal, and Optimizely would need to focus on the right customers in order to reach its next stage of growth.

Larson's team focused on learning which business customers were getting the most value from Optimizely's tools. These turned out to be businesses with lots of customer interactions (providing more data) and business models like e-commerce or subscriptions where experimentation drove measurable change in revenue. Further analysis found that these customers were already spending over $50,000 a year with Optimizely. Firms that spent less were getting less benefit from Optimizely and had much lower retention (a key metric for any SaaS business).

Larson decided to change the target market. Larson told his team there would be no more sales to "Joe's House of Wicker," and implemented a $50,000 floor for all new sales. Small-business clients were told they would need to pay more or find another product. Meanwhile, Optimizely shifted its focus to sell to companies that fit the highest-value customer profile.

As Optimizely homed in on its most valuable customers, it redesigned its products and services to meet their particular needs. Optimizely launched a new full-stack product that allowed clients to run experiments on their own software code, integrating much more of their operations than just websites and communications. In customer interviews, Larson's team discovered that the biggest barrier to clients' success was not a lack of experimentation tools but the challenge of building a more data-driven culture. Firms saw the value of experimentation, but they had to unlearn old habits of decision making. To address this need, Optimizely established a new customer success division focused on consulting services to help enterprise clients become more effective experimenters.

These changes made a huge impact on Optimizely's customers. Nike, for example, had started as a client when its marketing department was looking for a workaround to do website testing without going through their own IT department. Now, Nike began to use Optimizely's full-stack solution to run experiments not just on websites but also on its apps and services like Nike Run Club. Working with the customer success team, Nike broke down barriers between its own silos and brought teams together to look at e-commerce and understand individual customers' buy flow. Nike even used Optimizely to experiment on its own vendors, measure the ROI it was getting from each, and push them to work harder for Nike.

Larson also decided to revalidate Optimizely's pricing and revenue model. In examining customer performance data, he found a financial disconnect. The best clients, like the *Wall Street Journal*, were measuring revenue gains over $50 million a year thanks to Optimizely, but they paid less than 1 percent of that in fees. In response, Optimizely began to price its services differently, sometimes based on a split of their clients' revenue gain, and thus capture more value for the firm.

The results of refocusing and revalidating the business model on the most important customers were dramatic. Optimizely raised the average size of its new customers from $40,000 to $200,000. They eliminated customers with the lowest value and highest turnover rates. And they successfully pushed upmarket into the enterprise clients who could deliver sustainable growth into the future.

Validation for Every Stakeholder

As you continue to grow a new venture or business, strive to do validation for every stakeholder, treating each one as a customer whose needs must be met. In an interconnected world, your innovation will only succeed if you can bring the right partners to the table.

When Edison prepared his electric lighting business for the market, he did not focus only on the user of light bulbs at work or home. He focused on the whole ecosystem of electric bulbs, meters, power lines, stations, and generators—and on the individuals and organizations behind all of it. Edison aligned with industry partners on the technical standard for electrical current. He ran his first pilots near Wall Street to attract the interest of investors. And he used his fame and reputation to lobby support from regulators and overcome resistance from the lamplighter's union.[24]

As you scale your own venture, look to the external partners in your Rogers Growth Navigator and the allies that will be most crucial to your success. Include upstream suppliers and downstream business partners, technology standards and data suppliers, as well as policy makers and other influencers. A student of mine leading a consumer health start-up found it was equally important to validate and solve the top problems of her big-box retail partner as it was to validate and problem-solve for the end user of her product.

If your venture is facing resistance from your own organization, try applying the Four Stages of Validation on the inside. Treat every internal stakeholder—whether compliance, the sales force, or the CDO—as a customer. Then do validation on them: Who are they (i.e., job title and role)? What's their problem (i.e., the root cause why they may not support your venture)? What's your solution (i.e., how can you address their concerns to get them on the same page)? Yes, this means interviews with internal stakeholders, just like any external customer. This is particularly critical in stage 3 and stage 4 validation as you test how you will deliver your innovation and do it profitably. Always remember: Validation is not a stage of innovation. Validation *is* innovation.

Experimentation from the Bottom Up

Embedding this approach to innovation will require a change in how many leaders see their role. Innovation is no longer about a few important people coming up with, or signing off on, "the big idea." Instead, it is about lots of people coming up with lots of ideas and using a repeatable process to test and learn which of them could work and how. Effective leaders understand that ideas are easy, but validation is hard.

Experimentation also demands a different approach to decision making. In many organizations, decisions are made based on seniority and experience. In Silicon Valley, this is called decision making by the HIP-POs (highest paid person's opinion). To support a culture of experimentation, leaders need to refrain from opinion-based decision making and instead task others to experiment and find the right data. As Optimizely's vice president of customer success, Jennifer Ruth, told me: "If you have a leadership team who are just all gut instinct and believe that no one else in the world knows better than they do, then experimentation is not going to be successful."

Leaders must work hard to instill a culture of experimentation. This means encouraging others to place bets and take smart risks, to spend a little to learn a lot. It means celebrating "smart failures" like Walmart's Jetblack or its robot floor sweepers. In *The Digital Transformation Playbook*, I offered a four-part test for smart failures: Did you learn something important? Did you apply that learning to change your strategy? Did you share your learning in your organization? Did you fail as early and cheaply as possible? Leaders must make a point to celebrate failures that meet this four-part test.

Effective leaders focus on instilling the right mindset within their teams. They continually communicate and live experimentation's key principles: *Don't debate; validate. Think like a scientist. Get to market sooner to learn faster. Spend as little as possible to learn as much as you can. Test in minutes not months. All learning comes from the customer. Commit to the problem; be flexible on the solution.*

Just like strategy, experimentation should happen at all levels of the organization. It is not the case that one team "does strategy" and another team "does innovation" for the business. As we saw in chapter 4, strategy cascades up—every team hones its strategic P/Os in support of the P/Os of the teams above them. Every team should then be developing venture ideas based on its strategy and iteratively validating those ventures in the market.

The methods I have laid out for you—illustrative and functional MVPs, staged metrics, the Four Stages of Validation, the Rogers Growth Navigator—are all designed to work at every level of the organization. The same process of validation works whether you are building an entirely new business, revamping an existing product, or updating an internal process. Experimentation and continuous learning should be applied not just to product development but to every function: marketing, sales, human resources, risk management, supply chain, and so on. Of course, this is not what we see in many organizations. Innovation is often handled by a dedicated team in a special "island of innovation," exempt from the normal rules of business. As we'll see in chapter 6, experimentation from the bottom up requires a very different approach to managing growth throughout the company.

∼

At the start of a DX, no business, no matter how innovative, can know which digital products, services, or business models will succeed in the real world, delivering value to customers and capturing value in turn. Without experimentation, the greatest leadership commitment to "go digital" will end up in costly failures, like CNN+, which lost $300 million launching an idea pushed from the top. In Step 3 of the DX Roadmap, we have seen how any organization can avoid this fate by learning to validate new ventures to learn which ideas may work and how. You learned how to test your assumptions with iterative MVPs, each one designed to answer a specific business question. And you learned how to use the Four Stages of Validation to guide any venture on its path from an idea on the page to a business at scale.

As you start to apply the process of experimentation to digital ventures in your own business, you are now ready to begin the next step of the DX Roadmap: repeating this process at scale across your entire organization. Major challenges must be addressed. Which ventures should be funded? Who will decide when to shut some down? What rules should be waived for new ventures at the start? How will the successes be handed off to the core business? What will you do with digital ventures that don't fit your current organizational structure?

To scale the process of experimentation across your business, you will need a clear approach to managing resources and people across a portfolio of ventures aimed at different strategic opportunities. You will need a governance model that embraces digital innovations inside your core and beyond it, with both low uncertainty and high uncertainty. In chapter 6, we will see how to manage growth at scale so that digital transformation touches every aspect of your business.

6

Step 4: Manage Growth at Scale

GOVERNANCE

When Vanessa Colella was appointed Chief Innovation Officer for Citibank, her mission was to establish a new group called Citi Ventures to help drive innovation across the global company of 200,000 employees. The challenge was daunting: to help a legacy bank keep up with the ferocious pace of change being driven by emerging technologies, changing consumer needs, and the venture capital flooding into fintech start-ups.

Colella's team worked with the rest of the business to identify a set of problem/opportunity (P/O) statements that mattered most to the future growth of the bank—with themes ranging from cybersecurity to distributed payments, to adapting banking products to suit changing social trends. But the essential question Colella faced was, How do we pursue these strategic priorities across such a large corporation? What would be the best structure and governance for new ventures so we can move fast like a start-up but achieve scale and impact within a huge legacy enterprise? Should new ventures be managed inside the business units? In a separate lab? Outside the business entirely by investing in start-ups?

Colella decided from the outset that it was critical not to try to move ahead without the core business itself. "The era of innovation as a separate unit that then hands things over to the business is gone," Colella told me. Instead, Citi Ventures aimed to partner extremely closely with the business to ensure that its innovation process was deeply embedded, and it involved the very bankers who work and interact daily with Citibank's clients.

The first step was to establish D10X, an innovation accelerator for Citibank's existing business units. Its ambition is to support radical, transformative innovations that are still related to Citibank's core businesses. There are two D10X accelerators, one each for the Global Consumer Bank and the Institutional Clients Group. As Colella explains, "Employees in corporations like Citi also have fabulous ideas of how they can better serve their clients."[1] They just need a repeatable process and set of rules to turn those ideas into innovation with an impact.

That process starts with a pitch, just like a start-up seeking investment from a VC. Citibank employees of all ranks (from interns to senior vice presidents) pitch their innovation ideas to a panel of decision makers called a growth board. Ideas deemed promising are entered into the D10X program with a very small amount of seed funding. Employees are placed in small multifunctional teams, coached by a set of entrepreneurs-in-residence, and given a very short time frame in which to validate their ideas with clients to learn if they address a genuine market need. Rather than building a product, the initial focus is on validating the customer's problem. At the end of that short sprint, the team returns to the growth board to present its data, and—if the team thinks that data show a genuine opportunity—to pitch again for additional funding and time. These pitch sessions, called Deal Days, happen on a rolling basis. Teams return to them repeatedly, just like an independent start-up going back to investors for repeated rounds of investment as it proves the case for its business.

At any given time, 100 of these internal start-up teams may be at work in various stages of D10X. Teams from the consumer banking side have launched new customer experiences to transform budgeting, account management, and personal debt. On the institutional banking side, D10X projects have included CitiConnect for Blockchain, in partnership with Nasdaq, and a virtual proxy-voting platform for investors called Proxymity, which was so successful it was spun off as a separate public company.

But D10X is not the only approach to driving digital innovation at Citi. A division called Citi Ventures Studio was launched to pursue innovation outside the scope of Citibank's core business—where employees might not otherwise look to innovate. Citi Ventures Studio was started by Valla Vakili, a seasoned entrepreneur Colella hired to bring ideas from lean start-up and design thinking into the bank. One of Citi Ventures Studio's first ventures was Worthi, a free online tool that uses labor market data to provide personalized career development tools so individuals can explore new jobs, estimate salaries, and develop skills that match market needs. Another venture was City Builder, a data-driven platform to support investments in U.S. opportunity zones by bringing together investors, fund and wealth managers (at Citibank or elsewhere), and cities that are seeking investment to drive economic renewal.

Other programs at Citi Ventures look beyond Citibank's employees to spark innovation. The Citi University Partnerships in Innovation and Discovery (CUPID) program uses hackathons to engage students from leading universities in innovation efforts across Citibank. Citi Venture Investing invests directly in the start-up ecosystem, funding early-stage fintechs that have achieved product-market fit and are operating in one of a few focus areas for Citibank (payments, fraud, machine learning, customer experience, etc.). Investments have included highly successful fintechs like Docusign, which later had an IPO on the Nasdaq, and Honey, which sold to PayPal for $4 billion.

Despite the wide-ranging approaches that fit under Citi Ventures, Colella is clear about her team's mission: "We don't run innovation." Rather, they enable it across the enterprise. Citi Ventures is comprised of less than 100 people, but its influence is far-reaching. Many thousands of Citibank employees have participated in D10X, Citi Ventures Studio, CUPID, and other programs. Senior leaders from every business unit are actively involved in growth boards, overseeing a new approach to innovation. The mandate of Citi Ventures is not just to launch new ventures but to change the culture and practice of innovation in the whole enterprise.

Why Governance Matters

Rapid, iterative, customer-centric innovation is possible in large companies— but not if you carry over your traditional ways of working. Innovative ventures need innovative governance.

When BASF launched its Onono lab in São Paulo, Brazil, its mission was to accelerate innovation for the global chemical firm through rapid collaboration with partners and start-ups. But Onono's director Antonio Lacerda was told that the lab would have to follow the same data policies designed to secure the company's entire cloud infrastructure. As Lacerda explained to me, that would have made it impossible to partner quickly and nimbly with new start-ups. So, before launching Onono, he expended significant political capital to arrange an exception: a "sandbox" of separate data was created for the Onono team, with special permission to share APIs with new partners. Lacerda was able to customize governance to support Onono, but digital transformation (DX) cannot rely on a series of ad hoc decisions and waivers to business rules granted by higher-ups. It needs new management practices that scale and repeat.

In Step 4 of the Digital Transformation (DX) Roadmap, you take on the challenge of managing growth at scale. In Step 3, your task was to validate, adapt, and grow a single digital venture. Now your goal is to grow not just one venture but a portfolio of ventures serving a range of strategic priorities. In Step 4, you expand your focus to managing growth across an enterprise.

Designing repeatable processes for innovation is essential for the growth of any established business. Yet it is incredibly hard. Every talented executive I meet bears the scars of corporate innovation struggles. In too many organizations, new ventures are green-lit based on a single executive sponsor. Once started, ventures move slowly, managed by teams that sit in traditional silos. Resource allocation is slow too, and promising projects wait weeks or months for their next round of approvals. Because each project is backed by an influential executive, no one wants to shut it down, even when it shows little promise. Meanwhile, risk aversion leads businesses to fund only their low-hanging fruit—incremental improvements in the core that bring a guaranteed, quick ROI. This path will never lead to DX. Instead, you need governance that embraces uncertainty and supports growth both within and beyond the core. Table 6.1 shows some of the key symptoms of success versus failure in Step 4 of the DX Roadmap.

The challenge for Citibank, BASF, and any business seeking growth is to pursue a variety of new ventures in different business units and functions at the same time. These must include some ventures in the core and beyond the core, and low-risk ventures as well as highly uncertain ones.

Table 6.1.
What's at Stake—Step 4: Governance

Symptoms of Failure: Governance	Symptoms of Success: Governance
• A top executive must personally approve any new innovation.	• Established structures provide resources and governance for innovation.
• New ventures move slowly, led by traditional teams in functional silos.	• New ventures move fast, led by highly independent, multifunctional teams.
• Allocating resources to new ventures is slowed by the annual budgeting cycle.	• Resource allocation happens quickly through iterative funding.
• Innovation is limited to a few big projects, which are hard to shut down once they are started.	• A steady pipeline of innovations is managed with smart shutdowns to free up resources.
• The only ventures to gain support are low-risk innovations in the core business.	• Governance supports ventures with low and high uncertainty, both in the core and beyond.

Each venture must be supported by the right governance model so that it can succeed. This means developing not one but a mix of different structures—like Citibank's mix of internal accelerator, external investing, university partnerships, and innovation studio—designed to manage different growth opportunities.

For each structure, governance rules must be carefully designed to address several issues. The first is *oversight*. Who approves new projects? To whom do they report? And who shuts them down? Next is *funding*. How will you allocate resources across ventures and avoid "comparing apples to oranges" (where a long-term bet on growth must compete for funding with a critical infrastructure project)? How will you ensure funding is iterative rather than locked into annual budgeting? Equally critical are *people*. Who will decide that a talented executive will be pulled out of your core business to work on a new venture that has yet to turn a profit? How will teams be formed with the right multifunctional skills? Governance must also include *metrics*. How will you measure the progress of new ventures? How will you assess ventures that have different time horizons or different levels of uncertainty? There is also the crucial management of *compliance*. How will you help new ventures move fast while respecting safety, regulations, risk, and integration with existing technology? All these issues will be addressed in Step 4 of the DX Roadmap as we introduce the elements and tools you need for successful governance.

What's Ahead

In this chapter, we will see how any organization can design governance models to drive digital innovation across the enterprise. We will examine six essential elements to managing growth at scale:

- *Teams and boards*—How to ensure that they work together to accelerate innovation and allocate resources across a portfolio of ventures.
- *Green-lighting*—How to approve and start new ventures with minimal deliberation and minimal investment.
- *Iterative funding*—How to match investment to level of uncertainty, shift resources rapidly, and accelerate when the time is right.
- *Smart shutdowns*—How to manage your pipeline of ventures systematically and free up resources by shutting innovations down smartly.
- *Three paths to growth*—How to manage ventures that have different levels of uncertainty as well as ventures near and far from your core.
- *Innovation structures*—How to set up different structures (labs, hackathons, venture funds, and more) that provide pools of resources and tailored governance for different types of ventures.

After examining each of these six elements, we will introduce a strategic planning tool, the Corporate Innovation Stack—to help you to define the rules for your innovation structures, boards, and teams. Finally, you will learn why growth at scale requires a bottom-up approach that redefines the roles of every team and every leader.

Teams and Boards

For iterative, experiment-driven innovation to work at scale inside any organization, we require two different groups of people. The first group are the innovation *teams*: those who do the work of innovation by talking to customers, building iterative MVPs, running experiments to validate business models, and bringing a successful venture to market. The second group are the sponsors or, more specifically, the innovation *boards*: those who approve new projects, allocate funding, and oversee the progress of teams. To manage growth at scale, it is critical to understand the roles of teams and boards, and the management processes each will need to succeed.

Innovation Teams

There is a saying in Silicon Valley that "leaders vote with head count." As a veteran product manager explained to me, tech giants like Google and Meta have plenty of money to throw at new ideas. Their scarcest resource is good talent; so that is what matters most to a team. At Amazon, the clearest sign that Jeff Bezos was committed to a new venture was the caliber of people he would peel off existing parts of the business to work on the newer one.

Any team that is working on a new venture will, of course, need to be well versed in the mindset and methodologies of iterative experimentation, which we saw in chapter 5. But incredible talent and the best practices of lean start-up, agile, design thinking, and product management will not, by themselves, bring success.

For any team that sits within an enterprise, the rules governing that team are critical to its function. Many readers will be familiar with the idea of the small multifunctional team, which is central to the practice of agile and product management. But size and composition are only part of what sets up a team for success. By studying innovation in digital natives like Amazon and Google, and digital transformers like Citibank and Walmart, I have identified five essential pillars of team governance. Great innovation teams are:

- *Small*—Margaret Mead famously said, "Never doubt that a small group of thoughtful, committed citizens can change the world; indeed, it's the only thing that ever has."[2] Citibank's Vakili shares the same view: "I believe in the outsize productivity of small teams, if they can be equipped properly." Why keep teams small? Research by J. Richard Hackman and others has shown that smaller teams coordinate, communicate, and make decisions much faster.[3] And as we know, speed is essential to innovation. Small teams are foundational to agile methods like Scrum, which demand a rapid cadence of short sprints in which every team must deliver new working code, test and learn, and adjust priorities. At Amazon, innovation teams are called two-pizza teams because each one must be small enough to be fed by two pizzas (maximum of eight people). In traditional enterprises, I have heard objections to the idea of such small teams, with executives insisting their project is too important to move forward without the involvement of a dozen stakeholders or more. But I have never seen a team over the two-pizza limit succeed in rapid innovation.

- *Multifunctional*—Great innovation teams have diverse members who cut across functional silos (e.g., marketing, engineering, and design). Each team should contain among its members all the essential skills needed to do its work. Teams can then move fast because they are self-sufficient. Instead of constantly waiting for a report, data, or support from another department before taking the next step in a project, a multifunctional team should be able to act entirely on its own. The precise mix of team roles will depend on the organization. At Procter & Gamble, a typical team combines marketing, consumer insights, design, and R&D. At Walmart, a nine-person product team typically has six software developers. In start-ups, any team is usually multifunctional from the start, but for most large organizations, multifunctional teams are a big shift from the typical functional silos.
- *Single-threaded*—The best innovation teams have all their members dedicated full-time to the team's work. This is the model of classic agile teams, and it is how design firms like IDEO work, with every team member responsible for only one venture at a time. The term "single-threaded" comes from Amazon. It is a metaphor borrowed from computer science (for an application that executes only one part of a program at a time). At a minimum, any innovation team's *leader* must be single-threaded. They cannot be splitting their work week between the venture team and other projects. Leading the team is their full responsibility. Single-threaded leaders are the norm in a start-up (as are single-threaded teams, as soon as there is funding to pay salaries). Embracing single-threaded leadership is a challenge for most large organizations where every manager is committed to several projects.
- *Autonomous*—Innovation teams should have clear decision rights that give them the authority to work under their own direction. Teams should not need to get approval on their work from anyone outside the team—whether it is on product design, what tests to run next, or which customers to pursue. Autonomy also means there are no prohibitions on contracting resources from outside the company. As one innovation team told me, "We don't work with our company's shared services IT at all. We're outside that ecosystem for a reason." Complete autonomy is to be expected in any start-up, where investors are not managers, and board oversight is never day-to-day. But team autonomy will be a radical shift for large organizations that are wedded to top-down management.

- *Accountable*—Every innovation team must be accountable for the results of its work. This is what allows it to maintain total autonomy over how it achieves those results. Team accountability flows from two factors. The first is *a clear definition of success*—which is defined in terms of outcomes, not deliverables. That definition may include concrete metrics as well as qualitative principles, and it must be agreed on with leadership before the team's work begins. The second requirement is *transparency*. At any time, the team's results must be visible to anyone inside or outside the team. Every test run, every MVP built, and every metric tracked should be visible to anyone in the company. At Walmart Labs, transparent tools display each product team's members, what they are working on, and every piece of code published. Accountability and transparency are inevitable in a start-up (everyone knows when your marketing campaign is failing to acquire new customers). But this is a dramatic departure from corporate work. In most large organizations, accountability is diffuse and shaped as much by politics as by outcomes.

Table 6.2 summarizes these five pillars and shows their sharp contrast with the business-as-usual (BAU) management of teams in the predigital era. Too often BAU teams are sprawling, siloed, fractional, micromanaged, and political—whereas great innovation teams are small, multifunctional, single-threaded, autonomous, and accountable. This gulf between teams is not the result of different *people* but of different *governance*. Innovation teams have a different mandate than the functional teams in a legacy organization. BAU functional teams are designed either to execute a project with a fixed deliverable (e.g., "migrate our customer database to our new cloud service provider") or to carry out an ongoing function (e.g., "run marketing for our Southeast Asia market"). In contrast, innovation teams are designed either to pursue a new growth venture or to innovate for a persistent problem for a key customer or stakeholder. Team form follows team function.

Growth Boards

The other critical group for managing innovation at scale is the managers who will allocate funds and oversee the work of teams. One of the first questions I ask executives looking to scale their digital efforts is, Who

Table 6.2.
The Five Pillars of Innovation Teams Versus BAU Teams

Innovation team	To pursue a new growth venture or innovate for a persistent problem	BAU functional team	To execute a temporary project or carry out an ongoing function
Small	• Fewer than ten people on a team • Rapid cadence of communications and work	Sprawling	• Many team members with varying levels of involvement • Communication bottlenecks are frequent
Multifunctional	• Team members from different silos • Have all essential skills on the team	Siloed	• All members from a single function or silo • Work depends on the skills of others
Single-threaded	• Team leader is committed 100 percent • Team members have few or no other assignments	Fractional	• Everyone is working on the team part-time, juggling other priorities
Autonomous	• Team owns all decision making between funding milestones	Micromanaged	• Approvals are required for all major decisions (many people can say no)
Accountable	• Clear definition of success • Transparent metrics • Team is solely responsible	Political	• Deliverable is clear, but success is debatable • Access to metrics is restricted • Many people are responsible in theory, but none in practice

sponsors innovation at your organization? The most common answer is that new ventures are approved by a single sponsor. One or more executives may play this role and use their clout within the organization to support a new digital venture they deem strategically important and promising. The problem with the single-sponsor model is that it is inherently ad hoc, with decisions based on the instincts and judgment of different individuals. It also runs the risk of sustaining pet projects. Once a sponsor puts their name behind a project, it is very hard for them to let it die, no matter what market validation shows about its prospects.

The most successful model for sponsoring corporate innovation is the board. In the board model, a group convenes and deliberates together to decide whether to sponsor various possible innovation ventures—much like a group of VC investors listening to pitches from start-ups, or the judges of a hackathon picking a few winners out of dozens of teams. One board can sponsor multiple innovation teams at the same time. (The single-sponsor model, by contrast, is usually "one executive backs one team," which makes it extremely hard to withdraw support.) Diversity, agility, and impartiality make the board model inherently better at managing innovation as a repeatable process.

Corporate innovation boards are often dubbed growth boards, a term that Stephen Liguori coined at General Electric (GE) in 2014 to describe a small group that oversees funding decisions for internal innovation. Eric Ries, who was an adviser to Liguori at the time, helped popularize the term, which has been adopted at Citibank, Procter & Gamble, and elsewhere.[4] Other names for the same idea include venture board and growth council. Whatever the name, any corporate innovation board has four critical jobs:

- *Green-lighting new ventures*—The board must choose which ventures to green-light with an initial investment and an agreed definition of success. This initial investment may be an equity stake in an outside start-up or the seed funding for an internal team to begin validating its idea. When approving internal teams, the board must allocate head count and other resources, as well as budget.
- *Iterative funding*—Funding ventures is completely different from funding departments or operating units; it must be given iteratively, based on data. The board's second job is to review each team's progress regularly and decide whether to release the next tranche of resources to that team or to shut down the project and free up team members to work on other priorities.
- *Strategic guidance*—Between funding cycles, the board should meet regularly with each team to review each venture's progress. As the team learns from iterative testing and considers next steps to advance its innovation, the board should provide strategic advice.
- *Liaising and advocacy*—The board must also act as the liaison between the venture team and the rest of the parent organization, making introductions, connecting the team to company resources, and removing organizational obstacles whenever needed.

Having the right people on a growth board is essential to its success. As one business leader remarked to me, "You don't want a bunch of MBAs. You need people who think like VCs or entrepreneurs." Having observed growth boards in a variety of companies, I recommend the following characteristics for the best board composition:

- *Small*—Effective boards are small (no more than eight people), following the two-pizza rule that successful teams do.
- *Heterodox*—To support innovation, a board must be able to challenge company orthodoxy, advocate a long-term view, and bring in ideas from outside the industry. The best boards combine internal stakeholders from different divisions or business units, and at least one member with an external perspective. Experience in entrepreneurship or venture capital is a huge benefit.
- *Capable*—Teams need a lot of help from their board, so it should include members with knowledge of the market, topical expertise, and clout within the organization. If the board is to be an effective champion for its teams, it must wield real influence in the parent company.
- *Engaged*—Boards must meet frequently so that feedback and funding can be truly iterative. Every six or eight weeks is preferable, and quarterly meetings are the absolute minimum. Board members must be actively involved during and between meetings, whether in person or remotely. A golden rule for meetings is, If you don't attend, you can't vote.

The seniority of board members is important to get right. At least some board members must be senior enough to have real clout in the organization, but no members should be so senior that they are too busy to make time for board meetings. I have seen organizations that try designating the top executives of the entire company as their venture board to oversee innovations. Too often, these executives want to be the ones who green-light new ventures, but they simply don't have the bandwidth to track and counsel each team's progress. In some cases, top executives may be too far removed from the market to judge the team's work as well as others less senior.

Defining decision rights is critical for boards to work effectively with the teams they oversee. We can think of the roles of teams and boards as analogous to the roles of independent start-ups and their VC investors. Each side needs to have very clearly defined authority:

- *Team decision rights*—The innovation team, like a start-up, has autonomy, that is, complete control of its venture between funding milestones. While the board may provide input and advice, the team holds decision rights on what customers to pursue, what MVPs to develop, and what tests to run.
- *Board decision rights*—The innovation board, like a VC investor, has complete funding authority for each team in its portfolio. The board's decisions should be made in conversation with the team, as part of an open and lively debate, but the decisions remain with the board. Other senior executives, including the CEO, may advise and provide input to ventures, but they cannot vote on or overrule the board's investment decisions.

The board model is superior to the single-sponsor model for several reasons. The benefit to the team is that a board provides multiple coaches and advocates who can each offer the team different perspectives, technical expertise, and relationships inside and outside the company—more than any single sponsor can. The benefit to the company is that a board is designed to allocate resources based on results (i.e., how a venture validates and performs in the market) rather than based on personal conviction or pride—being unwilling to admit the idea you green-lit is not fit to continue. Where the single-sponsor model is inherently ad hoc, personal, and political, boards provide a sponsorship model that is repeatable, rational, and strategic.

Green-Lighting

The first critical process where boards and teams work together is green-lighting, where new ventures are approved for their very first round of validation. Approval of a venture comes with an initial release of resources from the board (typically including time, money, and people). The best green-lighting practices minimize the initial investment to each team and maximize the number of ideas that are approved to be tested.

In green-lighting, it is important to resist the urge to try to pick the "best" ideas among those submitted. First, you truly have no way of knowing which ideas will work. That knowledge can be learned only through validation (so don't try to guess!). Second, successful ventures often emerge from ideas that are initially flawed but evolve in response to testing, feedback, and iterative learning. As Colella explained to me, "Particularly in large corporations, people tend to think in buckets of good versus bad ideas. But . . . good ideas are often cloaked inside a bad idea!" Instead of trying to guess which ideas will work, I recommend judging ideas based on problem definition, strategic fit, and team mindset. When hearing first-round pitches for D10X, Citibank's growth boards listen for the problem to be solved, whether there is some unique take or insight into that problem, and whether the team has the right mix of passion plus an assumption of total ignorance about the future success of their idea.

Your goal should be to fund as many promising ideas (i.e., strategic, well-defined, and with the right team) as possible in the first round. Some companies use an open-door approach to green-lighting employee ideas. Google's famous "20 percent time" policy allows engineers to use 20 percent of their paid time to start working on any idea that piques their curiosity and see where early exploration might lead. At Adobe, any employee with an innovation idea can request a "Kickbox" that includes a $1,000 credit card to fund the very first round of testing of their idea. The box includes guidance on a five-step process to validate their idea before choosing whether to pitch it to senior management. The only requirement is that employees share the results of what they learn.[5]

The key to green-lighting many innovation ideas is to build a fast, cheap, and effective validation process. This must bring in the voice of the customer to rapidly test whether the venture is focused on a genuine problem (i.e., stage 1: problem validation). At Citibank, ventures often begin with a two- or three-day workshop in which employees explore a strategic P/O statement and have a chance to develop their own innovation ideas in a rapid, iterative fashion with actual customers. This approach allows Citibank to test hundreds of venture ideas within a program like D10X. As you increase the speed and drive down the cost of your early validation, you can afford to test and pursue more and more possible ideas for growth.

New ventures should be started with minimal deliberation and the smallest possible investment. But that initial investment should be focused entirely on *learning*—spending not to make a product but to test the hypotheses of the business model. If those early tests are promising (most often they are not), later stages can follow. Only after multiple rounds of learning and validation (or adapting the strategy until it begins to see validation), should any significant investment be made.

Iterative Funding

The next critical process for managing innovation is iterative funding, the process by which boards allocate resources to growth ventures after they have been green-lit. Iterative funding is designed to be extremely agile and responsive to market validation. To see how this works at scale in an enterprise, you need to look at investing under uncertainty, the role of learning, and how iterative funding differs from traditional budgeting.

Uncertainty, Net Present Value, and Option Value

Every new venture begins with a degree of uncertainty—in market demand, technological maturity, the willingness of partners, the approval of regulators, and so on. To master iterative funding, you must understand how that uncertainty shapes two kinds of value. *Net present value* is the value of a financial return on your investment over time. *Option value* is the value that comes from your right to take future action. Both kinds of value are critical to investing in innovation (see the box "Option Value Explained").

Option Value Explained

Rita McGrath defines option value as "the right, but not the obligation, to make a future decision."* Investing in strategic options, or "real options," refers to any investment that grants the opportunity to make a later strategic decision once more is known.

The value of options was first observed in financial markets—where an investor can pay for the right to buy or sell an asset at a future date at an agreed-on price. These agreements are extremely valuable but not in the traditional sense. They yield no direct return to the investor; instead, they create value by providing the option for a future purchase or sale if conditions are favorable.

A more familiar example can be seen in airplane tickets. Many airlines sell the same seat on the same flight at two different fares—often called economy versus

---

(*continued on next page*)

(continued from previous page)

economy flexible. The only difference is that the second fare includes the option to cancel and get your money back. The flexible fare costs more, even though the seat, meal service, and luggage allowance are all identical. What you are paying extra for is pure option value—the option, should you choose it, of not boarding the plane. Not surprisingly, the price of that option (the spread between the fares) is highest when the flight is still weeks away. The price difference narrows in the final days before the flight, when the option value (and the likelihood that you will change your plans) is lowest.

One more example can be seen in the game of poker. Each player, after receiving their first few cards, is asked to make an initial bet called an ante. Only if they do so will they receive their remaining cards and have the chance to bet further and thus the chance to win the pot of money wagered. That initial ante is pure option value—you pay for the option to bet again later, when holding your complete hand. Only in the final round of betting is there any present value, that is, the chance to make money.

In the VC funds that back Silicon Valley start-ups, the combination of option and present value is critical. For any VC, an early-stage investment in a start-up is viewed as mostly option value: the VC invests for the right to follow with more investment if the start-up turns out to have a viable business model. Only in later rounds of investment do VCs start to judge their portfolio companies on measures of present value—such as the start-up's revenue, customer acquisition cost, and operating margin.

* Rita McGrath has shed great insight on the importance of option value to innovation under high uncertainty. See Rita Gunther McGrath, "Falling Forward: Real Options Reasoning and Entrepreneurial Failure," *Academy of Management Review*, 24, no. 1 (January 1999): 13–30. Also, Rita McGrath, "A New Approach to Innovation Investment," *Harvard Business Review*, March 25, 2008, https://hbr.org/2008/03/a-new-approach-to-innovation-i.

Some innovations begin with low uncertainty, for example, using a known solution to solve an existing problem in your current business, with good benchmarks and clear metrics for success. Low-uncertainty investments are best judged in terms of their net present value (typically, ROI). This is the same logic used for investing in day-to-day business operations. If a project requires $50,000, it should be approved only if it will yield more value than putting that same cash to use elsewhere in the firm. Traditional budgeting is based entirely on present value and on a premise of predictable financial results.

However, many ventures that you will want to invest in will begin under high uncertainty. They may start with a poorly defined problem, unclear metrics, and no good benchmarks. They may require establishing relationships with new partners or serving new customers. In these cases, there are no predictable results! For innovations under high uncertainty, financial management based on present value is practically impossible. Investing under uncertainty *does* make sense, but only when it is understood as an investment in option value. When a growth board provides initial funding to an innovation team, it is not investing for ROI. It is investing to learn while retaining the right to invest further if testing shows promise in the market. The goal of your initial investment should be to validate an important assumption (e.g., "is this a genuine problem for a real customer?") and bring data back to the board as quickly as possible. Then the board members can decide whether to exercise the strategic option to pursue the venture further. That opportunity to take future action is the essence of option value.

To help visualize the relationship of uncertainty to option value and present value, I have developed a model called the uncertainty curve of innovation, which is shown in figure 6.1. The horizontal axis shows the level of uncertainty of a business venture. Within the same company, different innovations begin with more or less uncertainty. For example, a new digital business

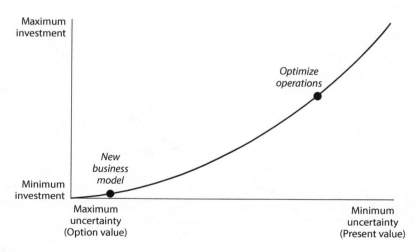

Figure 6.1.
The uncertainty curve of innovation

model applying an untested technology in a volatile market would start far to the left, at the point of maximum uncertainty. By contrast, an innovation that optimizes the operations of your current business using a well-known technology would start further to the right, with much less uncertainty.

The vertical axis in the figure shows the level of investment that is appropriate for a venture. The curved line shows the relationship between investment in a venture and the venture's uncertainty; as we follow the curve from left to right, we see that it bends upward. On the far left, when the uncertainty of a venture is at a maximum, the firm is investing purely in option value. In that case, the size of the investment should be very small. On the far right, when a venture's uncertainty is at a minimum, the firm is investing entirely in present value. In that case, the size of the investment can be quite large.

How Learning Shapes Funding

The whole point of validation is that uncertainty is not fixed because experimentation drives down uncertainty through learning. Figure 6.2 shows that a novel innovation will typically start as a "big idea" with great uncertainty (think of the brainstorming session where the Amazon Fire Phone was first conceived). The role of validation is to reduce that uncertainty with iterative experiments—things like customer interviews, wire frames shown to customers, and iterative prototypes or MVPs. Each of these tests,

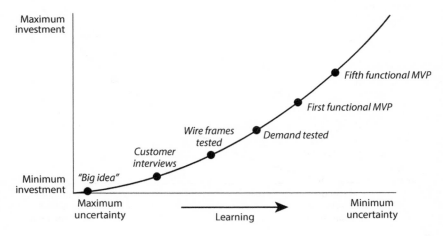

Figure 6.2.
Learning and the uncertainty curve of innovation

if designed right, will yield new insights that validate or invalidate crucial aspects of the planned innovation. At the bottom of Figure 6.2, you can see the arrow of *learning* pointing to the right. Only by validated learning can a business move a venture from high uncertainty to low uncertainty.

Look next at the uncertainty curve in figure 6.3, starting from the left side of the figure. A start-up in its first funding round will ask VC investors for only a very small initial investment because the business is so uncertain and any funds given are at maximum risk. Similarly, corporate teams working on uncertain ventures should be granted only a very small operating budget, limited time, and limited head count in their first round. Citibank's D10X grants as little as $2,000 to spend on initial validation. If the team invests those resources effectively in learning, it will reduce the venture's uncertainty—moving to the right in figure 6.3. The value of the venture will shift from pure option value to more present value, and the size of each funding round should follow the curve up. This is why each round of VC fundraising for a successful start-up will increase dramatically in size. As the start-up's business model is validated, the risk of failure declines, and the size of investment will grow exponentially.

Many corporate managers tell me how they struggle to get budgets approved for innovation. My advice is always to try asking for less money. Then use what you get on early experiments to validate if there is a profitable opportunity. If validation comes back positive, you will then be in a position to ask for the budget you originally wanted.

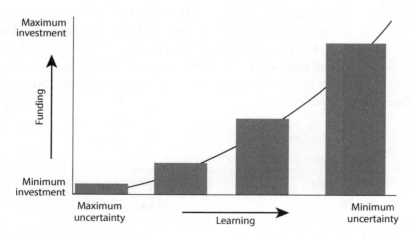

Figure 6.3.
Investment and the uncertainty curve of innovation

The uncertainty curve of innovation captures two final insights about managing innovation:

1. *For high-uncertainty ventures, milestones should be pegged not to time but to validation*—Notice that time does not appear anywhere in the uncertainty curve of innovation. In the traditional planning-oriented approach to management, time is dominant. Time appears on the horizontal axis in every Gantt chart and project management tool. When managing under uncertainty, however, a key mindset shift is to let go of arbitrary milestones of time and instead manage according to milestones of validation.

2. *In times of rapid change and uncertainty, speed of learning is your organization's greatest competitive advantage*—By mastering the process of experimentation, your firm will be able to validate, test, and learn much faster. By learning faster than your competitors, you can pursue the same strategy with less uncertainty. Thus, you can invest resources sooner, at less risk, and with a higher chance of success. In the digital era, those who learn fastest will always win.

Iterative Funding in Practice

The practice of iterative funding for growth ventures is based on the VC approach to financing start-ups. Colella explains how this works at Citibank: "Just like in a VC, [our] employees will test their ideas, validate the markets, and if they get positive results, they'll come back to the growth board and pitch again for additional funds."[6] This iterative process is quite different from traditional BAU budgeting in large enterprises, as shown in table 6.3.

Table 6.3.
BAU Funding Versus Iterative Funding

BAU Funding	Iterative Venture Funding
Slow, big start	Quick, small start
Long budgeting cycles	Short funding cycles
Decision based on executive opinion	Decision based on validation
Incremental growth	Exponential growth

Let's look briefly at each of the key differences between BAU funding and an iterative funding process:

- *Slow, big start versus quick, small start*—In traditional corporate budgeting, a new project will be granted a large initial budget (to show commitment to the project), but only after a long business case analysis—striving (misguidedly) to assess the chances of an uncertain new venture through third-party data and modeling. With iterative funding, the approach is the opposite. New ventures are given a tiny initial budget based on a quick assessment that asks only whether the opportunity is well defined and strategically relevant to the enterprise.

- *Long budgeting cycles versus short funding cycles*—The next difference is in frequency. In traditional corporate budgeting, projects and departments are funded annually through a complex process that takes months. A promising new venture can wind up waiting over a year to get resources for a four-week test. Iterative venture funding is made in short cycles of one to three months, providing a team with thirty to ninety days of resources before it must return and argue for further support.

- *Decision based on executive opinion versus decision based on validation*—The third change is in how funding decisions are made. In traditional budgeting, decisions are based on the opinions of senior executives—which can be influenced by personal conviction (pet projects) or the persuasive talents of team members. Instead, each round of funding should be decided entirely on a venture's validation data. As we saw in chapter 5, the key metrics will change as validation progresses. So, with each round of funding, the board must agree with the team on what data they need to bring to their next review. The Rogers Growth Navigator can be used to guide the discussion of what has been tried and learned, and what the team must validate next if the board is to continue funding.

- *Incremental growth versus exponential growth*—The rate of change in funding is quite different between the two funding processes. In most organizations, the default budget in the next cycle is an incremental change to the prior budget (e.g., "last year plus 3 percent"). With iterative funding, if validation is successful and the venture continues, the size of each investment round should grow exponentially. Human resources may also increase—either by adding head count or shifting employees from part-time to full-time on the project.

Any iterative funding process requires a great deal of flexibility. Boards must be ready to ramp up investment quickly in the ventures that prove themselves in the market. If a team's testing is extremely positive, it may request to meet with the board earlier for its next funding review, to accelerate the pace. For a board to be flexible, it will need a pool of resources that is funded up front (e.g., for a year). The board can then allocate those resources judiciously across a portfolio of projects. Within that portfolio, only similar innovations should compete for funds, for example, only high-risk innovations within a given business unit, or only innovations outside the core. (We will see examples of this kind of resource pool later in the chapter.) Fund the portfolio first, and then the ventures.

At some point, as a venture scales, the type of budget that funds it may need to shift, along with who makes the funding decision. In industries with complex physical products, a budget bump typically occurs when a team moves from testing with illustrative MVPs to functional MVPs, which cost much more. At Air Liquide, this happens whenever a team moves from building wire frames to building a working industrial product with live data. "It does not have to be a lot of money. Something in the low $100,000s range, significant enough to make it count," explains Olivier Delabroy, vice president marketing at Airgas, an Air Liquide Company. At Air Liquide, the source of funds changes then from an operating budget overseen by the CDO to a capital budget disbursed by an innovation board.

Any large successful corporate venture will eventually graduate from funding by the innovation board. If a thriving venture needs a $100 million infusion after a couple of years to reach its next level, this will likely go to the company's executive board to approve. Likewise, senior leaders may weigh in on any decision to expand from a minority stake in a start-up to buying it outright.

Smart Shutdowns

Of course, not every review will conclude with a decision to continue funding. One of the classic problems that bedevil corporate innovation is that companies learn how to start new projects but not how to stop them. For innovation to deliver results, firms must be ready to exit projects that prove unsuccessful or are insufficiently aligned with strategy. As Stephen Dunbar-Johnson, president, international of The New York

Times Company, told me, "It's easy to start new things. The really hard part is shutting them down!"

Shutting down ventures smartly—that is, systematically and regularly—is a critical job for growth boards. Every time a board meets for an iterative funding review, the question must be, Do we fund this venture further or shut it down? Whichever decision is made, it should be data driven. Table 6.4 shows common test results at each stage of validation that indicate serious trouble for a venture. Any one of the results listed in the table is a clear signal to either pivot (fundamentally change course) or end an innovation project and free up its resources.

Table 6.4.
Signals to Shut Down a Venture at Each Stage of Validation

Validation Stage	Common Signals to Pivot or Shut Down
1. Problem validation	• *No problem*—You can't identify a customer problem you are solving (i.e., you have a solution in search of a problem). • *Low priority*—Customers recognize the problem, but it does not make their top five list of priorities. • *Problem solved*—Customers are satisfied with existing alternatives for addressing the problem.
2. Solution validation	• *No urgent demand*—You receive polite praise for your solution ("that would be nice") but no requests to register, use, or buy. • *No killer feature*—None of your proposed benefits are enough to motivate behavior change by the customers. • *No competitive advantage*—Customers don't see a reason why they must choose your solution over existing solutions.
3. Product validation	• *Low usage*—Customers don't use your solution when offered or discontinue use after the initial trial. • *Too hard*—You have no clear path to deliver a solution customers will use (e.g., technology is not ready, regulation won't permit it, or you lack essential IP) • *Too easy*—Your solution works, but competitors can easily deliver the same thing as well or better than you.
4. Business validation	• *No value capture*—Customers like your offering but they won't pay for it, and you can't find another value stream for your firm. • *No path to profit*—You are capturing value, but costs are too high and won't go down enough to break even as you scale. • *Too small a prize*—The maximum upside is not large enough to merit a continued focus by your organization.

Overcoming the Barriers to Shutting Down

At legacy firms, the biggest barrier to shutting down innovation projects is often cultural. There is often an aversion to admitting failure and an irrational feeling that failure of any kind poses too much risk. As Citibank's Colella puts it, "Most people in large companies associate failure with something that has economic consequences or bad consequences for clients or somehow impairs the safety and soundness of the system." But failure in testing new ideas, if managed appropriately, is not risky at all—and it is much less risky than not pursuing innovation. According to Colella, "If we're testing an idea or a prototype and a client tells us this doesn't solve a problem they have, and they wouldn't buy it . . . we haven't lost anything other than the time and effort putting together the idea."[7]

By contrast, there are very *real* costs to the firm if your teams do not shut down ventures quickly and smartly. Without this discipline, your innovation will lack focus, your resources will be spread too thin, and you will run out of bandwidth for new experiments. You will be stuck with "zombie projects"—unsuccessful ventures that never shut down and continue siphoning off resources. As an executive at Axel Springer media group describes it, "You have millions of little projects going on forever and limiting your ability to try new things out . . . You need those people, money, to spend on other projects."[8] At Johnson & Johnson, an entire new series of innovations was funded by evaluating the existing portfolio and shutting down projects that no longer matched the company's updated strategy.[9]

Shutting down projects will become easier only if you make it a routine decision. Innovation boards with a regular calendar of funding reviews will make a huge difference. In GE's oil and gas division, projects were rarely shut down before its board was instituted. As soon as the board began, it easily shut down 20 percent of existing projects in its first ninety-day cycle. As the board and teams became focused on aligning to strategy, this rose to 50 percent of new ventures shutting down within sixty days.[10] At media giant Schibsted, the goal is to "take something out" whenever you are "putting something new in" the development pipeline. When a project comes up for review, set a high bar for yourself by asking, Why *shouldn't* we shut this venture down?

The following five practices are essential to achieving smart shutdowns in any organization:

1. *Plan a pipeline with survival rates*—Many corporate innovation programs find a survival rate as low as 50 percent, or even 30 percent, is typical in their first funding review—after a bright shiny idea has contact with real customers. In subsequent rounds, survival rates typically increase. Understanding your survival rates at different stages of validation allows you to plan a pipeline for the future. For example, if a growth board is expected to help launch three or four new ventures to market within a year, it needs to be sure to plant enough seeds at the start to have high odds for success. An executive at the *Washington Post* described this shift in thinking after the paper was bought by Jeff Bezos: "Before Jeff we were very cautious . . . We would do the absolute safest play because we would maybe develop one big new product a year, and it had to succeed. Now we'll do a ton of products and the majority of them won't succeed, but we'll figure out many ways of how not to do things . . . so it's leaning into risk."[11] Figure 6.4 illustrates this approach, showing a pipeline plan for a typical hackathon, with survival rates for each milestone. A pipeline plan could also show validation milestones: problem validation, solution validation, product validation, and business validation.

2. *Use your backlog to reassign swiftly*—Each innovation board should maintain its own venture backlog, a ranked list of ideas for ventures

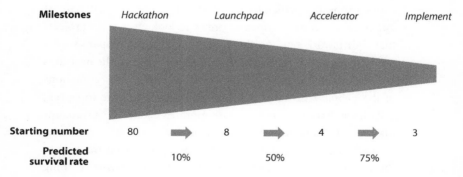

Figure 6.4.
Sample pipeline for an innovation hackathon program

that have been approved but not yet begun. Using this backlog in your review process will make shutdowns much easier. The point of a shutdown is not simply to kill a failing idea but to free the team and its resources to work on a more promising idea from the backlog. When you shutter a project, quickly reassign members to the best next idea. In many cases, your next step may be to refocus that team on a different solution to the same problem.

3. *Extract value from shutdowns*—When you decide to shut down a project, look to extract as much value as possible, whether financial value, option value, or strategic learning. In some cases, a company may be able to sell the venture to investors or another business. When Walmart's Vudu streaming video service was no longer a strong strategic fit, Walmart spun it off and sold it to media giant Comcast. Sometimes a venture will be shut down because it is promising but not yet workable at scale. By shrinking your investment, you may maintain the venture as a hedge against future options. After the failure of Google Glass as a consumer product, the company did not pull the plug. Instead, it shrank the initiative to an enterprise-only device (focused on applications on factory floors), where Google quietly continued to develop augmented reality technology.[12] Sometimes only a full shutdown makes sense, and the key value to extract is the learning gained from experimentation. When Amazon shut its unsuccessful Amazon Auctions and zShops services, it applied the lessons it learned for the subsequent launch of Amazon Marketplace to great success.

4. *Share learning widely*—Sharing what you learn from shutdowns is one of the key principles of smart failure, but it is the hardest one to follow. Most companies prefer to look away from projects that didn't work out. As the New York Times Company's 2014 report explained, "When we do shut down projects, the decisions are made quietly and rarely discussed, to protect the reputations of the people who ran them. As a result, lessons are forgotten, and the staffers involved become more risk averse."[13] Overcoming this reluctance was essential at the New York Times: lessons learned from its failed Times Select initiative paved the way to the paper's turnaround of its business model. Sharing learning from failed ventures is even more important as organizations become larger and more decentralized. The German affiliate of

Fédération Internationale de l'Automobile (FIA) ran an innovation lab where eight of ten projects were killed in a single year. Its biggest win? Sharing those results with other FIA affiliates around the world who were struggling with the same challenges in their own markets.

5. *Distinguish people from projects*—This is a final critical piece to building a culture that accepts and learns from failure. A strong review process will hold teams accountable for their results. But you should be careful not to associate a failed project with the merit of the individuals who worked on it. Those same team members could achieve tremendous success for you in their next project. Google's Susan Wojcicki helped launch two innovation projects within a year of each other: Google Answers and AdSense. Both faced significant risks. The first was shut down as a failure but provided lessons that were applied to future Google products. The second became one of Google's most profitable products of all time.[14] Be sure to encourage your innovators to keep working on their next idea!

To manage your venture pipeline, you will want to track the *rate* of failure at different stages. But to improve results, you should focus on measuring the *quality* of your failures. Six months after every shutdown, conduct a review applying the four-part test for smart failure: Did you fail as early and cheaply as possible? Did you learn from the failure? Did you apply the learning to strategy? Did you share the learning with others? The best-run innovation efforts track and evaluate failures against such criteria, and they recognize (and even reward) the best failures to show everyone how failure can be done well.

If your shutdowns are working, you will begin to see volunteering. When teams are truly focused on learning through validation, they will often suggest their own shutdown to the board, reporting, "Here's what we have learned and why we recommend shutting down now." This is what happened at GE Oil and Gas once the board process was established. Similarly, at Citibank, employees report to their D10X board, "It's with a heavy heart but a strong conscience that I recommend that you kill my project because here's what we learned when we went outside the building and worked with our clients . . . They don't really need this."[15] Those same employees will soon return to your board with another venture idea. It could be your next big breakthrough.

Three Paths to Growth

Many leaders feel comfortable focusing only on innovations that have low uncertainty and are closely aligned with their core business. But such a narrow focus will close off many of the biggest opportunities for growth in the digital era. To succeed in DX, any business must be able to manage innovations with varying degrees of uncertainty and at varying distances from the core. This means overcoming the challenges of both uncertainty and proximity, which we saw in chapter 2. Together, these two challenges point toward three different paths to growth—each with its own rich opportunities and its own management challenges (see figure 6.5).

Three Paths Defined

Let's take a close look at each of these three paths to growth to ensure that we can adapt our governance to support ventures to scale on each path. A summary is provided in figure 6.6.

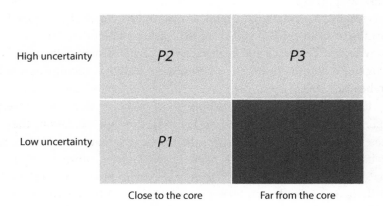

Figure 6.5.
Uncertainty, proximity, and the three paths to growth (*Note*: There is no fourth quadrant for "far from the core" plus "low uncertainty" because any innovation far from your core will involve great uncertainty for your organization to execute.)

• *In the core business*
• *Uncertainty low enough for core business to manage*

• *In the core business*
• *Uncertainty too high for core business to manage*

• *Outside the core business*
• *Uncertainty high (for your organization)*

Figure 6.6.
The three paths to growth

PATH 1 VENTURES

Path 1 (P1) ventures are innovations within your core—that is, they improve or solve a problem for an existing business unit or division. In addition, P1 ventures have low enough uncertainty that they can be effectively managed within existing business units and functions (e.g., marketing, HR, finance).

P1 innovations tend to address a known problem, have an easily agreed-upon metric for judging performance, and rely on established technical solutions. They are clearly doable with the skills and tools of your own organization or your partners. Still, these straightforward innovations can provide a lot of tangible value to your business, even if they are just fixing known problems or helping you catch up with peer competitors.

While P1 ventures do not deliver the kind of exponential or disruptive innovations that draw admiration in Silicon Valley, they are an essential part of the healthy growth of any mature business. And, yes, that includes digital titans like Google, Amazon, and Alibaba.

PATH 2 VENTURES

Path 2 (P2) ventures are also innovations to your core business, but they involve too much uncertainty to be managed effectively by the business units alone. P2 innovations may involve changes to your customer experience, your value proposition, or the delivery model of your current business.

It is often unclear exactly what you should build, whether customers will adopt it, how it will generate a financial return, or whether your organization can even deliver it.

P2 ventures are critical to the continued growth of any established business in a rapidly changing environment. Every P2 venture addresses a problem or opportunity that is directly related to the core business. But each venture requires relentless validation, prototyping, and discovery before it yields a solution that customers will adopt and that your business can deliver profitably.

PATH 3 VENTURES

Path 3 (P3) ventures are innovation opportunities that do not fit within the current core business of your firm. They typically serve new customers, use a new revenue model, or carry a different cost structure than your existing business.

P3 ventures may compete with the core, directly threatening it with replacement or cannibalization. Or they may pose opportunities in a whole new industry, serving different customers. P3 ventures pose great uncertainty and difficulty in management precisely because they do not fit within your normal operations. Yet P3 innovation cannot be ignored. Every truly successful business in the digital era has pursued P3 ventures by looking beyond narrow definitions of its products, customer base, or industry.

Recall the case of Amazon Web Services (AWS), a classic P3 innovation. When AWS began, Amazon was a pure consumer retail business. The new B2B cloud-computing service was a radically different business model, with a completely different type of customer, revenue model, and sales process. In time, AWS grew to become the biggest source of profits for the entire company.

Table 6.5 provides examples of ventures from each of the three paths to growth for companies in different industries.

Challenges of Each Path

As we have seen, all three paths hold the potential for growth for any business. At the same time, each path faces unique challenges for effective management and governance.

Table 6.5.
Examples of P1, P2, and P3 Ventures for Different Industries

Industry	P1 Ventures: In the Core Business Plus Low Uncertainty	P2 Ventures: In the Core Business Plus High Uncertainty	P3 Ventures: Outside the Core Business Plus High Uncertainty
Newspaper	Use truck route optimization software to cut delivery costs of print newspapers.	Personalize user notifications and recommendations through the mobile app. Teach editors to design articles with data and interactive elements to engage readers in complex topics.	Offer stand-alone non-news subscriptions (e.g., crossword or cooking apps). Offer weekly news series licensed to radio or streaming video. Offer paid online courses or live events.
Retail bank	Use new data to predict customer churn and optimize promotions to maintain customer loyalty.	Create an omnichannel customer experience that links branches, ATMs, website, and mobile app.	Create a mobile-only app that targets a new generation of customers with a value proposition of managing and sharing your data, goals, and money.
Insurance company	Use new sources of data in underwriting models to predict risk.	Create a mobile app for claims filing and tracking. Establish online communities for small-business owners.	Offer direct-to-policyholder insurance that is sold without independent agents.
Fashion brand	Shift paid advertising mix to include more digital platforms. Add 3D tools for product display on websites.	Grow e-commerce distribution with existing and new retail partners. Partner with Apple or Android OS to design and brand a luxury smartwatch.	Launch a new brand sold exclusively direct-to-consumer via an app. Launch a subscription giftbox service.

(*continued*)

Table 6.5.
(*Continued*)

Industry	**P1 Ventures**: In the Core Business Plus Low Uncertainty	**P2 Ventures**: In the Core Business Plus High Uncertainty	**P3 Ventures**: Outside the Core Business Plus High Uncertainty
Auto manufacturer	Use AI in factories to detect manufacturing flaws faster and more cheaply.	Incorporate new predictive safety measures for drivers (digital eye tracking, etc.). Connect in-car data to the owner's app to track their carbon footprint.	Create an urban ride-sharing network for cars, scooters, and bicycles.
Physical retailer	Use predictive analytics for selecting new store locations. Use robots for scanning store shelves to record inventory.	Offer preordering online for pickup in-store. Create a mobile app experience for loyalty rewards and in-store payment.	Build an online marketplace that brings together product brands, curators, and service providers.
Telco	Use AI for market segmentation to target customers with the right offer at the right time.	Provide cybersecurity tools for small-business customers already using broadband and phone packages.	Offer a home IoT and wearable device service to monitor customers' elderly parents at home. Provide a mobile payment platform for consumers whether or not they use our phone service.

P1 CHALLENGES

P1 innovation is the easiest path in some ways because it faces neither the challenge of uncertainty nor proximity. But there are two common traps in managing P1. The first trap is to pursue *only* P1—innovation aligned to your core business, and with low uncertainty. While this approach may feel comfortable and low-risk, it will close off many of the biggest opportunities for growth for your firm.

The other mistake is the opposite: to neglect P1 innovation and focus exclusively on big-idea innovations. A business must maintain a steady stream of P1 innovations in its digital pipeline—incremental innovations that are guided by strategy and that yield returns to the bottom line. Beware of anyone who wants to take innovation out of the hands of the business units. They may recite a skunkworks theory that mature businesses are incapable of innovation and that it must be left to separate teams of fast-moving iconoclasts. This is flatly wrong. As the director of an innovation lab at a global financial services company told me, "We don't own innovation. We have innovation assets we bring to the rest of the organization. But if we want to be an innovative company, we can't pretend that there's a place called Labs that owns innovation."

P2 CHALLENGES

P2 is inherently more difficult because it involves greater uncertainty. Many companies try to pursue P2 ventures within their core business units, but these units frequently lack the needed skills in iterative experimentation. As a result, they will make too many assumptions, reach for an "obvious" solution to every problem, and then rush to build it.

Other companies try to take P2 innovation out of the hands of the core so it can be managed by innovation experts. In these companies, the core business is encouraged to deliver a list of projects for a digital innovation team that develops solutions entirely on their own, before handing them off to the business. This "build it and throw it over the wall" approach leads almost inevitably to disappointment. Even if the outside team discovers a great solution, it will struggle to be accepted and implemented by the core business it was meant to serve. The result is a kind of organ tissue rejection that ends in failure.

Other governance challenges for P2 innovation relate to funding. The core business almost always lacks a process for iterative budgeting, which is essential for innovating under uncertainty. In addition, if the core is asked to pay for P2 ventures, it will underinvest in them—precisely because they are risky and unlikely to pay off in the near term (when the core is held accountable for quarterly results). But if the core is not asked to pay anything toward a P2 venture, it will have no "skin in the game" for an innovation that is meant to work in its own business unit. That sets up the venture for weak sponsorship and lack of adoption later.

P3 CHALLENGES

The first challenge facing P3 ventures is that they do not fit anywhere within the existing organizational structure. Without a logical home in any existing business unit, they lack a power center. As a result, these innovations will struggle to attract sponsorship and support. If the organization is focused exclusively on current customers and the metrics of its current business, a P3 opportunity that addresses a different market will be ignored or neglected entirely.

If the central company leadership does choose to sponsor a P3 venture, it will often be derided as a distraction from the real work of the company. Investors famously chided Jeff Bezos to give up his AWS project and get back to focusing on his retail business. A 2006 cover of *BusinessWeek* declared, "Bezos wants to run your business with his Web technology. Wall Street wishes he would just mind the store."[16]

In addition, P3 ventures often breed resentment or backlash in the organization. Those working hard in the core business complain about the attention given to these new, unproven ideas: "Hey! We're the ones making the money that funds you with your experiments!" In other cases, a P3 venture faces active resistance if it is perceived as cannibalizing sales for the core business.

Governance for Each Path

Despite the challenges discussed above, all three paths lead to tremendous growth for the companies that manage them right. But succeeding in each path means adapting your governance model for each path. Table 6.6 provides a summary of how to manage each path to meet its particular challenges. Let's look at the governance of each path in more detail.

P1: INSIDE THE CORE

A P1 innovation should be managed inside the core using your standard functional (or matrix) teams—for example, it is run by the IT department, the marketing department, or a local operations team in a geographic business unit. P1 innovations can be managed with the standard metrics and planning that are well established in the core business. Because their uncertainty is low, P1 innovations can be funded by traditional budgeting based

Table 6.6.
Governance for the Three Paths to Growth

Governance	P1: In the Core Business Plus Low Uncertainty	P2: In the Core Business Plus High Uncertainty	P3: Outside the Core Business Plus High Uncertainty
Summary	*Inside the core*	*Partner with the core*	*Outside the core*
Starting point	Inside the core business	Separate unit, in close partnership with the core	Separate unit, with loose ties to the company
Teams	Standard functional (or matrix) teams	Multifunctional innovation teams	Multifunctional innovation teams
Work	Standard planning	Iterative experimentation	Iterative experimentation
Metrics	Standard business metrics	Staged validation metrics	Staged validation metrics
Funding	Standard budgeting process	Iterative funding approved by a growth board	Iterative funding approved by a growth board
Sponsorship	Funded entirely by the core	Funded partly by the core to start, later funded entirely by the core	Funded entirely by a separate budget
Trajectory	Starts in the core, stays in the core	Handed off to the core after key validation milestones	Starts outside the core, eventually merges with or becomes a new business unit

on net present value. All funds for P1 ventures should come from the core business, out of normal operating budgets.

P2: PARTNER WITH THE CORE

A P2 innovation should be managed within a dedicated innovation unit working in close partnership with the core business unit that the innovation is meant to serve. That starts with defining the goals of the venture with sponsors from the core who will ultimately own the project. "First, you have to align everyone," says Olivier Delabroy. "You have to put the business in the driver's seat and have a committed plan . . . If you want to scale your ideas, you need, from day one, to embark with the business."

After that initial alignment, the business must continue to partner with the innovation team throughout testing and validation. Work is done by a multifunctional innovation team, including members from the core alongside experts trained in iterative experimentation. Funds are disbursed by a growth board, following iterative funding practices, to account for the high uncertainty of the venture. To ensure buy-in, any P2 innovation must be financially sponsored by the division that will eventually own it. The funding may be subsidized at the early stages (e.g., from a central innovation budget), but the sponsoring division must have "skin in the game" from the start.

After uncertainty has been reduced (typically based on milestones of problem validation and solution validation), a decision is made whether the venture should continue. If the decision is yes, the venture will be handed off entirely to the business division that sponsored it to scale and launch it in the market. At that point, the business unit takes over all funding for the venture and will reap all profits from it.

P3: OUTSIDE THE CORE

A P3 innovation should be managed outside the core in a separate unit, much like an independent start-up that the parent company provides with seed capital (in some cases, that may actually be what you do). A P3 venture should be set up under the sponsorship of corporate leadership but with maximum independence from the core business. This setup allows it to attract entrepreneurial talent and gives it the chance to compete directly with your own business, if that is truly necessary. At the same time, a P3 venture should never be 100 percent separate from the organization. Where needed, there should be a mandate for resource sharing and collaboration— including support such as access to data, branding, supply chain partners, or a talent pipeline.

P3 innovations must be managed for high uncertainty, just like P2 innovations. This means a small multifunctional team that applies iterative experimentation to rapidly validate and adapt to market learning. And it means iterative funding by a dedicated growth board. P3 projects should be funded entirely by the parent company and not out of the operating budgets of any existing business units. Eventually, if a P3 venture is successful, a leadership decision must be made either to merge it with an existing business unit or to establish it as a new permanent division of the company.

PLAN WHERE TO LAND

Whatever its path, every new venture that succeeds eventually ends up in the core: P1 starts in the core; P2 hands off to the core; P3 joins or becomes a new unit in the core. Planning early for this eventual home is critical. As Mario Pieper at BSH Home Appliances explained to me, "You need to know not just the business model, but also have an idea for a landing spot— somebody in the organization whom you have to work with."

THE NEED FOR ALL THREE PATHS

Managing all three paths to growth is essential for long-term growth in the digital era. Many companies mistakenly try to manage innovation on only two paths (see the box "Why Dual Transformation Falls Short"). Only with separate governance models for all three paths, however, can your business achieve real and continuous transformation.

Why Dual Transformation Falls Short

I have seen many companies attempt a dual-path approach to transformation, which is given various names, including champion/challenger, battleship/speedboats, or (in the banking sector) run the bank/change the bank. In each case, the first term refers to the core business and the second to an independent unit focused beyond it. In the boat metaphor, the battleship is the legacy business, which can only be turned slowly toward a digital direction. The speedboats are small teams that move swiftly in pursuit of digital opportunities because they are untethered to the core.

James G. March provided early thinking on the tension between exploiting the core and exploring beyond it.* His ideas were built upon by Charles A. O'Reilly and Michael L. Tushman's writing on the ambidextrous organization.† Although their work identifies an important problem—what I describe as the challenge of proximity—the two-part solution they offer is still incomplete.

In practice, I have seen the dual-path approach to transformation lead to frustration. In many companies, the core languishes, with its organization and culture unchanged because it is given an excuse to move slower. Meanwhile, the independent teams generate many ideas but struggle to scale them to have a real impact. These teams drift farther from the main business over time and lose leadership support.

There is a reason for this trouble. Even when executed well, a dual approach is simply a model for managing P1 (battleship) and P3 (speedboat) innovation. But for most businesses, P2 is where the most valuable growth happens! That's right: most digital growth comes from P2—new ventures that are related to your core business and customers but involve a significant amount of uncertainty. In a dual-path organization, these ventures are managed as if they were either P1 or P3. Either case is a recipe for trouble.

(*continued on next page*)

(continued from previous page)

When you treat a P2 innovation as if it were P1, you send it to the core to die. You treat an uncertain opportunity as if it were a well-defined, everyday business project. That means running it within an existing division and applying traditional project management, business case analysis, and budgeting. In the best case, these P2 innovations are underfunded (because they can't prove an ironclad case for their profitability) and are left to wither on the vine. In the worst case, they are approved and overfunded, and become expensive and embarrassing digital failures when initial planning turns out to be riddled with assumptions.

When you manage a P2 innovation as if it were P3, you spin it out on its own to die. You treat a new innovation that is inextricably linked to your current business as if it were a stand-alone start-up. That means handing it off to an independent team that operates without the core business. These teams often generate promising business ideas, but their ideas inevitably fail when they have to integrate with the core business—whether it is due to resentment ("not invented here" syndrome), a failure to understand the needs of the business ("our customer would love that, but it will bankrupt our P&L"), or some other source of misalignment ("this doesn't match our product roadmap"). The result is innovations that never scale to have a meaningful impact on the goals of the firm.

* James G. March, "Exploration and Exploitation in Organizational Learning," *Organization Science* 2, no. 1, Special Issue: Papers in Honor of (and by) James G. March (1991): 71–87.
† Charles A. O'Reilly and Michael Tushman. *Lead and Disrupt: How to Solve the Innovator's Dilemma* (Stanford, CA: Stanford Business Books, 2021).

Governance, Not Ideation

When I introduce the three paths to executives of large enterprises, a certain misplaced enthusiasm often arises along with a particular question: Should we use the three paths as a springboard for generating new ideas? That is, should managers start out by envisioning P1 ventures, P2 ventures, and P3 ventures? The answer is no. The three paths to growth is a model for innovation governance, not for generating innovation ideas.

As we saw in chapter 4, idea generation is a strategic process. For new ventures to have the greatest chance of delivering real value, we must begin by looking at customers and the business and identifying the most important problems and opportunities for each. Use the strategy tools in chapter 4 to guide your search for innovation ideas. Use the three paths once you have a new venture in mind to pursue. Only then are you ready to identify the governance model that will give that new venture its best shot at success.

Innovation Structures

Too many organizations start innovating without the resources and governance in place to carry ideas through to scale. They approve new projects or organize hackathons with no support structure to build on the ideas they generate. For innovation to drive growth at scale, businesses must establish *innovation structures* that bring teams and boards together and provide them with the resources and management they need to succeed.

I define an innovation structure as *a pool of funding and talent for innovation, with defined sponsorship and governance rules.* This pool of dedicated resources, funded in advance, allows a growth board to fund a portfolio of either P2 or P3 ventures iteratively—shutting down some ventures and accelerating investment in others—without needing to pause work constantly to seek funding or staff for the teams that board oversees.

An innovation structure is where P2 and P3 innovation come to life inside an organization. (P1 innovations are managed within the core itself, so they do not need a separate structure.) Innovation structures come in many forms and with even more names. Some of the most common types are the following:

- *Digital accelerators*—Also called centers of excellence or digital factories, these structures are set up to accelerate the development of innovations within the company's core business.
- *Innovation labs*—Also called innovation studios, these structures focus on launching new ventures outside the company's current core business. Teams are granted autonomy to move as quickly and as independently as possible.
- *Innovation challenges*—Often called hackathons, these contests solicit ideas from a wide pool of participants who may have access to a shared data set or tool base. A challenge may be open to employees, business partners, university students, or the public. After an initial round with many participants, a few winning teams receive funding for iterative testing and validation.

- *Start-up incubators*—Also called start-up accelerators, these focus on partnering with and growing external start-ups that are relevant to the company's strategy. Direct investment may happen, but the focus is on collaboration.
- *Corporate venture capital*—Corporate venture funds invest in external start-ups, managing a portfolio of investments over time and taking an equity stake, much like a traditional VC fund.
- *Mergers and acquisitions (M&A) teams*—M&A is a major part of the digital strategy of many firms, where acquisitions bring in new digital business models as well as digital talent.

As these examples show, an innovation structure may be internal (utilizing only company employees) or external (partnering, acquiring, or investing in outside start-ups), or the structure may bring together internal efforts with outside support and partners.

Governance and Design Matter

Beware of setting up any innovation structure without giving careful attention to its governance and design. Providing innovation resources without governance will lead teams to run amok. I have heard companies lament over setting up an innovation lab that is funded by the central headquarters but does not have clear operating rules. These efforts typically serve solely as a corporate branding exercise ("Look, we have a digital innovation lab you can visit!"). No ventures emerge that deliver real value to the business. This leads quickly to resentment from the core business, and the lab is ultimately shut down.

Equally bad is an innovation structure with a clear purpose but whose design does not match its mission. One disastrous example of this was GE Digital, a unit set up by GE in 2015 to pioneer a completely new business model—a software operating system called Predix to power the machines of the industrial world. This was a classic P3 innovation mandate: a new unproven business model outside anything GE had done before. It should have called for a lean and independent structure: a small, dedicated team that experimented, validated, and found product-market fit before seeking to grow. Instead, it was assigned to a legacy division that provided IT services to GE's core business units (aviation, power, transportation, etc.). The legacy division was given the new mandate for business model reinvention ("build Predix!"), but it was still led by its prior CEO, and it still retained its old responsibilities to internal GE customers. As a result, GE Digital launched with a huge staff (1,700 employees within its first year) and massive overhead costs. With a quarterly P&L and revenue demands to meet, it was forced to focus almost entirely on serving internal customers rather than pursuing new markets. The result was predictable: GE Digital utterly failed at its reason for being—to build Predix as a new business model to drive GE's future growth.[17]

Before launching any innovation structure, it is critical to align on a few key elements:

- *Mandate*—Any stand-alone innovation structure, beyond the business units themselves, must have a clear reason for being. This rationale should include the benefits that the structure is meant to provide to the rest of the organization, and the strategic problems and opportunities it is meant to pursue.
- *P2 or P3*—It is critical to decide if the structure is focused on P2 or P3. Is the structure meant to support innovation within the core business or beyond it? If you don't know this answer from the start, it will be impossible to define clear rules on who sponsors projects, who holds decision rights, and what (if any) are the roles and obligations of business units in the core.
- *Funding source*—Who will fund the structure? If it is focused on P3, its funding must come from the central headquarters. But if it is focused on P2, its funding should be split: you will need to decide how much is paid by relevant business units and how much by headquarters. The innovation structure should be funded up front on an annual basis. Then its growth boards can allocate resources flexibly across different venture teams.
- *Goals and metrics*—It is critical to decide in advance what success will look like so everyone has the same expectations. If you don't agree on goals at the outset, your structure will be hobbled by conflicting expectations (e.g., an innovation lab thinks it is investing in ten-year bets, but it is funded by a committee that expects new products to launch in year one). Choose metrics to match your goals. A P2 structure could be measured on the impact of its innovations after they are handed off to the business and scaled up. A P3 structure might measure results like a venture capital fund—tracking its financial return on a portfolio of bets that pay off over several years.

Most importantly, you should start small and expect each innovation structure to evolve as you learn what works best and as the needs of your business change. Ford's Smart Mobility unit (a P3 structure pursuing new business models beyond car ownership) started with just twelve people. BASF's Onono lab intentionally began with only two full-time employees because its P2 mission was to spark innovation by bringing together business unit leaders with start-ups and customers. The last thing Antonio Lacerda wanted was for Onono to head off pursuing innovation ideas on its own. He explained, "With only the two of us full-time, we knew that nothing could happen at Onono without the involvement and support of our business units."

Spotlight on Two Innovation Structures

The following two cases provide examples of smart governance and design in innovation structures from companies in two very different industries: industrial manufacturing and financial services.

P2 Spotlight: United Technology Corporation's Digital Accelerator

United Technologies Corporation (UTC) launched an innovation structure in Brooklyn, New York, called the Digital Accelerator to enable digital innovation in its four core business units. Vince Campisi, the company's CIO and CDO, knew the firm was adept at using technology to increase productivity within its operations. But he saw it struggle to harness the data in its industrial products to add value for customers and transform the user experience. Campisi brought in Steve Serra, formerly an outside innovation consultant, to establish UTC's Digital Accelerator to support this P2 innovation in the core business.

Given its mission, Serra knew that no venture should start in the Digital Accelerator without explicit sponsorship approval from the core business. As a P2 innovation structure, the Digital Accelerator uses a split funding model: 20 percent of its budget comes from corporate seed funding, and the rest is from the four business units themselves, with each unit funding a particular "studio" supporting its ventures.

Venture teams are comprised of innovation experts working full-time at the Digital Accelerator, combined with representatives from the core business. Campisi explains: "When a business unit president shows up with their staff at our Digital Accelerator, our first question to them is, 'What are your priorities, your business objectives and outcomes?'" Those objectives are quickly translated into a problem statement, which kicks off a process of rapid experimentation. If validation shows there is a real business opportunity, the team moves ahead quickly with MVPs and prototyping.

Every venture begins with a plan for its handoff back to the business unit. Early stages of validation are done at the Digital Accelerator, but when product-market fit is found, the innovation is transferred to the business. Serra pointed to the example of a digital product designed to monitor the health of an aircraft engine for the company's Pratt & Whitney business unit. The Digital Accelerator worked with Pratt & Whitney to develop the first functional MVP and put it into real-world use with customers in a limited test. "We released the software to our first customers and saw how they used it. We trialed it with scores of users, not thousands." The team waited until they had three business customers and until they "knew what was working, what was not, and what additional things customers wanted" so they could define a product roadmap. At that point, Serra explained, they were ready to move ownership to the business, which would continue to refine the product, scale it, and integrate it into their operations.

For an accelerator like UTC's, the right talent is critical, as is the balance of newcomers and people with long experience in the parent company. As Serra told me, "More outsiders mean you will move faster. More insiders mean you can integrate faster." UTC placed the Digital Accelerator in Brooklyn to tap a prime talent market while staying on the flight path between the company's two headquarters in Connecticut and North Carolina.

The vision for the Digital Accelerator was dynamic from the start. In addition to seeding innovations, it was meant to change the culture of innovation at the core. Campisi stressed, "We can't do enough highlighting of the pioneers who were willing to make the leap of faith with us—to show how digital is a vehicle for solving important needs for customers." Since its launch, the Digital Accelerator has continued to evolve, adapting to the changing needs of UTC, which was later rebranded as Raytheon Technologies after a merger. Digital Accelerator employees moved into the business units they had previously supported, further driving innovation in the core. Meanwhile, the focus of the Digital Accelerator shifted from customer-experience design to data-driven value creation.

P3 Spotlight: Mastercard's Start Path

One of Mastercard's innovation structures is Start Path, which was designed to seek growth opportunities beyond Mastercard's core with the help of fintech start-ups. Partnering with start-ups is a popular tactic for legacy companies seeking to drive

(*continued on next page*)

(*continued from previous page*)

digital innovation, but without a clear focus, it rarely yields lasting results. Mastercard developed Start Path with a clear focus: to learn about the fast-moving fintech landscape and build partnerships early—both for its own core business and for the global network of banks and merchants that are Mastercard's customers.

Start Path is a free, one-year accelerator program for fintech start-ups around the world. Mastercard's learning about emerging trends and opportunities is fed each year by seeing the pitches of 2,000 applicants who seek to join Start Path. That learning continues with the forty start-ups who are accepted into the program, as Mastercard helps nurture them through their next stages of market testing and validation.

Mastercard is careful to define the growth stage of start-ups it will consider for Start Path. Because its goal is to learn from businesses that already have product-market fit, Mastercard makes a conscious decision not to accept applications from start-ups at the idea-on-a-napkin stage. Instead, it focuses on finding what it calls *real actual businesses building interesting tech* (RABBITs).

These start-ups already have many options for raising capital. So, rather than investing in every Start Path member, Mastercard focuses on the commercial benefits it can connect them to, which means matching each start-up with the banks and merchants in Mastercard's network. By introducing start-ups to this top-tier client list, Mastercard has become the preferred partner for some of the world's best fintech start-ups. At the same time, Mastercard offers access to its Start Path ecosystem as a value-added service to its own business customers around the world.

Two case examples of well-designed innovation structures are described in the box "Spotlight on Two Innovation Structures."

One Company, Multiple Structures

It is important to recognize that there is no single perfect innovation structure. Too often, I have seen executives convinced there is a magical silver bullet for innovation in their business (whether a digital factory or a moon-shot lab like Google's). Your goal should not be to pick one structure but to develop multiple structures to pursue different growth opportunities. The most innovative companies that I have seen all use multiple innovation structures to support P2 and P3 while continuing to pursue P1 innovation in their core. Table 6.7 lists examples of companies that use a

Table 6.7.

Firms with Different Structures for Managing P2 and P3 Innovations

Company	Structures for P2	Structures for P3
Citibank	**D10X**—This internal accelerator solicits venture ideas from employees in Citibank's consumer and institutional businesses, pairs them with mentors, and helps them build digital innovations within the core. Projects have included Proxymity and CitiConnect for Blockchain. **CUPID**—The hackathon program engages students from leading universities around the world to support ongoing innovation projects across Citibank.	**Studio**—This lab incubates new digital ventures outside the current business that focus on Citibank's strategic P/Os. Ventures include Worthi and City Builder. **Venture Investing**—This fund invests in external start-ups that have product-market fit, offer strategic value to Citibank, and can benefit from Citibank's global commercial relationships. Exits include Honey and Docusign.
Air Liquide	**Digital Fabs for business units**—Four teams focus on accelerating DX in Air Liquide's four business lines. Ventures include a predictive maintenance data project within the Large Industry line. **Digital Fabs for business functions**—Two teams focus on digitizing the global finance function and the HR function. **ALIAD**—This corporate VC fund invests in start-ups that the core business partners with as a customer. The portfolio focuses on sustainable energy, AI, and IoT—with start-ups like Plug Power and Avenisense.	**i-Lab**—This innovation lab explores digital business models in areas new to the business, including energy stewardship, home health care, and air pollution reduction. **M&A**—Acquisitions have been used to expand into new product areas (such as biogas) and to acquire digital capabilities (such as Alizent, providing IoT solutions across the firm).
BSH Home Appliances	**Sprinter Model**—BSH Digital partners closely with the core business to test and rapidly scale digital innovations that leverage assets of the core. **BSH Start-Up Kitchen**—BSH partners with start-ups (Series A and B) looking to work with the home appliances industry. After an early pilot-test, BSH leverages the scale of its core business to accelerate the growth of these partners.	**Company Builder Model**—This model is used to launch new ventures whose business model is distinct from BSH's core business. Examples include We Wash, a digital service for community laundry, with IoT-connected machines for urban dwellers. **Strategic Venturing**—BSH surveys the market when a new digital venture is proposed to see if a solution already exists. If a match is found, BSH explores options to acquire, invest, or partner. Examples include Chefling (AI for pantry management) and Kitchen Stories (recipe app). **BSH Future Home Accelerator**—This start-up accelerator runs in partnership with Techstars. Its goal is to grow the ecosystem of start-ups focused on future home living (cooking, AI assistants, sleep management, etc.).

combination of innovation structures to drive growth and transformation across their business.

Tool: The Corporate Innovation Stack

We are now ready to introduce our next strategic tool, the Corporate Innovation Stack. The purpose of this tool is to manage innovation at scale in any established business. To do this, we need to define governance rules for innovation at three different layers (see figure 6.7):

- *Innovation structures* (e.g., digital accelerators, innovation labs, or corporate VC funds), which provide resources and oversight for P2 and P3 innovation.
- *Innovation boards* (or growth boards), which green-light, advise, and provide iterative funding to a portfolio of different growth ventures.
- *Innovation teams* (small and highly independent), which do the work of ideating, validating, and growing a single venture through rapid experimentation.

The tool is comprised of three different "charters" for the three different levels (a charter for each structure, each board, and each team). Each charter is meant to define governance and rules for that level of the innovation stack before its work can begin (see figure 6.8).

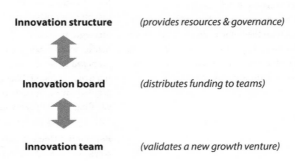

Figure 6.7.
Three layers of the Corporate Innovation Stack

1. Structure's Charter

Structure: Mission				Structure: Process	
Mandate	P2 versus P3	Goals and metrics		Talent pool	Recruiting
	Resources	Leadership		Independence	Learning

2. Board's Charter

Board: Members		Board: Process		
Composition	Abilities	Pipeline	Portfolio	Resources
	Responsibilities		Iterative funding	Handoffs

3. Team's Charter

Team: Members		Team: Process	
Composition	Commitment	P/O statement	Metrics
	Incentives	Experimentation methods	Decision rights

Figure 6.8.
The Corporate Innovation Stack

1. Structure's Charter

Step 1 of the Corporate Innovation Stack focuses on crafting a charter for each innovation structure. The charter spells out its mission and the processes that will guide its operations. This charter must be defined for each P2 or P3 innovation structure before any resources are given to it.

STRUCTURE: MISSION

- *Mandate*—Why is this innovation structure needed? How will it benefit the organization, and how should it influence the organization over time? What strategic P/Os does it hope to address?
- *P2 versus P3*—Is this structure focused on P2 (innovation in the core) or P3 (beyond the core)? If it is focused on P2, which of your core business units or functions will it support? How will it partner with them?

- *Goals and metrics*—How do you define success for this innovation struc-ture? What is its time frame? What metrics will you use to measure its long-term impact? What metrics will measure its near-term progress?
- *Resources*—For a P2 structure, what share of the initial funding will come from the business units and how will that be budgeted? For a P3 structure, how much funding will it receive from the central orga-nization and how will it be budgeted? What other resources will the organization provide (access to data, to customers, to channel part-ners, etc.)?
- *Leadership*—Who oversees the innovation structure? To whom do they report?

STRUCTURE: PROCESS

- *Talent pool*—Will this structure's innovation be pursued by internal teams, external teams, or a collaboration between both? What mix of skills will you need? What is the minimum head count (for venture teams plus administration)?
- *Recruiting*—What proportion of its staff should be new hires versus internal recruits? Will internal recruits be permanent or on short rotations to work in the structure? Will you procure external talent through partners (consultants, universities, etc.) or M&A?
- *Independence*—What sandboxes will the structure be given for compli-ance (security, risk management, data access, regulation, etc.)? What independence will it have from normal corporate functions such as IT (going outside the existing tech stack) and HR (different hiring and compensation)?
- *Learning*—What mechanisms will be used to capture learning (both suc-cesses and failures)? How will that learning be shared across the organi-zation? How will shutdowns be evaluated and smart failures celebrated?

2. Board's Charter

Step 2 of the Corporate Innovation Stack focuses on crafting a charter for each growth board. This charter defines the members the board will need and the process of their work. The charter must be created by the innova-tion structure before a growth board's members are recruited or resources are given to it. Depending on a structure's size, it may use one or more boards.

BOARD: MEMBERS

- *Composition*—How many members will serve on each board? What mix of seniority will you seek? Where will members come from inside the organization? (Any P2 board must represent the business unit its ventures will support. P3 boards should draw from across the enterprise for a diverse perspective.) Will you recruit any board members from outside the company?
- *Abilities*—How will you ensure that board members understand the principles of iterative validation and funding? What other skills will you seek in your members (subject-matter expertise, VC or entrepreneurial experience, internal influence in the business, etc.)?
- *Responsibilities*—How frequently will the board meet? A regular cadence is important, and meeting every four to twelve weeks is preferable. How will you define board members' key responsibilities? What does the board need to report to the structure's leaders (e.g., after each funding decision)?

BOARD: PROCESS

- *Pipeline*—What milestones will define every venture's progress? What percentage of ventures do you expect to drop off at each milestone? What is the expected time from green-lighting until a venture is handed off to grow on its own?
- *Portfolio*—How many ventures will the board oversee at one time? How many successful ventures do you want at the end of your pipeline? Given attrition, how many ventures should you have at the start? Will you use a venture backlog—approving ventures in advance, so they are ready to launch when resources are ready?
- *Resources*—For internal teams, what resources will you allocate (operating budget, head count, fractional time per person, etc.)? For outside teams, what funding and other resources will you provide? For startups, what investment stake will you seek?
- *Iterative funding*—What criteria will you use to green-light a new venture? What is the size of a typical first-funding round? What criteria will you use at each milestone to decide whether to continue to fund? How quickly will funding grow at each milestone? How will you track shutdowns and measure the quality of "smart failures"?

- *Handoffs*—For P2, when do you hand off a venture to the sponsoring business unit? What are the key validation milestones? For P3, when does a successful venture graduate from the board and go elsewhere for continued oversight or funding?

3. Team's Charter

Step 3 of the Corporate Innovation Stack focuses on crafting a charter for each innovation team that defines the roles of the team's members and the process of their work. Every team must have a charter, created with and approved by the board, before the team is green-lit to begin work.

TEAM: MEMBERS

- *Composition*—What size should the team be? What skills will its members need for the team to work completely independently? For P2 structures, what members of the team will come from the core business unit?
- *Commitment*—Will the team's leader(s) be single-threaded to the venture? Will other team members be single-threaded? If they are not full-time at the start, when will they shift to a full-time commitment?
- *Incentives*—What kind of upside stake (e.g., equity or performance bonus) will team members be given in the success of their venture? How will you ensure that team members have a viable career path in your organization?

TEAM: PROCESS

- *P/O statement*—What problem or opportunity is the team committed to? Who is the key stakeholder (a customer or someone in the business)? What outcome are you seeking? How will achieving this outcome create value for the firm (e.g., revenue, cost savings, or another value driver)? What tenets should serve as guiding principles for the team's work?[18]
- *Metrics*—What metrics will you use to measure success? What guardrail metrics will you use to avoid unintended consequences or risks? How will you share these measures transparently across your organization?

- *Experimentation methods*—What cadence will the team use (e.g., daily stand-up meetings and biweekly sprints)? What artifacts will the team use (e.g., Rogers Growth Navigator, kanban boards, user stories)? How many illustrative versus functional MVPs will you expect to build? What innovation methods (e.g., lean start-up, Scrum) will the team draw on?
- *Decision rights*—What can the team decide without any approval from the growth board or any other external party?

Remember that any good innovation structure should evolve to meet the changing needs of the business. A board or a team, learning from experience, may discover ways to improve how it works. All three charters—for structures, boards, and teams—should therefore be revisited from time to time to update them for continued success.

Governance from the Bottom Up

The model of governance we have seen throughout this chapter—innovation teams, boards, and structures—represents a shift from top-down management toward a more bottom-up organization.

The governance of *innovation teams* is designed to support bottom-up decision making and autonomy. These teams' small size and multifunctional skill set allow for independent action. Transparent metrics and a clear definition of success allow each team to hold decision rights over its work, without sign-off from other parties. An example can be seen in the governance of Amazon's two-pizza teams, which are allowed to operate with complete autonomy once an agreement is reached on what they are seeking to accomplish. As longtime Amazon executive David Glick explained to me, a team's metrics, sometimes called its fitness function, provide "a mathematical description of what you're trying to optimize." Before any staff member is assigned to a new team, these metrics are hammered out in a discussion between the team leader and top management. In the early days, "Jeff [Bezos] used to review every single fitness function," Glick recalled. Once an agreement is made on the metrics, they are tracked, shared transparently, and used to judge the team's work and hold its leadership accountable.

The governance of *innovation boards* is designed to support a more bottom-up approach to leadership. Digital-native businesses focus on pushing decision making down the organizational chart, with leaders making far fewer decisions on the day-to-day work of those below them. Pushing decision making down is precisely what growth boards are designed to do. Rather than micromanage teams pursuing innovation, boards are designed to empower them. They do this in three important ways. They ensure that teams have resources—budgets, head count, and the right mix of multifunctional skills. They align processes—metrics, decision rights, compliance rules—to help rather than hinder the work of teams. And they advocate for teams internally and connect them to others outside the firm.

The governance of *innovation structures* is designed to engage people at every level of the organization and in every function. Whether in a hackathon or a program like Citibank's D10X, these structures can surface and accelerate growth ideas pitched by anyone, from senior vice presidents to the newest junior hire. Meanwhile, structures like Mastercard's Start Path bring in insights and ideas from outside that can point the business in new directions. Remember that P2 innovation structures should not only support your business units with new products and commercial innovation. They should also support your functional silos—HR, marketing, customer service, supply chain, and so on—to solve problems in their work and create value for the firm.

∼

For DX to deliver lasting impact to any organization, it must involve more than a few teams operating in isolated pockets of innovation. Without new governance models to allocate resources and manage new ventures, the potential for growth will always fall short. In Step 4 of the DX Roadmap, we have seen how any organization can design its governance to manage growth at scale. We have seen how teams, boards, and structures can scale experimentation across the enterprise. We have learned how to manage the three paths to growth to pursue opportunities of varied uncertainty within your core business and beyond it. And we have seen how iterative funding and smart shutdowns are essential to investing wisely and maintaining a pipeline of innovations.

With a shared vision, strategic priorities, a process for validating new ventures, and a governance model to manage growth at scale, you are now ready to turn to the final step of the DX Roadmap and grow your capabilities. As you began work on your first digital ventures, you will likely have discovered some gaps in the capabilities of your organization. These gaps may include your technology and data infrastructure, your employee talent and skills base, and the culture and mindset of your organization.

To build a strong foundation for the future of your business, you will need to invest in the digital capabilities of your organization. In the next chapter, you will learn how to define the capabilities that will be most critical to your digital future and grow them to deliver on the promise of transformation.

7

Step 5: Grow Tech, Talent, and Culture

CAPABILITIES

When the first of Volkswagen's ID.3 electric cars rolled off the assembly line in Zwickau, Germany, CEO Herbert Diess was joined by Angela Merkel, who was chancellor of Germany at the time, to commemorate the milestone. After five years and $50 billion in development, the German auto industry's answer to Tesla had finally arrived. But the following spring, Volkswagen's top executives were forced to postpone the launch of the ID.3 to customers. The car's software was rife with bugs, and many of its digital features—including a cutting-edge heads-up display—were not working properly. When the car finally did launch in the fall, its first 50,000 customers were told they would have to return to the dealership for a software update as soon as it was ready. These updates were meant to happen over the air, but Volkswagen decided that the operating system was not yet safe enough because it might be exposed to online hackers. As the ID.3's leader, Thomas Ulbrich, explained, "Updating the vehicle's core software is a complex process and we have to make sure at any time that our vehicles are safe."[1] The ID.3's rollout made painfully clear that the company's digital capabilities were not yet prepared to deliver on its strategy.

As the largest automaker in the world, the Volkswagen Group has long prided itself on its skill in hardware engineering and design—reflected in brands ranging from VW and Audi to Porsche and Lamborghini. But as Volkswagen shifts from gas-powered to electric vehicles and works on future autonomous vehicles, the relative importance of hardware and software to the business has shifted. The capabilities that define a great car company are different in the digital era.

These new capabilities start with digital technology. Traditional gas-powered cars were built with software but only for running secondary functions like heating, maps, and entertainment. These simple applications were coded onto separate chips implanted in parts throughout the car. They were easily outsourced to suppliers and plugged in when the vehicle was assembled. But with the shift to electric vehicles, software is now in the driver's seat. It runs the entire powertrain, brakes, battery, and lights—the most critical systems of any car. The hundreds of applications in an electric vehicle cannot be built as separate widgets; they must be part of an integrated operating system. Just as important, the software must be continually updated over the life of the vehicle, just like a smartphone's operating system and apps. Volkswagen's ambition is to build an entirely new software platform called VW.os 2.0 that will be used by every vehicle brand from VW to Porsche, to Skoda. But to get there, the company will need more than just new technology.

To pursue its strategy, Volkswagen also needs a transformation of its talent. Volkswagen and its peers have long outsourced their IT needs to suppliers. "Over the past 20 years, the auto industry became more integrators than developers," observes Alexander Hitzinger, a former member of Volkswagen's board.[2] This kept costs down but required giving up control. To achieve its electric vehicle strategy, Volkswagen set a five-year goal to shift from 10 percent of its vehicle software being built in-house to 60 percent.[3] That meant insourcing deep technical knowledge that formerly resided in partners. It also meant bringing together thousands of programmers previously scattered across Volkswagen's divisions to work in a centralized fashion. Dirk Hilgenberg was hired from competitor BMW to lead this centralized software unit—a new company under the Volkswagen Group named CARIAD.

For Volkswagen to succeed, however, it needs more than digital technology and talent; it needs a digital culture. As Hilgenberg sees it, the company's biggest challenge is the mindset of its people. "The global transformation of the industry will take roughly 10 years—with or without Volkswagen,"

Diess declared in a LinkedIn post. As CEO, he pushed back against the complacency he saw in senior executives. Rather than grading themselves on traditional measures where VW excelled, he pushed them to look at new metrics—such as battery range and advanced computing—where it was far behind.[4] In addition, CARIAD's software teams need a more agile culture, like a tech company. To build VW.os 2.0, they must adopt collaborative ways of working with technology partners like Continental. Tech companies like Diconium have been acquired not just for their technical talent but for the culture they bring. To attract even more talent, Volkswagen needs a culture that enables teams to innovate around customer needs and continuously ship new software. In Diess's words, "a culture which is customer-oriented, fast and agile."[5]

Shifting the technology, talent, and culture of Volkswagen is essential to its digital transformation (DX). But it will not be easy, and it will not happen overnight. As Danny Shapiro, VP of automotive at chipmaker Nvidia, says, "You can't just flip a switch and be a software company."[6]

Why Capabilities Matter

In Amazon's early days, when it was still known as a website selling books and household goods, Jeff Bezos remarked to employees that "Amazon is not a retailer. We're a software company." He went on to explain, "Our business is not what's in the brown boxes. It's the software that sends the brown boxes on their way."[7] One of the questions I hear legacy businesses struggle with in their DX is some variation on this: "Are we a car company? Or are we a *tech company* that sells cars?" Whatever you call yourself, what matters is whether you have the capabilities that are most critical to your strategy for the digital era.

In every industry, the defining capabilities of a great company are shifting. As every business pursues its own DX, these capabilities will distinguish tomorrow's winners from its also-rans: new technologies, new skills, and new cultural mindsets. We can see the interplay of these different kinds of capabilities in the model of a modular organization. Modular architecture has been a major trend in IT throughout the digital era. Its software is composed of loosely coupled, independent pieces of code called microservices. Each one acts as an independent building block that performs a discrete business function and can be updated without risk to the rest of the system. This provides technical benefits of resilience and scalability. But the biggest impact of modular architecture is how it affects the organization itself. By turning the work of a business into individual components, modular architecture allows teams to operate with much greater independence.

As companies like Walmart have migrated to modular IT systems, they have transformed their organizations with independent teams that innovate much more rapidly. Research by Mark J. Greeven, Howard Yu, and Jialu Shan has shown the widespread benefits of modular architecture in reducing organizational complexity.[8] In a modular organization, getting what you need from another department becomes a self-service process. The extreme degree of this can be seen in Haier, a manufacturer of home electronics, from refrigerators and washing machines to televisions. Taking advantage of modular IT, Haier has reorganized its entire company into 4,000 microenterprises (MEs) of ten to fifteen people. Some MEs deliver final products to consumers; others provide internal services like staffing, product design, or manufacturing to other MEs. Each one operates with independence and autonomy, and all coordination is managed through an internal cloud-based platform.[9] The culture of Haier matches this new organizational model as well: it is bottom-up, risk taking, and collaborative, with each team having a clear sense of ownership of its work.

In the fifth step of the Digital Transformation (DX) Roadmap, your objective is to grow the right mix of technology, talent, and culture to support the digital growth trajectory of your business. The challenge for Volkswagen, Haier, and any established business is to ensure that its capabilities match the ambition of its digital strategy.

Why not start the DX Roadmap with growing capabilities as the first step? Many consultants propose a DX agenda that focuses first on capability building—such as moving to the cloud, establishing data governance, and hiring engineers. But building capabilities is not a strategy! The truth is that there is no generic digital organization and no universal blueprint for the capabilities every business will need. Only when you have some clarity on your vision for the future and have started to pursue your first digital ventures will it become clear which capabilities are most important to build first.

Growing your digital capabilities can be the hardest, longest, and most costly work of any transformation effort, but the investment is essential. Without it, progress will be thwarted by inflexible software, incomplete data sets, and systems that can't communicate with each other or with partners. Your workforce won't have the skills needed to build and grow your digital ventures. Your teams will be held back by a culture that is rigid instead of

Table 7.1.
What's at Stake—Step 5: Capabilities

Symptoms of Failure: Capabilities	Symptoms of Success: Capabilities
• Inflexible IT systems reinforce silos and limit collaboration.	• Modular IT systems integrate across the organization and with outside partners.
• Data is contradictory, incomplete, and inaccessible to managers in real time.	• Data provides a single source of truth to managers across the company.
• Centralized IT governance causes bottlenecks for new projects.	• IT governance provides oversight while keeping innovation in the hands of the business.
• Employees lack digital skills, so digital projects must be outsourced.	• Employees can build and iterate digital solutions themselves.
• A top-down culture and bureaucracy stifle employees, breeding cynicism and inertia.	• An empowering culture and processes help employees drive bottom-up change.

flexible, siloed instead of collaborative, and tentative instead of confident about taking risks. If these deficits are left unaddressed, every new digital innovation you pursue will be limited in its impact.

Building the right digital capabilities for your business is not easy, but it is the only way for transformation to deliver real change in the long term. Table 7.1 shows some of the key symptoms of success versus failure in Step 5 of the DX Roadmap.

What's Ahead

In this chapter, we will see how any organization can build the foundation it needs for its unique digital future. We will examine three essential types of capabilities for the digital era:

- *Technology*—including IT infrastructure, data assets, and governance systems.
- *Talent*—including technical skills like data science and nontechnical skills like design thinking.
- *Culture*—the mindsets and norms that shape day-to-day behavior throughout the firm.

The chapter will introduce two new tools: the Tech and Talent Map, which identifies and closes gaps in your technology and skills, and the

Culture-Process Map, which defines, communicates, and enables the right culture at scale in your organization. Finally, we will see how the right capabilities are critical to bottom-up change and transformation.

Technology

The right technology capabilities are essential to any digital strategy, but many legacy businesses are held back by their limits in this area. Among the symptoms are software that is slow to adapt, data that cannot be accessed in real time, technology silos that match organizational silos, and systems that don't talk to each other or outside partners. As you pursue your digital strategy, it is essential that you work closely with your CIO to assess your current technology capabilities and identify your most critical gaps. Specifically, I see three main areas that organizations need to assess: IT infrastructure, data assets, and tech and data governance.

IT Infrastructure

Any organization must constantly assess its technology infrastructure to identify the capabilities it needs to support its future strategy. This may include decisions about cloud computing—for example, whether to use public, private, or hybrid cloud models or on-premise solutions to meet the needs of the business. It includes system architecture, such as microservices and application programming interfaces (APIs) to connect to different parts of the business and outside partners. Data storage, using models like data lakes or data warehouses, is crucial to storing data for effective use and retrieval. Just as important are the applications that run key business processes—for example, pricing and inventory for a retailer, content and subscriptions for a publisher, and customer analytics for almost any business. Having the right IT infrastructure for your particular needs is essential to your DX success.

Recall the example of the National Commercial Bank (NCB) from chapter 3. NCB's strategy to become the top digital bank in Saudi Arabia was to build a best-in-class mobile banking experience and thus free client-facing employees to drive an expansion into unbanked markets. The biggest obstacle to this strategy was the bank's legacy IT, which operated on a snarl of 160 different systems with a complex web of integration. Multiple points of integration failure called for constant intervention by back-office personnel. In a multiyear effort, NCB rebuilt its core banking technology in a modern architecture of just fifteen systems supporting seamless digital operations. The result was a reliable, best-in-class customer experience that made NCB's banking app number one in the country. Customers shifted over 98 percent of their transactions to digital self-service, driving cost savings and top-line growth for the bank.

TECHNICAL DEBT

NCB's story is a clear illustration of the concept of technical debt. Technical debt is any future cost to the business caused by suboptimal technology.[10] The term applies to both software and hardware; it can range from poor HTML code that slows down a webpage to systemwide deficits in networking, data integration, or cybersecurity. Technical debt has many causes, from deferred maintenance of aging systems to changing technology standards, to poor initial design. It can even be the result of an intentional decision to "move fast and fix later." CTO Fiona Tan explained to me that Walmart may delay integrating new business acquisitions into its existing tech stack if its strategy is to prioritize growth and speed-to-market of the new business in the near term.

Left unaddressed, the costs of technical debt are many. It saps resources, diverting IT budgets into maintenance rather than supporting new growth. It slows down business teams and entire organizations. Most important, technical debt impedes strategy whenever infrastructure hinders innovation, as experienced by Volkswagen and NCB.

A common mistake is for companies to fix infrastructure problems with patches and workarounds that sustain inflexible legacy systems. Just like a loan with interest, however, unaddressed technical debt will *grow over time*. Instead of patching over the underlying problems, a strong IT organization insists on periodically "paying down" technical debt to improve the efficiency and agility of the business. Paying down technical debt is hard. It means spending resources without gaining any new products or functionality. But the benefit of rebuilding is to make your IT faster, more reliable, more secure, more flexible to updates, and better able to integrate with other systems. This process, called refactoring, takes time and investment, and the payoff is not immediate. But as NCB learned in refactoring its IT systems, it is essential to future growth.

MONOLITHIC VERSUS MODULAR IT

One of the key types of IT refactoring today is a shift from monolithic to modular architecture. In a traditional monolithic architecture, the software—whether an app, a website, or a bank's entire retail operation—is built as one integrated program. This can work well on a small scale, for example, when quickly building an MVP. But as a monolithic system grows, it becomes increasingly rigid and inflexible. To change one part of an application, you must test the impact on the whole system or risk bringing it down. Updates of any kind become slow and painstaking. This is why enterprise computing systems from the 1990s and 2000s are famously hard to customize or adapt to changing business needs.

In modular architecture, the same software is rebuilt as a set of modules called microservices. Each of these software modules communicates with the others through an automated interface called an API. Within a single company's architecture, hundreds or thousands of microservices can interact this way, each one managed and developed by a single team.

When Amazon.com started, its architecture was monolithic. The entire website ran as a single, integrated piece of software. After a few years of rapid expansion, the site had grown to millions of lines of code whose limitations were impacting growth. As CTO Werner Vogels explained, "Whenever we wanted to add a new feature or product for our customers, like video streaming, we had to edit and rewrite vast amounts of code on an application that we'd designed specifically for our first product—the bookstore."[11] In 2002, Amazon began a shift to a new architecture. According to legend, Bezos issued a memo mandating that henceforth, all teams would have to write their code in microservices that would communicate with each other and with the outside world through APIs.[12] The transition took several years, but it laid the foundation for what became Amazon Web Services (AWS), and it served as a pioneering example to other businesses.

Modular architecture hosted in the cloud brings numerous benefits: it is more scalable, secure, and flexible. But perhaps its most important impact is on organizational speed and flexibility. Under Amazon's original architecture, if one team wanted to add a line of products to the store website, it needed to coordinate with numerous other teams (marketing, warehousing, web design, etc.) through meetings, phone calls, and emails. With microservices, everything one team needs from another can happen through an automated software interface. Vogels describes the impact: "We were able to innovate for our customers at a much faster rate, and we've gone from deploying dozens of feature deployments each year to millions, as Amazon has grown."[13]

Today, a shift from a legacy monolithic computing system to a modular architecture in the cloud is increasingly seen as essential. Years ago, Netflix transitioned its entire website to a modular architecture, hosted on Amazon's cloud-computing service.[14] Microsoft, Google, and others now compete with AWS in providing these services. Modular computing is now used in all kinds of legacy businesses, from large enterprises like Walmart to smaller players like Acuity that have built their own technology stack and APIs.

Data Assets

The second area of tech capability critical to any DX is data. As explored in *The Digital Transformation Playbook,* data is now a key strategic asset for any business. Every organization needs a strategy for how it will invest in and grow its data asset over time. This data asset should include customer data (e.g., individual customers' profiles and behaviors, including purchase, usage, and other interactions). It should include data on the firm's internal operations, people, and assets (e.g., supply chain data, inventory records, employee information, and more). And it should include data from all its products and services—both underlying service data (e.g., mapping data for a navigation app, or financial data for a brokerage service), as well as product use data (which features are being used when, where, and how).

If it doesn't capture data effectively and grow data as an asset, any organization's DX will stumble. The New York Times Company found its early digital efforts were hampered by a failure to capture essential data, including data on archived articles going back over 100 years. Deficiencies in the data "tagging" of past articles made it impossible for teams to find and leverage content easily from this enormous trove. The Times watched digital-native publishers like the Huffington Post do a better job repackaging *New York Times* content—using historic *Times* stories to engage readers around events like the death of a political figure or the release of a movie. Meanwhile, the Times also struggled to automate the sale of its historic photos and spent years trying to create a useful recipe database. Eventually, with strong investment in its data assets, the Times began to reap rewards—from enhanced journalism to new subscriber services, to increased traffic from outside channels. Adding structured data to its cooking recipes, for example, increased traffic to the *Times* from search engines by 52 percent.[15]

In the digital era, data is generated at an unprecedented rate and from proliferating sources—including social media, mobile devices, and the web of sensors that make up the Internet of Things (IoT). But they are also being generated by new business models, like software as a service (SaaS), which allows companies to observe customers' use of their digital products directly over time. Growing your data asset is not just a matter of putting cookies on your website or purchasing data from third parties. Rather, it must be part of the planning and design of your products and services themselves.

One global energy utility I have advised is rethinking its operations after realizing that it was collecting data on electricity use only at the level of power meters—when what it wants is individual customer-use data. As Nike shifted from being a brand selling products through brick-and-mortar channels to an omnichannel brand that sells more and more directly to the consumer, data has become central to its success. From the design of its apps to its newer subscription business models, to its partnerships with physical retailers, Nike plans at every stage how best to gather and deploy data about its customers, products, and business.

Tech and Data Governance

The third area of tech capabilities that is essential to DX is governance systems for both your data and your technology assets. Any governance system must address the needs of internal stakeholders (different business units and functions) as well as external stakeholders (customers, regulators, business partners, etc.). Whether defining the rules for data sets or tech infrastructure, any governance model should address a few key issues:

- *Access*—who accesses what, under which conditions, and with what permissions and constraints.
- *Integration*—how data and software connect across technical systems and organizational silos.
- *Quality*—how the integrity of data, software, and other assets is assessed and improved continually.
- *Security*—how assets are protected from malevolent actors and other risks, inside and out.

Yana Walker, a former student of mine, led the design of one such governance model at Bristol Myers Squibb. Its purpose was to integrate the data from three different divisions: manufacturing, quality management, and regulatory affairs. The project had technical goals—consolidating data from the divisions, harmonizing and standardizing the data, and ensuring data quality (with a focus on remediation of aging and incomplete data sets). The project also had organizational goals—providing access and transparency to the right stakeholders, ensuring data security, and ensuring regulatory compliance for every country where the data's servers were housed. The governance system was implemented ultimately in two parts. An automated system was built to manage the data, following more than sixty business rules to handle most issues. And a data governance council was established—with representatives from each division—to address inconsistencies and questions that fell outside the business rules.

Governance systems enable the kind of data sharing and collaboration that are essential to DX. An executive at the Sony Group explained to me how, by linking customer data across its different divisions, Sony gained powerful market insights and built better predictive models. But data integration can only happen with effective data governance. Integrating all of Sony's data would never have been allowed if it meant, for example, that Sony Pictures could use all the individual-customer data from Sony's PlayStation Network to bombard gamers with emails promoting its next movie release. Before data sharing can happen, rules on access, quality, and security are essential.

Another critical function of governance is to help large organizations establish a common set of data on which to make decisions—what is commonly called a single source of truth. One of Walmart's key digital investments has been to create a single view of the customer through data and make it available as a service to managers across the company. Shared KPIs are incredibly powerful in aligning an organization around a strategy, but they hinge on everyone agreeing on the same shared data. Unless internal stakeholders trust that data, they will use their own or start collecting data elsewhere. Shared, trusted data is essential to organizational alignment.

One more critical aspect of governance is how much to centralize key assets and capabilities. In too many organizations, I have seen an overcentralized model, where all projects must go through a central IT division located at a distant headquarters. The result is innovation rigor mortis. The desire for strong governance must be balanced with the need to keep innovation in the hands of the business, where it is closest to the customer.

The best governance models I have seen manage to strike a balance. Data is stored in more than one location but synchronized across the entire business. New areas of technical expertise (such as machine learning) may temporarily sit in a central unit but are then pushed out to the businesses. And software applications remain in the hands of local business units but with a bias toward funding applications that can be reused across the organization.

Build Versus Buy

One of the most common questions around technology in DX is this: Should we build the capability we need (e.g., a new microservices architecture) with our technology teams, or should we procure it from an outside partner via technology purchase, license, or SaaS? The choice between these two options is commonly referred to as "build versus buy."[16]

In recent decades, there was a strong tendency toward "buy"—as companies outsourced technology to partners and focused their employees on industry-specific work. At most firms, technology was deemed outside their core competencies and treated as a cost center. IT departments evolved into vendor management units. In the digital era, we have seen a big shift in thinking as technology capabilities have become core to every business strategy. Companies like Volkswagen discovered the limitations of outsourcing 90 percent of their software as they face digital-native rivals like Tesla. Jeff Lawson, the cofounder of Twilio, reframes the choice for incumbents as "build versus die."[17] In other words, no company will survive long term if it does not develop the capabilities to build its essential technologies.

A "build" strategy has several inherent advantages. It provides greater control and the ability to customize a solution to the specific needs of your business. PepsiCo's chief strategy and transformation officer Athina Kanioura found that even the best software it purchased was too generic— lacking enough business-specific data and alignment with PepsiCo's business goals. So Kanioura followed a "build" strategy and established digital hubs for the company in Dallas and Barcelona to bring more capabilities in-house.[18] A "build" strategy also provides a greater ability to integrate with partners. At Acuity Insurance, CEO Ben Salzmann has invested for years in building the company's core IT systems and APIs to allow fast and seamless integration with any insurtech partner—what Salzmann calls "nimbleocity." He gives an example: "Google came to work with us because our peers will take months and months to do anything with them. We can partner with any technology vendor in two weeks." One more benefit of a "build" strategy is that it allows the business to retain ownership of technology IP. This in turn generates greater profits from any technology that is important to competitive advantage.

A "buy" strategy can have compelling advantages as well. If technology solutions already exist in the market, deploying these (rather than "reinventing the wheel") can allow a firm to get to market much faster and at much less cost. A "buy" strategy may bring less risk—particularly if the company can try the solution in a pilot before committing to it. And it may bring much less maintenance cost, for example, in the case of a SaaS solution. So there are inherent trade-offs to the build versus buy decision. You can't and shouldn't try to do it all yourself.

Therefore, it makes sense to use both "build" and "buy" strategies for at least some of your tech capabilities. My friend Anand Birje, president of digital business at global services firm HCL Technologies, suggests that you start by asking which technology capabilities are most important to your competitive differentiation. If a technology will enable you to compete and command a premium in the market, you should build it yourself in a microservices architecture that you own. On the other hand, if a technology is a simple cost of doing business, then you should look for a solution that you can purchase on a flexible SaaS basis where you pay only for what you use. Birje calls this "composable" versus "consumable" tech.

Finally, be sure to assess the technical uncertainty around any solution you are considering. Is this something—like public cloud infrastructure—where solutions are widely deployed in the marketplace, with ample third-party research on their costs and benefits? Or is this a new, cutting-edge area where solutions will use unproven technology? If technical uncertainty is high, pursue a "try before you buy" approach—whether this means a limited early deployment with a service provider (before an ongoing contract), or a pilot project with a tech start-up (before buying them or building your own version).

Staging the Journey

Whether you build or buy, none of this work happens overnight. Paying down technical debt on your infrastructure, building your data assets, and establishing good governance models all take time. There is no amount of funding or leadership commitment that will let you snap your fingers and get these things done overnight. But be careful: as you proceed down a long road of capability building, your organization's needs and priorities will inevitably change over time. Given this reality, growing your tech capabilities should be planned as a multistage journey, with flexibility to adapt as you go. Think of the organization as a train in which you are rebuilding one car at a time, applying temporary patches and duct tape to other cars until you get to them, all while the train continues down the tracks.

NCB, for example, took three years to build its new core systems from retail to corporate banking and another two years to migrate to them while running the business. Volkswagen has planned a five-year evolution of its VW.os operating system, moving in stages from version 1.0 (a limited release, with open source code and software from outside vendors) to 1.1 (used by more vehicles), to an ultimate 2.0 (with advanced features and deployed across all the company's brands).[19]

At Bristol Myers Squibb, Walker's team built its data governance model through a carefully staged journey. This began with six months of developing a prototype to demonstrate to leadership that there would be enough data to answer important business questions. In the next phase, a robust test environment was deployed to test the logic of business rules for the new system. Final migration happened with a "post-go-live" period where the old data processes were run in parallel with the new integrated one—to sift through numerous scenarios and gain full confidence in the new system's resilience and reliability. The whole process took over a year. But the timing largely depended on the number of systems being integrated. Walker's advice? "Start early, start early, start early!"

As you plan your journey, remember to put a premium on modularity. A more modular design will allow for more flexibility and quicker updates as your needs continue to change.

Talent

As important as technology is to any digital strategy, having employees with the right capabilities is just as critical. No organization can build its own apps and infrastructure if it lacks skilled engineers. No business can pursue a direct-to-consumer strategy if it lacks people with digital marketing skills. It cannot reorganize into small, multifunctional teams if it lacks training in product management and agile methodologies. And no business can become a data-driven organization if it lacks skills in data science and analytics.

As you pursue DX, it is essential that you work closely with HR leaders to assess your current talent capabilities and to identify critical gaps. Skills to look for include technical and nontechnical skills in different combinations and different parts of the organization. Closing your talent gaps requires managing the entire talent life cycle—from hiring and acquiring talent to training your workforce, retaining them, and exiting those who are not aligned with your strategy while minimizing attrition among those who are.

Technical and Nontechnical Skills

Any new strategy for the digital era is likely to demand that your business grow its capabilities in several *technical skills* areas, including software engineering skills with differing focuses on applications, platforms, networks, and more. They also include skills in data science and business analytics, and skills in emerging and fast-changing fields such as machine learning and cybersecurity.

As Johnson & Johnson's (J&J) vice president of human resources, enterprise technology, Juliana Nunes is responsible for digital talent. It's her job to ensure that J&J has the skills it needs as the company rapidly shifts strategy, products, and services for the digital era. Nunes has partnered with IBM to assess the current technical skills within J&J's global workforce—using machine learning to analyze each employee's digital footprint and infer what skills they have and at what level of maturity. Among the technical skills they found that J&J needs to grow are data science, cybersecurity, and intelligent automation. "We know you can't predict the future," Nunes says, but with the right skills "we believe we can be better positioned for it."

Any organization also needs to assess which *nontechnical skills* it will need to support its DX efforts. Nontechnical skills typically include innovation skills—such as training in product management, agile methods such as Scrum, design thinking, or lean start-up. It may include new go-to-market skills—such as digital marketing, e-commerce, online sales, and channel management. Depending on the problems they are solving, your multifunctional teams will need skills from other disciplines, too—such as communications and design (storytelling, graphic design, user experience

[UX], etc.) and the social sciences (economics, sociology, psychology, anthropology, etc.).

Amazon is known for hiring PhD economists and spreading them across two-pizza teams throughout the company to aid in running controlled experiments at the level where work is being done fastest.[20] When Imran Haque was CDO at the global shipping firm CMA CGM, one of his first initiatives was to design a new digital product serving the needs of small and midsize shipping businesses. But CMA CGM had never sold to these kinds of customers in the past, and so it lacked any relevant sales experience. One of the keys to pursuing the new strategy was first to acquire skills in digital marketing to help reach this very different audience.

Different Levels and Combinations

Addressing your talent needs will require more than just a shopping list of skills in broad categories. Many leaders speak about the total number of programmers they are targeting to hire for their DX. (Recall from chapter 1 the *New York Times*'s publisher boasting that they have "more journalists who can write code" than any other newspaper.) But what matters more is which specific kinds of programmers you have and need in various specialized fields (network engineering versus application programming, etc.).

It is equally important to recognize that your organization will require different people with different skill levels in the same domain. For example, you may need fifty expert data scientists to support your digital efforts—but what about businesspeople who know how to talk with these data scientists? You will likely need far more managers in other functions (marketing, finance, operations, etc.) to acquire a basic knowledge of data science so that they can collaborate effectively with these scientists.

In a large organization, your talent needs are likely to vary considerably across different business units and functions. When J&J analyzed its own talent needs, it found several areas like data science that were critical to teams across the company. But other skills were needed only in specific business units—such as e-commerce skills for its consumer business, and robotics skills for its medical device business.

Many organizations find what is important are *combinations* of different skills, including both technical and nontechnical. Nunes at J&J spoke to me of the value of combining data science skills with deep experience in the health-care sector—sometimes from different members of a team but ideally in the same person. Many digital-native companies like Meta look to hire product managers who are "T-shaped" thinkers: people with real depth in one domain but an ability to collaborate across several others.[21]

The Talent Life Cycle

Addressing your talent needs is about more than just hiring new people with digital-era skills. It is just as critical to ensure that they have an attractive future and career path in your organization. In its early days of DX, the New York Times Company found that many of its best digital talent hires were quick to leave the company. As one of them explained, "I looked around the organization and saw the plum jobs . . . going to people with little experience in digital." Another departing talent observed, "When it takes 20 months to build one thing, your skill set becomes less about innovation and more about navigating bureaucracy . . . If there's no leadership role to aspire to, staying too long becomes risky."[22] Thus, the challenge is not simply to find the right people and plug them into your various departments. Growing the right capabilities means managing the entire talent life cycle: hire, acquire, train, retain, exit, and partner (see figure 7.1).

HIRE

Recruiting new talent is critical to bridging talent gaps. But one common mistake I see is to focus on star hires—bringing in a few leaders from Google or Amazon and expecting them to transform your teams from

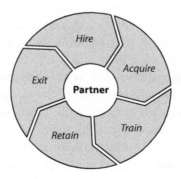

Figure 7.1.
The talent life cycle

above. DX typically requires a critical mass of new talent. (One McKinsey analysis estimated that traditional automakers need to grow their software talent by 300 percent to meet the shifts in their industry.[23])

How can you compete with skilled digital talent in such high demand? One key is to broaden your geographic lens. Instead of headquartering your digital operations in Silicon Valley, you may opt to build it in a tier-two or tier-three market where you can be a top-choice employer for technical talent. Another key is to be willing to hire from outside your industry. Nunes says of J&J, "We knew that, in order for us to bring the skills that we need, we needed to look beyond the traditional health care companies." Today, that means J&J hires from tech firms, telcos, financial services, and beyond.

ACQUIRE

Another important way to bridge talent gaps is through buying another firm that has people with the capabilities you need—what is called an acqui-hire. This strategy can be effective for speeding up a big shift in skills, for example, McDonald's acquisition of the AI firm Dynamic Yield with its 200 employees.[24] The value of such an acquisition is often in the firm's talent even more than the value of its revenues, customer base, or proprietary technology.

For large firms seeking to accelerate the growth of digital talent, a larger anchor acquisition may be more effective than a series of smaller acquisitions. Bringing onboard a critical mass of hundreds or even thousands of employees with digital skills and a digital mindset can jump-start a broader change in the entire firm. After the anchor acquisition is fully assimilated, it should be easier to integrate smaller acquisitions of digital-native talent.[25]

TRAIN

The next step in bridging your talent gaps is training. It is essential to develop and grow the capabilities of the people already in your organization. Training is commonly thought of in terms of upskilling and reskilling. Upskilling refers to building on the skills an employee has in their current role (think of your long-time marketer learning new digital tools and tactics). For an employee whose old role is disappearing, reskilling means giving them the foundational skills for a new job (think of a customer service representative whose job is replaced by bots and is training for a new role in sales). Reskilling programs are vital to employee morale, but they depend on the individual employee's willingness to embrace a bigger change.

RETAIN

It is essential that your organization also have a strategy to hold onto employees with critical capabilities. At J&J, Nunes asks: "How do I create the best growth experience so that people are going to be willing to stay here with us? Top talents are recruited by other companies all the time. So how do I create an experience for them so they feel they are continuously growing?"

Daniel Pink's model for intrinsic motivation of employees is apt. He stresses three elements: autonomy (the opportunity to direct your own work), mastery (the opportunity to learn and grow through your work), and purpose (the opportunity to benefit others through your work).[26] Each of these elements is critical to employee retention. As Nunes observes: "We need to create an environment for our talent to flourish. If they feel that they are in the middle of a bureaucracy that won't allow them to do what they want to do, they are going to leave."

EXIT

No employee will stay with your firm forever. I have seen many leaders struggle with employee exits as part of DX. Sometimes the challenge is orchestrating the departure of senior executives who are no longer aligned. In other cases, it is shifting resources spent on one type of employee toward hiring more of another type.

The first kind of exits to plan for are *voluntary exits*—how much attrition do you want? Turnover rates that are too high can be costly. But attrition can also become too low, making it difficult to bring in new talent. Beware of creating "golden handcuffs" for employees, where no one leaves because they are incentivized to stay for life. As Philipp Wohland, chief people and transformation officer at Virgin Media O2, explained to me, "During transformation, incentive systems that cause a 'playing to stay' mentality are counterproductive. Instead, you want to enable a 'playing to win' spirit." Be sure your own incentives reward the outcomes you are seeking rather than rewarding employee tenure. The second kind of exits to plan for are *involuntary exits*—whether targeted removals, across-the-board buyouts (which may be paired with layoffs to reach a target), or reorganization (where an entire unit is dissolved, but its staff are allowed to apply for positions in a redesigned unit).

Perhaps the most important factor in employee exits is alignment. Leaders need to focus on communicating where they are going as a business and why, how current employees can be a part of that journey, and what it will require from them. In my observation of organizations going through major transformations, the highest turnover rates happen at the most senior levels (as much as 70 percent leaving), and these exits are largely voluntary. When a new direction is articulated clearly, employees who have been around longer are often less willing to change and will instead opt to take a buyout offer.

PARTNER

Effective leaders grow talent not just with their employees but with an eco-system of partners. You should make build versus buy decisions for your talent, just like you do for tech capabilities. Ask yourself, "Which of these needs should I fill in-house, and which can be better filled with outside partners?"

The best partner relationships should not just compensate for skills you lack on the inside. They should support each stage of your talent life cycle. This can include training (great partners work with your employees and help grow their skills in the process). It may lead to hiring (recruiting individuals from an outside partner as permanent hires). In some cases, a great partner can become the target of an acqui-hire.

Great digital-era organizations design themselves to be open and permeable. They fluidly deploy teams that combine internal hires and outside partners. They cultivate networks of past employees whom they continue to work with in the future. And they encourage individuals to move across the perimeter of the organization.

Tool: The Tech and Talent Map

Our next tool is the Tech and Talent Map (see figure 7.2). The purpose of this tool is to help any organization develop the technology and talent capabilities it needs to thrive in the digital era. The tool guides leaders through assessing the capabilities they need for the future, identifying gaps and prioritizing them, and devising strategies to bridge those gaps over time. The Tech and Talent Map can be applied at the enterprise level, but it can just as easily be applied to an individual business unit or department. It can even

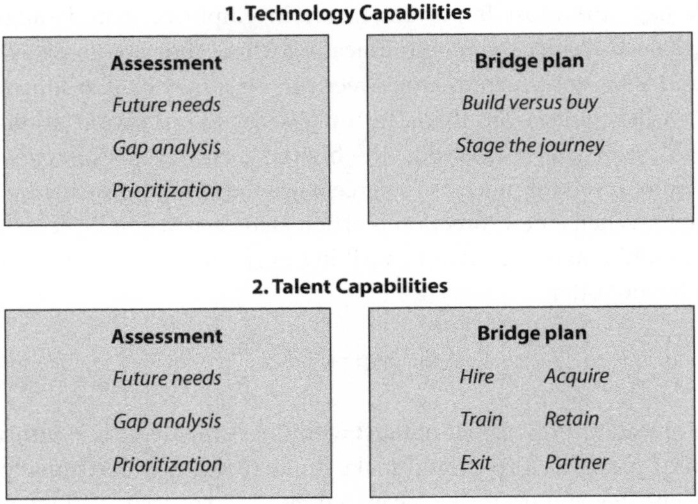

1. Technology Capabilities

Assessment	Bridge plan
Future needs	*Build versus buy*
Gap analysis	*Stage the journey*
Prioritization	

2. Talent Capabilities

Assessment	Bridge plan	
Future needs	*Hire*	*Acquire*
Gap analysis	*Train*	*Retain*
Prioritization	*Exit*	*Partner*

Figure 7.2.
The Tech and Talent Map

be used to assess the capability needs of a single team. Regardless of the scope of its application, the process is the same.

1. Technology Capabilities

Step 1 of the Tech and Talent Map focuses on technology needed to support the DX of your organization, business unit, or team. It should be completed in close partnership with your IT leadership, who can speak with expertise on subjects like computing infrastructure, security, or data integrity; as well as business and functional stakeholders, who will best understand the needs around decision making, customer experience, legal compliance, and so on.

ASSESSMENT

Begin with an assessment of your future technology needs to support your evolving digital strategy. Be sure to focus on these elements:

- *Tech infrastructure*—Do you have plans for a shift to cloud computing? What kind of architecture and APIs will support your business growth?

Should data be stored in data lakes or data warehouses? What kind of applications do you need to run your core business processes?

- *Data assets*—What kind of data do you need in order to support your business strategy? What data do you need on customers? What data do you need from your operations? What data do you need to power your products, and what data should they be capturing?
- *Tech and data governance*—What systems will you need to manage access to your data and IT infrastructure and to ensure its security, quality, and integration?

Next, you should conduct a gap analysis, comparing your future needs with your current tech capabilities. Identify your biggest gaps in each of the above areas. As you do so, be specific about where your current capabilities fall short. For instance, do not state that you want just "better IT infrastructure." Instead, state, "We need more robust APIs that connect with our sales channel partners."

Prioritize each of these capability gaps. Again, be sure to gather input from all your relevant stakeholders (IT, business, and functional). I suggest asking each stakeholder to rate the gaps with a score of 1 to 5, where 1 indicates a severe lack of capability holding back the business, and 5 indicates an area needing only minor improvement. By combining these ratings, you can create a prioritized list of tech capabilities to grow for the future.

BRIDGE PLAN

Next, you will need to develop a plan for how you will bridge gaps in your tech capabilities. This requires consideration of a build versus buy approach:

- *Build*—Which capabilities are strategic, that is, they give your business a unique advantage in the market? How can you best build those yourself, with a flexible architecture and IP that you own?
- *Buy*—Which capabilities are purely operational? Can you find a solution to buy that will allow you to perform as well as your peers? How can you ensure flexibility to customize or change your solutions in the future?
- *Test first*—How much technical uncertainty is there in each solution? Is the technology well established with clear performance benchmarks? If not, how can you test it in a limited deployment before committing to use it across your business?

You should also plan for how you will stage your journey to close the gaps in your technology. Tech capabilities take time to build or buy, and the business must keep operating while the new capabilities are put in place. As you stage your journey, focus on these considerations:

- *Business impact*—Which investments are most urgent to your business needs? How should you invest in technical debt today to avoid costly impacts on your business tomorrow?
- *Iterative process*—How can you use MVPs to validate the business problems you aim to solve and whether stakeholders will use your solutions?
- *Modular development*—Can you break a complex solution into smaller pieces, following the agile imperative to continuously deploy increments of working code?
- *Parallel tracks*—How will you plan for a period of migration where old and new systems run in parallel and thus ensure resilience in the real world?

2. Talent Capabilities

Step 2 of the Tech and Talent Map focuses on the talent needed to support the DX of your organization, business unit, or team. It should be conducted in close partnership with HR leaders as well as business and functional leaders, who will each have different insights into the talent needs of your organization.

ASSESSMENT

Begin with an assessment of the technical and nontechnical skills that are most essential to your DX. As you assess your future needs, look broadly and include these areas:

- *Software engineering*—For different areas such as application development, networks, infrastructure, security, and hardware.
- *Data and analytics*—Including data science, data integrity, decision systems, and business analytics.
- *Emerging technologies*—Such as machine learning, robotics, cybersecurity, and automation.

- *Innovation skills*—In methodologies like product management, Scrum, design thinking, or lean start-up.
- *Go-to-market skills*—In e-commerce, digital advertising, influencer marketing, and so on, to support entry into new markets.
- *Other domains*—For example, UX, storytelling, market research, and economics for your multifunctional teams.

Next, you should conduct a gap analysis—comparing your future needs with your current talent. Work with HR, using both quantitative and qualitative data, to define your current skills and identify your biggest gaps in each of the above areas.

- *Specific skills*—What particular skills are you most lacking (not "coders" but the specific kinds of developers, and not "data skills" but "machine-learning expertise")?
- *Distribution*—Which skills are needed across the organization? Which skills are needed only in particular business units or departments?
- *Skill level*—Where do you need high expertise in a particular skill? Where do you need more general familiarity and basic knowledge?

Next, you should prioritize each of the talent gaps you have identified. Ask each of your stakeholders to rate the gaps that they have insight into with a score of 1 to 5, where 1 indicates a severe talent deficit holding back the business, and 5 indicates an area needing only minor improvement. Combine their ratings to create a prioritized list of talent needs that you can work with human resources to grow for the future.

BRIDGE PLAN

You need to develop a plan to bridge these gaps in your talent and support your future growth. Your plan should encompass each of the six steps of the talent life cycle:

- *Hire*—How will you recruit new talent to meet your capability needs? Where will you look (company, industry, geographic location), and how will you attract people to work with you?
- *Acquire*—Can an acquisition help close your talent gaps? If so, what kind of firm might you target? How will you manage its integration to accelerate the change you need and not lose what is best in the acquired company?

- *Train*—How can you best grow the capabilities of your current people? What upskilling can benefit them in their current roles? Where can reskilling enable you to redeploy talented people whose current roles are winding down?
- *Retain*—How should you engage your best talent so they don't walk out the door? Do they have a compelling career path with you? How can you ensure their work has autonomy, mastery, and purpose?
- *Exit*—How much turnover is healthy for the pace of change you are seeking? Is your voluntary attrition too high, or is it too low? Should you realign incentives to avoid the "golden handcuffs" that keep the wrong people in place? What combination of buyouts, layoffs, or reorganization is required to align resources with the talent you need most?
- *Partner*—How will you look beyond your team or organization for your talent needs? Which partners can support your strategy? How can you best work with them, learn from them, hire from them, or possibly acquire them? How will you design the best ecosystem of talent inside and outside to help your business thrive?

Culture

Growing the right capabilities for DX cannot stop with technology and talent. It is just as critical to include culture. The right organizational culture will be essential to the long-term success of any DX effort. Having studied digital efforts at scores of businesses around the world, I am convinced that it is impossible to achieve a lasting DX without culture change. Fortunately, I have seen effective leaders who prove that growing a digital-ready culture is possible in even the most long-established business.

Aftenposten's *Journey*

When I met Espen Egil Hansen, he was a rising star at Schibsted, a Scandinavian media conglomerate aggressively steering its portfolio of news and advertising businesses to adapt to the digital era. Hansen had recently led a digital start-up for Schibsted called VG Nett, where he built a thriving and profitable online business. For his next challenge, Hansen was tapped to transform one of the oldest and most cherished news institutions in northern Europe, the Norwegian newspaper *Aftenposten*. When Hansen took control as the new CEO and editor-in-chief, he knew that he faced huge cultural barriers to change. He was dealing with a proud institution with a history dating back to 1860; he knew that it had a strong sense of tradition and what Hansen called "one of the most conservative cultures anywhere—like a church!" Hansen knew that transforming the business of *Aftenposten* for the digital era could only happen if key changes were made to its culture. Specifically, *Aftenposten* needed a culture that was:

- *Entrepreneurial*—With a bottom-up mindset where everyone contributed ideas.
- *Collaborative*—Where employees worked across the traditional barrier of editorial versus business and across silos of different reporting desks.
- *Data-driven*—Where decisions were made based on data and testing rather than on the verdicts of the highest-ranking editors.
- *Customer-focused*—Where work centered on the customer's evolving digital experience rather than *Aftenposten*'s historic print product.

On his first day as CEO, Hansen attended the editors' morning meeting. *Aftenposten*'s most senior editors gathered to review the prior day's paper and discuss what lessons should be learned. As Hansen recalled to me, "I'm sure this meeting has been in place more or less the same since 1860. I listened only. Then, at the end of that meeting, I said 'This has been very nice. From tomorrow we will try something new.'" After 150 years, he canceled the editor's morning meeting. The next day, he introduced a new meeting that would start each day going forward. Everyone was invited— the entire editorial team and every single reporter but also the advertising sales team, the subscriptions team, the technologists, and even the janitors. Everyone was asked to be part of an open and frank discussion of what *Aftenposten* did well the day before and to share their ideas on what could make it better.

Other changes quickly followed. To foster collaboration across traditional roles, Hansen introduced multifunctional teams that combined journalists and technologists and gave them a mandate to collaborate with readers and try new forms of data-driven journalism. He took advantage of *Aftenposten*'s long-planned building move to design a space that would support a more collaborative culture. In the old building, employees had been spread throughout ten floors, with offices clustered in the corners. "We had 40 corners, and it was like 40 subcultures at *Aftenposten*," Hansen told me. For the new building, he pushed to bring everyone onto two large floors and to create a central space on each one—not only for morning meetings but also as the only location for coffee machines and trash receptacles. "The whole idea was to fuel spontaneous meetings of different people in the organization. It was not only symbolic—it really works!"

To support a shift to data-driven decisions, Hansen instituted a new model where metrics from each department were distributed openly and transparently among all employees. To push everyone to focus on the customer's digital experience, he stipulated that news stories shown in meetings should appear in their mobile screen format—to remind the editors (many who started in print) that this was how most readers read their stories.

When Hansen stepped down after six years, *Aftenposten*'s business was radically transformed. "We turned the business model upside down—from 80 percent advertising revenue to 80 percent subscriptions. Not many companies survive that kind of change," he explained. But just as important, the culture was changed too. "We have gone from being a business that was a monopoly in effect, back to market competition. We have become a data-driven organization from not being one." And the old hierarchical mindset had given way as well: "Very little at *Aftenposten* today is decided from the top." Hansen stressed when he shared what he had learned from the DX, "The hard part is not getting the technology right but changing our culture."

Culture in DX

The centrality of culture is not unique to *Aftenposten*'s DX. At the New York Times Company, culture was the Achilles heel of the paper's early digital efforts. Its infamous *Innovation Report* diagnosed that its transformation was being held back by a risk-averse mindset in the newsroom, a culture of silos, a woefully outdated focus on the print edition, work that was organized around old traditions rather than the changing habits of readers, and a failure to share and learn from mistakes. It was only when the Times's culture started to change that its transformation began to truly show results.

It is impossible to drive real DX without building the right culture. If a business is driven only by financial results and lacks a customer-focused mindset, it will never spot the next customer problem to be solved. If its teams rely on seniority rather than data to make decisions, efforts to "test and learn" will simply become "test to confirm." If its people are afraid to fail or admit mistakes, they will never be able to iterate, pivot, and adapt their innovations.

Even the biggest changes to process and governance will fail if they are not accompanied by changes in culture. Dániel Nőthig, who coaches large organizations on adopting agile software development, described to me how many clients want to focus only on the mechanics of agile. They diligently adopt all the right processes (daily scrum meetings, two-week sprints, kanban boards, etc.). But the essential mindsets of agile—to be iterative, self-directed, problem-focused, and customer-centric—are never communicated or embraced. Nőthig calls this, "Let's do the process, but not the culture." In all his coaching experience, he has never seen it work.

Digital-native businesses around the world are obsessed with the importance of culture to their success. If you spend time in Silicon Valley, you will quickly find that leaders there talk a lot more about their company culture than about their technology. When Satya Nadella assumed the role of Microsoft CEO, he was chosen by the board to implement a dramatic shift in strategy—from a servers-based offering to a cloud-based one, and from Windows-only to partnering with any operating system. Yet when he assumed leadership, Nadella spoke most passionately about his efforts to change the culture of Microsoft. As Nadella told shareholders a year into leading the turnaround, "Our ability to change our culture is the leading indicator of our future success."[27]

Microsoft is not alone. All the dominant digital titans that arose in the internet era—Amazon, Alphabet, Meta, Tesla, and Netflix—exhibit a similarly intense focus on culture. Each company has its own codification of its guiding principles, and each goes to great lengths to tie its stated culture to the actual day-to-day workings of the company.

Culture as Behavior

What is culture? The word has grown increasingly popular in business, but its meaning is often fuzzy and ill defined. Discussions of organizational culture often lapse into vague and imprecise language untethered to clear action or business needs. For years, this vagueness made me skeptical of the term "culture," but my thinking changed as I studied organizations where culture had become a powerful lever for transformation and growth. I saw that each of these organizations defined their culture in terms of everyday things that people do.

One famous definition of organizational culture comes from Herb Kelleher, cofounder and CEO of Southwest Airlines: "Culture is what people do when no one is looking."[28] Kelleher's wonderfully concise definition captures two ideas: that culture is behavior ("what people do") and that it is established by a mindset and norms rather than rules ("when no one is looking"). As one executive put it to me, "Our company's culture is the behaviors that we revert to by default."

How do the people in your organization interact and collaborate? What do people in your organization spend the most time on? How do they make decisions and run meetings? The Silicon Valley venture capitalist Ben Horowitz wrote an entire book about culture, which he titled *What You Do Is Who You Are*. Culture is all about our daily habits, interactions, and how we prioritize what gets done first. As Horowitz points out, the typical corporate mission statement offers no guidance on the kinds of decisions that employees make every day—yet these small choices will define your organization and determine its ultimate success or failure.[29]

How can you define the culture you want and make sure that culture takes hold? In early start-ups, culture is defined by the founders and their initial hires. As organizations grow, culture may be shaped by how the founders talk about the business to employees and how they model behavior. But what happens as a company grows larger, and the founding CEO can no longer stand on a chair and address the entire organization at the start of each morning? How do we shape culture in a large and complex organization?

To reinforce and embed culture at scale, you need to examine process. As Vince Campisi, CDO of United Technologies Corporation (UTC), told me, "In large organizations, process codifies culture." When a leader tells me about their vision and expresses frustration that their organization is not moving in that direction, I always ask them about process: What are you doing to change what you measure, what you reward, and what you ask people to do daily?

Building a customer-centric culture is impossible if all your metrics are based on short-term financial performance and not on the value gained by your customers. A collaborative culture is impossible if your organization is designed in functional silos, and your procurement office takes eight months to approve a two-week pilot with a partner. Entrepreneurial thinking and risk taking will be seen merely as buzzwords if your bonuses and incentives punish employees for project shutdowns and reward them for predictable results. For culture change to take hold, processes must be carefully designed to support transformation and not impede it.

In studying leaders like Hansen who transformed their organization's culture, I have observed a common pattern. Leaders who shape culture do three things:

1. They *define* the culture they seek in a clear set of principles and the behaviors they demand.
2. They *communicate* that culture with stories, symbols, and actions that bring it to life.
3. They *enable* that culture with processes that support the right behaviors.

Define Culture in Principles and Behaviors

Effective leaders *define* the culture they seek by consciously crafting their organization's principles. Google has its Innovation Pillars[30] and its "Ten things we know to be true."[31] Tesla has six leadership principles, which are taught to all new employees in its training programs.[32] Southwest Airlines encourages employees to "Live the Southwest Way" and "Work the Southwest Way," clearly identifying the components of that ethos (Warrior Spirit, Servant's Heart, FunLUVing Attitude, etc.).[33] And as Ford Motor transforms for the digital era, it has defined its "Five Rules of the Road," including "Respect Knowledge Over Hierarchy" and "Solve the Problem."

A clear set of cultural principles describes the behaviors that everyone in your organization should aspire to in their day-to-day actions, interactions, and decisions. Well-written principles provide a shared touchstone and a common vernacular among employees. They are a means to hold each other accountable. Two of the best examples I have seen are from Amazon and Netflix.

Amazon is famous for its sixteen Leadership Principles, which define the unique culture of the company. These principles—which include "Customer Obsession," "Think Big," and "Bias for Action"—have been refined over the years and are published on the company's jobs website.[34] Each principle is paired with a brief description of what it means in everyday work. But the Leadership Principles are not just published to be read. They are brought up in daily meetings when decisions are debated on any aspect of the business. The principles are "deeply embedded into the culture and the lens through which candidates, employees, and teams are evaluated and rewarded," in the words of one former employee. "Meet an Amazonian and I guarantee they can name them from memory and give an example of demonstrating them in their time there."[35]

Netflix's thinking on its culture was made famous by a 124-slide PowerPoint deck posted publicly by CEO Reed Hastings and viewed online more than 1 million times. That early manifesto described the nine behavioral traits that Netflix looked for in hiring and promoting its people. At turns humorous, philosophical, and practical, it explained why "brilliant jerks" would not be tolerated, laid out how employee compensation should be calculated, and described a Keeper Test (asking, "which of your direct reports would you fight for if they received an outside job offer?").[36] Netflix's latest statement of its cultural principles, at over 4,000 words, is full of stories about the principles that define Netflix's culture and what these principles look like in action. The principle of "Freedom and Responsibility," for example, ties employees' creativity to the company's practice of minimal rules and oversight: "In general, we believe freedom and rapid recovery are better than trying to prevent error . . . [O]ur biggest threat over time is lack of innovation . . . We are always on guard if too much error prevention hinders inventive, creative work."[37]

As you start to define your cultural principles, focus on the following eight qualities, all part of the best cultural principles:

- *Shared*—Known by everyone in the organization.
- *Discussed*—Referenced as a part of day-to-day discussions, debates, and work.
- *Actionable*—Giving guidance in decisions, especially when priorities compete and trade-offs must be made.
- *Nuanced*—Defined with some complexity as to what they mean for your particular organization and what they look like in action.
- *Dialectical*—Existing in tension with each other, including slight contradictions that can lead to healthy debate rather than settled dogma.
- *Relatable*—Described in language that resonates with employees from different geographic locations, genders, ages, identities, and backgrounds.
- *Tribal*—Helping to define who you are and to instill a sense of group identity: this is who we are; this is what makes us unique.
- *Intrinsic*—Defined in service of something beyond profit, whether for the benefit of customers, employees, or society at large.

During times of change, an organization's culture may be described best in terms of a shift "from X to Y." After stepping up as CEO at Microsoft, Nadella spoke about changing the organization from a "know it all" culture, where employees gained status through proving their expertise, to a "learn it all" culture, where people are driven by curiosity and humility to pursue constant learning and personal growth.

Think about your organizational culture. What is your culture today— that is, how do your people currently behave? What ideas or principles guide that behavior? Is that behavior in line with your shared vision of your digital future? If not, how does your culture need to change?

Table 7.2 lists seven shifts that I have observed most often in organizations seeking to realign their culture to support their DX. If you work in a legacy firm today, one or more of these profound cultural shifts will likely be vital to your success in the digital era.

Communicate Culture in Stories, Symbols, and Symbolic Actions

Effective leaders do more than define the culture they want; they constantly *communicate* what that culture is and why it matters. They do so in a way that captivates employees' thinking so that the culture is embraced over time in habits and actions. As leaders communicate about culture, their most powerful tools are not diagrams, graphs, or bullet points. Instead, they communicate best through stories, symbols, and symbolic actions. These are the best tools to shape how people think and behave in organizations.

Table 7.2.
Common Cultural Shifts During Digital Transformation

From Predigital Culture . . .	To Digital Culture
• From expert driven . . .	• To data driven
• From siloed . . .	• To collaborative
• From cautious . . .	• To risk taking
• From planning is everything . . .	• To experimentation
• From top down . . .	• To bottom up
• From committee led . . .	• To ownership
• From solution focused . . .	• To customer obsessed

STORIES

Human brains have evolved to process stories, and thus stories are essential to leading culture change. As the Nobel Prize–winning psychologist Daniel Kahneman has said, "No one ever made a decision because of a number. They need a story."[38] Aristotle knew that only a good narrative—rather than facts or rote instructions—can communicate complex meaning and connections in a way that humans will readily and lastingly absorb.

Stories can shape organizational culture in many ways. They may tie a cultural principle to the company's guiding mission or root it in the history of the firm. They may illustrate the consequences of failing to practice a cultural principle and inspire greater vigilance. Or they may spotlight unsung heroes whose day-to-day behaviors embody the culture to which the business aspires.

Nadella has used stories in all these ways to reinforce culture change at Microsoft. He underscores the company's commitment to empowering others by telling the story of Microsoft's very first product: a BASIC interpreter for the Altair. In the 1970s, this was a critical tool for the emerging community of computer hobbyists. As Nadella explains, "Our mission of empowering every person and every organization on the planet to achieve more is really a look back to the very creation of Microsoft."[39] To underscore the impact of Microsoft's work today, Nadella used a Super Bowl ad about a very niche product, an Xbox Adaptive Controller for disabled gamers. The device, which came out of a hackathon, became a passion project for its team, which spent a year designing the packaging so that kids with no hands could open it themselves. On watching the Super Bowl ad, one engineer commented, "I genuinely have never felt so much pride saying, 'I work at Microsoft.'"[40] As Nadella pushes employees toward a growth mindset, he often retells the story of his company's missteps in mobile and search, two huge opportunities that Microsoft failed to pursue early enough. His message: stay humble and never stop learning.

SYMBOLS AND SYMBOLIC ACTIONS

Symbols can also communicate the desired culture of an organization. Objects, words, and actions that illustrate an idea can be powerful vessels for shared meaning. By choosing the right symbols, leaders can continually remind an organization of the cultural norms it seeks to uphold.

These symbols sometimes take the form of a *ritual* whose power comes from repetition and shared experience throughout the company. Amazon has a tradition of designating one empty chair at every meeting to represent the customer. The chair serves as a reminder to everyone to argue for the perspective of the customer in their discussion—further ingraining the Amazon principle of "customer obsession." Under CEO Jim Hackett, Ford Motor held a Viking funeral whenever an innovation project was canceled to commemorate the team's valiant efforts. This sent a clear signal that failed ventures are still admirable—vital to learning and to the future of the business.

Chosen carefully, *language* can be a powerful symbol—with meaning carried by the words we use and those we avoid. At the *Washington Post* newspaper, executive editor Marty Baron declared that no job titles would be allowed with the word "digital" in them. Baron's point was subtle: he and his team talked constantly about "digital" when discussing the strategy of the business. But by allowing it in no one's job title, he signaled that digital was now everyone's job—not the specialty of a specific division or group of new hires.[41]

Physical *objects* that appeal to our sense of sight and sound can also be powerful symbols. As founder of Blinds.com, Jay Steinfeld wanted to push his employees to take risks and not be afraid of making mistakes as they worked to grow the business. He installed five-foot-tall test tubes in the office and instructed employees to drop in a clear marble every time they tried a new tactic to reach customers. If a test proved successful, a colored marble was also added; if it failed, the clear marble was left by itself. As Steinfeld kept pushing employees to experiment, a pattern emerged for all to see: there were many more clear marbles (attempts) for each colored one (success). The message: take risks and don't expect to get it right every time.[42]

A *leader's actions* can be powerful symbols as well when chosen to be visible and surprising and to demonstrate the culture you are seeking. Recall how, on his very first day as CEO at *Aftenposten*, Hansen canceled the 150-year tradition of a senior editors' meeting. That move was meant to cause a ruckus—and communicate to everyone that change was coming fast to that history-laden institution. Walt Disney was famous for picking up trash whenever he walked around Disney theme parks.[43] That simple action spoke louder than any speech about the importance of everyone's care in shaping the customer experience. When Hackett instituted Viking funerals for innovation projects at Ford Motor, he made sure to preside over them himself, in full Viking helmet and dress.

Enable Culture with Processes

Defining your culture and communicating it to everyone in the organization is critical, but it is still not enough to drive change. Effective leaders *enable* the culture they seek by ensuring that processes support—rather than hinder—the right employee behaviors. This becomes increasingly important as organizations grow larger and more complex. Leaders must continually look at the processes used to run their business every day and ask, Are these processes helping or hindering the culture we want?

When aligning processes with culture, I suggest starting with what I call the big three: incentives, metrics, and resource allocation. In 1975, Stephen Kerr published his classic management article, "On the Folly of Rewarding A While Hoping for B."[44] The article identifies the greatest source of internal resistance to most change efforts: employees are rewarded for behaviors you want them to stop doing (defending legacy operating models, lobbying for political decisions, etc.) and punished for the behaviors you want (taking smart risks, pursuing new areas of growth, etc.). The good news is that aligning incentives with the behavior you seek can have a dramatic positive effect on culture.

Culture change should also be baked into the metrics companies use to define, measure, and guide their work. This includes business-level metrics and KPIs, as well as metrics for work at the team level. If you want your employees to be more customer-centric, for example, are you measuring how much time they spend talking to customers?

Resource allocation is equally critical to driving culture change. If you want a culture of speed and flexibility, ask yourself, Is your financing frozen in an annual budgeting cycle, or is it allocated more frequently? Just as critical is how you allocate head count and shared services (e.g., IT support, marketing campaigns, or legal counsel). Guidelines for easily accessing outside resources can also prevent bottlenecks and keep teams operating the way you wish.

The big three—incentives, metrics, and resourcing—are essential to scaling culture, but they are only the start. Many other processes shape culture as well: criteria for hiring and promoting talent; reporting lines, approval processes, and accountability; communications and how meetings are run; employee access to data and analytics tools; as well as the design of office space and guidelines on hybrid and remote work. All these processes and more can reinforce or undermine the culture you are seeking. Leaders

must thoughtfully review every process that touches, constrains, or encourages employee behaviors if they want to reshape culture at scale.

We can see many examples of how process enables culture in successful
DX. *Aftenposten* enabled a more collaborative and data-driven culture with
its all-hands meetings, cross-functional teams, transparent data, and redesigned office space new employees:

One of Ford Motor's key cultural principles is "Solve the Problem." As
Marcy Klevorn, chief transformation officer, explained to me, this principle
means that if you see something is not working, "you don't pass the problem
to somebody else; it stops with you." One process Klevorn established to
support this in Ford Motor Company's culture was a daily meeting called
"Office Hours," led by a cross-functional group of leaders appointed by
Klevorn. "Every morning they gathered for an hour and anyone around the
organization could bring a problem to them. My only rule was the problem
had to be solved in that hour. I said, 'As long as you don't break any laws, I
don't care what you do to solve that problem, I will back you 100 percent—
even if I don't agree with you. Whatever you did to solve their problem, don't
let them leave without a solution to get them to move forward. And I will
back you!' They even called me, 'Are you sure?' Yes, just go do it. I believe
you guys will make great solutions. And guess what, of course, they did!"

Digital-native companies also offer powerful examples of using processes to enable culture. To emphasize the importance of speed in action at
Tesla, it was declared that meetings should have as few attendees as possible.
To encourage this, Tesla instituted a rule that any employee should leave
in the middle of any meeting as soon as they conclude that their presence is
not adding value. While shocking at first, this behavior soon came to be
seen as the normal way to run a meeting.[45] As part of Netflix's culture of
"freedom and responsibility," the company operates with minimal controls
on contract signing and expenses, leaving managers free to use judgment
rather than wait for sign-offs. It applies this same principle to transparency
around company documents. "Nearly every document is fully open for
anyone to read and comment on, and everything is cross-linked. Memos
on . . . every strategy decision, on every competitor, and on every product
feature test are open for all employees to read."[46]

Amazon is particularly famous for using process to ingrain its unique
culture. We have seen how its two-pizza teams with clearly designed
metrics drive a culture of agility and accountability, and how its API mandate ensures flexibility across the business. In addition, Amazon's culture
of "customer obsession" is reflected in the metrics the company reports to

shareholders each year, which emphasize customer growth, repeat business, and brand—rather than short-term financial results.[47] The company's entrepreneurial culture is enabled by a single sign-off process for innovation ideas: rather than needing to work her way up a line of command, a manager needs approval from only one senior executive to begin the first steps on a new project.[48] Perhaps most famously, Amazon banned PowerPoint presentations from meetings throughout the company. Instead, every presenter must prepare a written six-page narrative laying out their proposal and offering data arguing both for and against. The first half-hour of every meeting is set aside for everyone to read the memo in silence, take notes, and write their follow-up questions. The six-page memo was instituted precisely because it forces a more thoughtful and data-driven approach to decision making.

Tool: The Culture-Process Map

Our final tool is the Culture-Process Map (see figure 7.3). The purpose of this tool is to help any organization grow a culture that supports its strategy for the future and reflects its unique character. The Culture-Process Map guides leaders through three essential tasks: defining the culture they need, communicating that culture to others, and enabling that culture by aligning business processes.

1. Define Your Culture

Step 1 of the Culture-Process Map is to define your desired culture in terms of a set of clear principles and the behaviors they require. (Think of Ford Motor Company's principle, "Solve the Problem," and the required behavior, "don't pass the problem to somebody else; it stops with you.") Focus on the most important principles that will have the greatest impact. Some of these may be long-standing, but others should be new principles that define important shifts in culture for the future.

FROM . . . TO

Start by defining a few shifts in culture that are most needed for your organization to thrive in the future. In every legacy organization that I have

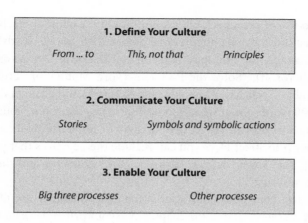

Figure 7.3.
The Culture-Process Map

worked with, the pre-digital-era culture has needed to evolve for the digital era. Try writing these culture shifts as "from . . . to" statements. Think of Nadella's push to change Microsoft from a know-it-all culture to a learn-it-all culture. Review table 7.2 for the list of common culture shifts in DX. Are any of these shifts relevant to your organization? In most legacy businesses, you'll find more than one.

THIS, NOT THAT

Next, identify aspects of your current culture that you want to keep and reinforce. What makes your culture distinctive and powerful? Try writing contrasting statements in the form of "We are this, not that." One example is, "We have a bias for action, not for deliberation." Think of these as hiring criteria that would help ensure a culture fit for new employees: if you are "this" you can thrive here, but if you are "that," you won't do well, even if you are skilled and talented. Avoid generic statements that would be universal to any company, for example, "we are hard-working, not lazy." Your "that" should be a quality you will avoid but that a different organization might choose to prioritize in its own culture and hiring.

PRINCIPLES

Combine all of the positive ideas from what you wrote (your "to" from each "from . . . to" statement and your "this" from each "this, not that") to create one list of principles you aspire to. Give a name to each principle on your list. Pick a short, memorable phrase (two to five words) that uses simple language, for example, "Customer Obsession" (Amazon), "Learn It All" (Microsoft), "Solve the Problem" (Ford Motor), or "Freedom and Responsibility" (Netflix). Then, for each principle, add a longer description of 50 to 500 words about what it looks like in the context of your business. What behaviors do you expect people to do or not do in their work? What should they prioritize? Here you can include the negatives that you seek to avoid (e.g., the "from" in your "from . . . to" statements and the "that" in your "this, not that").

Next, test your principles against the eight qualities of cultural principles that we saw earlier in the chapter. Are your principles *actionable*? Are they *relatable* to anyone in your organization? Do they have *intrinsic* value and motivation? Revise or eliminate any principles that don't measure up well to these qualities. Pick the principles that are most important to your culture. If two seem closely related, try combining them. Try for a short list (e.g., five to ten principles). Your goal is to focus on a few critical levers of culture, not a laundry list of everything about your organization.

2. Communicate Your Culture

Step 2 of the Culture-Process Map is to communicate your principles in ways that bring them to life as more than just slogans. By linking them to memorable stories, symbols, and actions, your cultural principles become something employees will recognize and strive for in their actions. Think of Ford Motor Company's Viking funerals or Microsoft's story of its first product, which exemplifies the principle of empowering people.

STORIES

Look for specific stories you can tell to bring your cultural principles to life. Some stories may relate to a single principle, but others may illustrate more than one. Look for different types of stories, including these classics:

- *Origin stories*—Relate your aspirations today to the early beginnings of your organization.
- *Mission stories*—Express your culture through the impact of your work on others.

- *Failure stories*—Capture when you fell short of the culture you aspire to and remind everyone of the work to be done.
- *Spotlighting stories*—Highlight the everyday actions of people throughout your organization and how these uphold your culture and make an impact.

SYMBOLS AND SYMBOLIC ACTIONS

Look for symbols to illustrate your cultural principles and make them visible every day at work. Look for examples from each of these types of symbols:

- *Rituals*—Actions you regularly perform together that symbolize some aspect of your culture.
- *Language*—Words and names that you consciously use or omit to reinforce a point about your culture and mindset.
- *Sights and sounds*—Objects, images, or media seen regularly by employees that remind them of a cultural principle.
- *Symbolic actions*—Actions you can take as a leader to surprise and draw the notice of others and that clearly illustrate one of your cultural principles.

3. Enable Your Culture

Step 3 of the Culture-Process Map is where you align your organization's processes with the culture that you seek. This starts with assessing your current processes. Where are they enabling your cultural principles? Where are they blocking or hindering them? Remember that process is critical to scaling culture change. Think of Netflix's open document policy or Amazon banning PowerPoint from its meetings.

BIG THREE PROCESSES

Start with the big three processes and consider how each one currently shapes your culture:

- *Incentives*—What are you rewarding employees for doing? What are you recognizing and praising them for? What do you punish them for? Where do these incentives match your cultural principles, and where do they differ?

- *Metrics*—What are the metrics you use to manage your business? What metrics do you use to evaluate individual and team performance? Where do these metrics align with your intended culture, and where do they diverge from it?
- *Resource allocation*—How, when, by whom, and on what basis is funding disbursed? What about head count or other scarce internal resources? Do these processes enable the culture you are seeking, or do they pose obstacles?

For each process, write a stop/keep/start analysis:

- *Stop*—What current process is impeding the culture you want? How will you change it?
- *Keep*—What current process is reinforcing the culture you want? How will you spread it more broadly?
- *Start*—What new process could you add to enable the culture you want? How will you implement it?

OTHER PROCESSES

Next, look more broadly at any other rules or processes that shape behavior in your organization. Again, consider how each one promotes or contradicts your cultural principles. These should include the following:

- *Hiring and promoting*—How do you hire and acquire new talent? How do you choose whom to promote into leadership? How can these processes strengthen your culture rather than dilute it?
- *Accountability and approvals*—Who signs off on important decisions? Where does decision making reside? Does this support the culture you want among employees and teams, or does it undermine it? Where do bottlenecks occur, and when do the costs outweigh the benefits?
- *Communications and meetings*—What processes do you use for daily communication? How are meetings typically run? Who attends these meetings and why? How does this match or not match the culture you want?
- *Tools and data*—What tools do employees have access to for their work? How is data shared across teams, silos, and divisions? Do employees have what they need to do their best work and live up to your cultural principles?

- *Workspace*—What is the design of your workspace, both physical and virtual? What work do employees do virtually versus in person? What written and unwritten norms are set for this? How does that enable or hinder your culture?

Again, try writing a stop/keep/start analysis for each process. What processes do you need to stop, keep, or start in your organization to support your culture fully?

How to Use the Culture-Process Map

Unlike other tools, the Culture-Process Map should not be applied in the same way at every level of the organization (company, business unit, team) because your cultural *principles* should be shared by the entire organization. You do not want a different culture in each part of the business! Therefore, in step 1 (defining your principles), top leadership must guide the process. They should involve as many stakeholders as possible from all levels, bringing their input and perspectives to what the firm's culture should be. But the final principles should be approved at the top and shared throughout the firm.

By contrast, step 2 (communicating the culture) should be everyone's job. Each business unit, function, and team should continually look for stories and symbols that illustrate the cultural principles. And each should share them so different parts of the organization can learn from each other.

Step 3 (enabling the culture through process) should also be everyone's job. At every level, leaders should be looking at processes and asking how they align with the desired culture. I recommend a formal review once a year, with input from stakeholders inside and outside the company. Ask your customers and your partners, How is it to do business with us? Where are we upholding our professed culture in our interactions with others? Where could we do better? Culture is a journey that is never complete!

Capabilities for a Bottom-Up Organization

Any digital strategy for the future requires investing in and growing new digital capabilities. But for real transformation to happen, businesses must focus on capabilities that will enable them to operate in a more bottom-up fashion, with change driven by employees at every level of the organization. Rather than building capabilities in service of a top-down master plan, this calls for building capabilities that foster a more empowered organization.

A bottom-up organization calls for investing in specific kinds of *technology* capabilities. This means modular IT architecture with APIs and microservices that are not just scalable and resilient but that offer greater flexibility for every team to work faster and connect with others outside the firm. It means data assets that are not just rich in data from diverse sources but synchronized and accessible to people across the organization. It means IT governance that provides oversight from the center but allows application and innovation by every team at the edge of the organization.

A bottom-up organization calls for growing specific *talent* capabilities as well. This means embedding new digital skills throughout the organization rather than hoarding them in central functions. It means staffing teams with the diverse mix of skills that they need to be self-sufficient and training teams in iterative experimentation with methods like agile, lean start-up, and design thinking. And it means attracting and retaining the best digital talent by giving them autonomy, mastery, and purpose in their work.

A bottom-up organization also calls for cultivating the right *culture*. This means defining cultural principles and behaviors for bottom-up action—such as risk taking, autonomy, and responsibility. It means engaging everyone in discussing and debating those principles, applying them in every project and meeting, and telling their own stories about them. And it means shaping every business process to enable employees to show initiative and act independently in support of your shared vision and strategy.

No digital transformation can succeed in the future if it relies on the capabilities of the past. Without capabilities that match the ambition of your digital strategy, the best vision for transformation will forever remain a distant goal, just out of reach. In Step 5 of the DX Roadmap, we have seen how any organization can grow the technology, talent, and culture it needs to deliver lasting growth. We have seen how the right IT infrastructure, data, and tech governance can transform work and unlock the potential of teams at scale. We have learned why digital skills require managing the entire talent life cycle. And we have seen the power of building a culture that is aligned with your digital vision, and that is embraced by all and enabled by every business process.

At the start of this book, I identified five steps to successful digital transformation—vision, priorities, experimentation, governance, and capabilities. Over the last five chapters, we have seen how the DX Roadmap can enable any organization to master each of these critical elements and find its unique path to growth. Through the five steps of the DX Roadmap, your organization can define a shared vision of your digital future, pick your most important strategic priorities, rapidly validate new ventures, manage growth at scale within and beyond your core, and grow the capabilities essential to your long-term success.

As I have emphasized throughout this book, the DX Roadmap is not a linear process, with centralized planning leading to completion at an ordained end date. DX has no finish line because its goal is to create a more adaptive organization able to respond to waves of change that will not abate. The Roadmap process itself is therefore iterative: you adapt your vision, priorities, ventures, governance, and capabilities as you go, based on what you learn.

Real DX must engage every level of the organization and every business function. Each step of the Roadmap, properly applied, should work in service of building a more bottom-up organization—where leaders push decision making down, where insights flow from the bottom up, and where strategy and innovation happen at every level. In the book's conclusion, we will return to this theme of the bottom-up organization and reflect on the dramatically different kind of leadership it demands in our dynamic digital era.

Conclusion

Three truths appear in all the stories we have seen about companies on the path to digital transformation (DX).

First, DX is iterative. It cannot start with a long planning process followed by dutiful execution of predetermined steps. Instead, successful transformation starts small, learns from what works, and adapts as it goes.

Second, DX has no end date. It is not a two- or three-year project to complete. DX is an ongoing evolution to become a more adaptive organization, one that can thrive in an era of accelerating change.

Third, DX must happen from the bottom up. It cannot be centrally planned and directed by a CEO or CDO acting alone. It must be driven at the same time by the vice president of supply chain, the head of a country unit, the email marketing manager, and the lead of a single product team. Change must come from every part of the organization and every job title.

This last point is particularly critical. Throughout the book, we have seen how each step of the Digital Transformation (DX) Roadmap is based on the idea of a bottom-up organization: a shared vision "cascades up" the organization, not just down. Strategic problems and opportunities are defined at every level. Digital ventures start in every business function and are given the resources and governance to scale. Every team is empowered by having access to data and technology, the skills to move fast, and a shared culture of ownership and accountability.

From Top-Down to Bottom-Up

The bottom-up model is a radical shift from the top-down model of management that defined large organizations in the twentieth century. Top-down management theory was built on an inherent trade-off. It sacrifices agility and speed for command and control. It is inflexible by design, with fixed processes and employees slotted into siloed roles. Work is designed to ensure predictability, consistency, and efficiency at scale. Numerous cross-departmental meetings are required to approve any change in standard practice. In many large organizations, the biggest impediment to speed is not resources or external constraints but the decision-making process itself. That trade-off of speed for consistency may have made sense in a more predictable, slow-changing business environment. But in the digital era, organizations need a different model that enables rapid change.

Today, we see leading organizations switching away from the top-down style of management. The U.S. military was famous for management by command and control; indeed, it was where many twentieth-century management theories were first tested. But that same top-down decision making is untenable in our twenty-first-century world of volatility, uncertainty, complexity, and ambiguity (VUCA). As described in Stanley McChrystal's book *Team of Teams*, unpredictable threats and competitors forced the U.S. Army to shift to a new model based on bottom-up decision making from small teams that are highly aligned but loosely coupled.[1]

Digital-native businesses like Amazon, Netflix, and Alibaba have all embraced the bottom-up model. As they grew from start-ups, these companies achieved speed and flexibility at scale by embracing three key principles:

First, *decision making is pushed down to the lowest level*. One of the bedrock principles of agile software methods is the use of self-organizing teams that, once given clearly defined goals, are allowed to figure out on their own how to best achieve them. Netflix's culture document states: "We pride ourselves on how few, not how many, decisions senior management makes." It goes on to explain, "We believe we are most effective and innovative when employees throughout the company make and own decisions."[2]

Second, *information flows up and down the organization and from the outside in.* The most critical market knowledge sits at the periphery and is usually sensed first in the lower levels of the organization chart. Intel's former CEO Andy Grove told the story of how his frontline marketers and plant supervisors detected a shift in customer demand away from memory chips—and even started responding to this shift—fully two years before his top management team recognized what was happening. "Our most significant strategic decision was made . . . by the marketing and investment decisions of frontline managers who really knew what was going on."[3]

Third, *innovation and change originate at every level.* Digital-native businesses embrace a model where leadership sets high-level strategy, but it is up to individual teams to set the mission, vision, and strategy for individual products. Amazon's most profitable business, Amazon Web Services (AWS), started with an idea from a junior-level engineer, Benjamin Black, sketched in a six-page memo. The *New York Times*'s approach to data-driven journalism was kicked off by an intern named Josh Katz when he took an assignment to write an article on a scientific paper and turned it into an interactive quiz that became the most-read article of the year. As Jeff Bezos of Amazon explains, "Distribution of invention throughout the company—not limited to the company's senior leaders—is the only way to get robust, high-throughput innovation."[4]

Rethinking Leadership for the Bottom-Up Organization

If the digital era requires a shift from prioritizing control to prioritizing speed and autonomy, then our old model of leadership must change as well. In the past, the leader was decider in chief. But in the digital era, the goal of a leader should be to make as few decisions as possible. Every leader will inevitably have to make *some* decisions—but these should be only the toughest and most important ones, when that level of leadership is truly required.

But what does that leave for the leader to do? In my own work and research, I have identified three essential jobs of leaders in successful bottom-up organizations: defining, communicating, and enabling. We

Table C.1.
The Three Jobs and Three Roles of Leaders in the Digital Era

Job of Leaders	Role of Leaders
Define a vision of where we are going and why	Leader as author
Communicate that vision in words, stories, symbols, and actions	Leader as teacher
Enable others to bring that vision to life	Leader as servant

have seen examples of each of these leadership roles throughout the DX Roadmap, from vision to priorities, experimentation, governance, and capabilities and culture. Together, these jobs define a new, emerging model of leadership in the digital era, as shown in table C.1.

Define

The first job of a leader is to define a vision of where the organization is going and why. This could be a statement of purpose or North Star impact that the business wants to achieve, a statement of strategy with key opportunities or problems to be solved, or a statement of the culture that the organization is striving for. The aim is to provide guiding direction to the efforts of others and to inspire them with a clear sense of purpose for their work.

A great leader will articulate where you are going and why—but not how you should get there. They set the context for others to act—but do not craft their operating plans. They will vigorously debate questions of strategy but trust others to execute and choose the right tactics. "If I say 'alignment,' you could think that means 'Do as the leadership tells you,'" Espen Egil Hansen says. "But that is not it at all. What you don't want is leaders that go into details that hinder innovation and learning and speed."

In defining the organization's vision, the leader takes on a role much like an author. They start by studying and learning from many inputs, inside and outside the organization. This requires getting in the trenches and listening to the perspectives of customers, partners, and employees at every level. Steve Jobs was famous for reading and answering email sent to steve@apple.com so that he could learn from customers directly. The leader must then work to synthesize all these perspectives and insights. Then they must simplify them—looking for common themes and a central thread—to define a future vision that will guide the actions of others.

Communicate

The second job of a leader is to communicate their vision to every stakeholder inside and outside the organization. Effective leaders communicate both what their vision is and why it matters. Or, as Lucy Kueng summarizes it, "This is our problem, where we are going, and why it is necessary."[5]

Leaders communicate these ideas in carefully chosen words, stories, and symbols to make sure the ideas are clear and unforgettable. In his very first letter to shareholders in 1997, Bezos introduced the phrase "Day 1," which became a rallying cry within Amazon for long-term thinking and a mindset that Amazon is always at the start of its journey. As Bezos wrote two decades later, "Day 2 is stasis. Followed by irrelevance. Followed by excruciating, painful decline. Followed by death. And that is why it is always Day 1."[6]

Leaders not only communicate; they overcommunicate. They don't just tell their story to employees on the biggest stage at their largest annual meeting. Leaders communicate through every tool and means possible—in public forums and private conversations. They repeat the same ideas and themes over and over. They are relentless. At Acuity Insurance, CEO Ben Salzmann is in a perpetual state of communication with employees and partners alike—from social media posts to company meetings in a theater built in-the-round in their headquarters, to his weekly "gossip" audio messages sent by voicemail to every employee.

Great communicators don't just speak; they ask questions, and they listen. Rather than declare "We need to do X!," leaders ask "How might we achieve Y?" They are approachable and regularly step out of their office to seek the perspectives of customers, partners, and employees at every level. By listening, they find out if others have heard them—and if not, why not? What barriers remain? Leaders remember the adage "The single biggest problem in communication is the illusion that it has taken place."[7]

Through it all, leaders recognize that every interaction they have—with an employee, a customer, or a shareholder—is a chance to teach what they believe about their organization. As social entrepreneur Wendy Kopp says, "Leadership is teaching."[8] Or, in the words of Antoine de Saint-Exupéry: "If you want to build a ship, don't drum up the people to gather wood, divide the work, and give orders. Instead, teach them to yearn for the vast and endless sea."[9]

Enable

The third job of a leader is to enable others to bring their vision to life. This, too, is a reversal of command-and-control leadership. Bottom-up leaders lead less by their own actions than by enabling the actions of others.

The first way that leaders enable others is by removing obstacles or roadblocks to their work. As Citibank's Valla Vakili, puts it, "Legacy processes, legacy ways of working. These are often just very simple things that get in the way of the creativity and productivity of the people you already have." It is a leader's job to align every process they approve—from compensation to organizational structure, to metrics and KPIs—with the vision they have defined and communicated. Processes carelessly chosen or unthinkingly inherited can undermine culture, strategy, and the most purposeful efforts of your employees.

Leaders enable the work of others through their choices of who to hire and who to promote to key positions. Leaders give those people the autonomy to act and provide them with the tools and technologies that will make a difference in their work. Leaders help their people grow their own abilities, developing the talents they need to realize the goals they set for themselves. And leaders advocate internally for those who need support to make change happen.

Leaders empower others by getting them the resources they need. This starts with the allocation of financial capital in support of strategic priorities—that is, putting their money where their mouth is. They also empower by allocating human capital—the most vital resource for any new initiative. The last resource a leader must allocate is their mental bandwidth. When the New York Times Company committed to a digital-first future, one of the key changes was to reallocate the attention of top leaders. The paper's long-cherished print edition, would continue to be produced (because its subscribers were among the most loyal, and its advertising business was profitable though declining). But the company was reorganized so that news would be developed in a digital-first approach, with a separate team pulling from that digital content to assemble each day's print edition. A few experienced managers were charged with overseeing the declining print operation. This allowed the rest of the Times's leadership to focus all their attention on future growth areas such as audio, video, paid apps, and the all-important digital news subscriptions.

By enabling others—through attention, resources, advocacy, and the removal of obstacles—leaders act in service of others in the organization. This third job of leaders resembles Robert K. Greenleaf's concept of "servant leadership"—which defines leadership as service to the needs and growth of others.[10]

Rethinking leadership around these three roles—author, teach, servant—may be hard for longtime leaders. Those who have risen under an older model may feel they are giving up power and influence as defined by the old model of control. But a deeper understanding of bottom-up leadership reveals that power and influence are simply reconfigured in the three roles.

A leader's instinct to act as decider in chief can be especially hard to resist during a digital transformation, as countless new decisions must be made—related to investments, hiring, workflows, technologies, products, and more. But instead of lapsing into old habits, leaders should focus on pushing these responsibilities down in the organization. Find your most talented people to do the highest-level planning. And push all individual decisions down to the level of the people who are actually doing the work. By defining a vision, communicating it powerfully, and enabling others to bring it to life, the leader plays an essential role in driving change.

∿

In the digital era, the need for transformation is inescapable. But while DX is hard, it is possible for any organization. By following the five steps of the DX Roadmap—defining a shared vision; picking the problems that matter most; validating new ventures; scaling change with new governance; and growing tech, talent, and culture—any organization can grow and transform for the digital era.

I wish you well in your own efforts as you find your path forward. Remember, as you pursue new digital ventures, always focus on impact and value creation, never on technology for its own sake. And as you work to transform your people, processes, and culture for the future, remember that the journey never ends. Change is always ahead.

MORE TOOLS FOR YOUR BUSINESS

You can find additional resources for applying the Digital Transformation (DX) Roadmap by visiting www.davidrogers.digital and subscribing to my newsletter. These resources include the following:

- Downloadable PDFs of the strategic tools in this book and my prior books
- Video tutorials on applying key concepts from the DX Roadmap
- New case studies, interviews, and research
- My latest advice on leading digital transformation

I hope you will subscribe, send me your questions, and keep in touch!

SELF-ASSESSMENT:
Is Your Organization Ready for DX?

This assessment tool is designed to uncover areas of strength versus weakness in your organization as it seeks to adapt and grow in the constantly changing digital era.

Who should complete the assessment?
I recommend having a wide range of managers and executives complete the assessment tool while keeping their individual identities and responses confidential.

How to complete the assessment?
Each question is presented as a pair of contrasting statements. Read each pair and reflect on the current state of your own business. Choose the number on the scale from 1 to 7 that you think reflects where your organization stands in relation to the two statements: 1 indicates fully aligned with the statement on the left, 7 with the statement on the right.

How to score the assessment?
Questions with a low score (1–3) indicate current weakness in the organization that will pose challenges for any DX effort. Questions with a high score (4–7) indicate an area of greater strength in the organization.

As you combine responses from multiple employees, be sure to capture not just the average score on each question but also the range of scores and frequency of each score. Some of the greatest insights may come from a question that produces divergent answers (e.g., many responses of 1 or 2, and many of 6 or 7).

Discussion and insights:

After creating a report on the numerical answers, convene a forum with those who completed the assessment tool. Use an independent moderator to review the scores and lead a discussion about why respondents answered as they did. This guided discussion should reveal important challenges facing the organization that may not be apparent to senior leadership. The insights from this assessment tool can then be used to focus your own efforts to implement the Digital Transformation (DX) Roadmap.

Vision (Step 1)

Our employees fear change and lack a clear sense of where the firm is going.	1 2 3 4 5 6 7	Employees at every level of our business understand our digital agenda and push it forward.
Backing for our digital investments is weak from investors, CFO, and P&L heads.	1 2 3 4 5 6 7	Support for our digital investments is strong from investors, CFO, and P&L heads.
Our digital initiatives are generic, following the examples of peers.	1 2 3 4 5 6 7	We only invest in digital initiatives where we have a competitive advantage.
We use generic digital maturity metrics to guide efforts.	1 2 3 4 5 6 7	The business impact of our digital efforts is clearly defined, with metrics to measure and track results.
Our firm follows the market, reacts to others, and is surprised by new entrants.	1 2 3 4 5 6 7	Our firm leads the market, alert to critical trends while there is time to choose a course.

Priorities (Step 2)

Our digital transformation is a series of scattered projects with no clear direction.	1 2 3 4 5 6 7	Clear priorities provide direction to digital transformation across our organization.
Our digital efforts are defined by the technologies they use.	1 2 3 4 5 6 7	Our digital efforts are defined by the problems they solve and opportunities they pursue.
Our digital efforts are focused solely on operations, cost cutting, and optimizing our current business.	1 2 3 4 5 6 7	Our digital efforts are focused on future growth as well as improving our current business.
A few people in our organization drive digital while the rest stick to old ways of working.	1 2 3 4 5 6 7	Each of our departments is pursuing its own digital ventures, with a backlog of ideas to try next.
Our transformation is disconnected from business needs and losing support over time.	1 2 3 4 5 6 7	Our transformation is linked to the needs of the business and gaining support over time.

Experimentation (Step 3)

Our approach to innovation is focused on coming up with a few great ideas.	1 2 3 4 5 6 7	Our approach to innovation is focused on testing many ideas to learn which work best.
Important decisions are made based on business cases, third-party data, and expert opinion.	1 2 3 4 5 6 7	Important decisions are made based on experimentation and learning from the customer.
Once our teams start a project, they are committed to building the solution in full.	1 2 3 4 5 6 7	In any project, our teams stay focused on the problem but flexible on the solution.
We view failures as costly, so our fear of taking risks is high.	1 2 3 4 5 6 7	We keep our failures cheap and maintain a bias toward risk taking.
Even our good ideas move slowly and don't seem to move the needle on our business.	1 2 3 4 5 6 7	Our good ideas grow fast and deliver business value at scale.

Governance (Step 4)

A top executive must personally approve any new innovation for it to happen.	1 2 3 4 5 6 7	We have established structures that provide resources and governance for innovation.
Our new ventures move slowly and are led by traditional teams in functional silos.	1 2 3 4 5 6 7	Our new ventures move fast and are led by highly independent, multifunctional teams.
Allocating resources to new ventures is slowed by our annual budgeting cycle.	1 2 3 4 5 6 7	Our resource allocation happens quickly through iterative funding.
Our innovation is limited to a few big projects, and they are hard to shut down once they are started.	1 2 3 4 5 6 7	We have a steady pipeline of innovations, and it is managed with smart shutdowns to free up resources.
The only new ventures that gain support are low-risk innovations in our core business.	1 2 3 4 5 6 7	Our governance model supports ventures with low and high uncertainty, both in our core and beyond it.

Capabilities (Step 5)

Our inflexible IT systems reinforce our silos and limit our collaboration.	1 2 3 4 5 6 7	Our modular IT systems integrate across our organization and connect easily with outside partners.
Our data is contradictory, incomplete, and inaccessible to managers in real time.	1 2 3 4 5 6 7	Our data provides a single source of truth to managers across the company.
Our centralized IT governance causes bottlenecks for new projects.	1 2 3 4 5 6 7	Our IT governance provides oversight while keeping innovation in the hands of the business.
Our employees lack digital skills, so digital projects must be outsourced.	1 2 3 4 5 6 7	Our own employees can build and iterate digital solutions.
Our top-down culture and bureaucracy stifle employees and breed cynicism and inertia.	1 2 3 4 5 6 7	Our culture and processes empower employees to drive bottom-up change.

CASES AND EXAMPLES BY INDUSTRY

Agribusiness
Deere & Company

Airlines
Southwest Airlines

Automotive
Ford Motor Company
Tesla
Volkswagen

Banking and Financial Services
Citi
Intuit
Itaú Unibanco
Mastercard Inc.
Nasdaq
National Commercial Bank (NCB)

Consumer Durables
BSH Home Appliances
Haier

Consumer Electronics
Apple
Nokia
Samsung Group

Consumer Internet
Facebook/Meta
Google/Alphabet
Zoom

Consumer Packaged Goods
PepsiCo
Procter & Gamble

Design
IDEO

Energy
Schlumberger

Fashion and Apparel
Nike

Government
U.S. Army

Health Care
Bristol Myers Squibb
Johnson & Johnson
Merck Animal Health
Pfizer
Zoetis

Hospitality
Airbnb

Industrial Manufacturing
Air Liquide
BASF
General Electric
United Technology Co./Raytheon
Technologies

Insurance
Acuity Insurance

Journalism
Aftenposten
Huffington Post
New York Times
Wall Street Journal
Washington Post

Logistics
CMA CGM

Marketing Technology
Adobe
Optimizely

Media and Entertainment
Axel Springer
CNN/Warner Bros. Discovery
Netflix
Schibsted
Sony Group
The Walt Disney Co.
YouTube

Membership Services
AARP
Canadian Automobile Association
FIA

Nonprofit
The Gates Foundation

Restaurants
Domino's Pizza, Inc.
McDonald's
Panera

Retail
Alibaba
Amazon
Walmart

Start-Ups
Blinds.com
Colombier Group
CupClub
Diapers.com
Muuse
Qikfox
VG Nett

Technology Hardware
Intel
Thomas A. Edison, Inc.
Xerox

Technology Services
Amazon Web Services
Ant Financial
Cisco
HCL Technologies
IBM
Microsoft
SAP

Telecom
Safaricom
Virgin Media 02
Vodafone

Transportation
Uber
Waze

VISUAL OVERVIEW OF THE DX PLAYBOOK AND DX ROADMAP

Domains	Strategic Themes	Key Concepts
Customers	*Harness customer networks*	• Reinvented marketing funnel • Path to purchase • Core behaviors of customer networks
Competition	*Build platforms, not just products*	• Platform business models • (In)direct network effects • (Dis)intermediation • Competitive value trains
Data	*Turn data into assets*	• Templates of data value • Drivers of big data • Data-driven decision making
Innovation	*Innovate by rapid experimentation*	• Divergent experimentation • Convergent experimentation • Minimum viable prototype • Paths to scaling up
Value	*Adapt your value proposition*	• Concepts of market value • Paths out of a declining market • Steps to value prop evolution

Figure A.1.
The DX Playbook overview

DX Roadmap Steps		Key Concepts
Vision 	**1. Define a shared vision**	• Future landscape • Right to win • North Star impact • Business theory
Priorities 	**2. Pick the problems that matter most**	• Problem/opportunity statement • P/O Matrix • Venture backlog
Experimentation 	**3. Validate new ventures**	• Four Stages of Validation • The Rogers Growth Navigator • Illustrative versus functional MVPs
Governance 	**4. Manage growth at scale**	• Teams and boards • Iterative funding process • Three paths to growth • Corporate Innovation Stack
Capabilities 	**5. Grow tech, talent, and culture**	• Tech and Talent Map • Modular architecture • Culture-Process Map

Figure A.2.
The DX Roadmap overview

NOTES

1. The DX Roadmap

1. Rachel McAthy, "Pulitzer Goes to New York Times 'Snow Fall' Journalist," April 16, 2013, https://www.journalism.co.uk/news/new-york-times-digital-snowfall -feature-wins-pulitzer/s2/a552683/.

2. Kyle Massey, "The Old Page 1 Meeting, R.I.P.: Updating a Times Tradition for the Digital Age," *New York Times*, May 12, 2015, https://www.nytimes.com/times -insider/2015/05/12/the-old-page-1-meeting-r-i-p-updating-a-times-tradition-for -the-digital-age/#more-10891.

3. Gabriel Snyder, "The *New York Times* Claws Its Way into the Future," *Wired*, February 12, 2017, https://www.wired.com/2017/02/new-york-times-digital-journalism/.

4. Joshua Benton, "The Leaked *New York Times* Innovation Report Is One of the Key Documents of This Media Age," *Nieman Lab*, May 15, 2014, https://www.niemanlab .org/2014/05/the-leaked-new-york-times-innovation-report-is-one-of-the-key-documents -of-this-media-age/, 44.

5. Amy Watson, "New York Times Company's Revenue 2021," *Statista*, March 21, 2022, https://www.statista.com/statistics/192848/revenue-of-the-new-york-times-company -since-2006/.

6. "NYT Innovation Report 2014," *Scribd*, March 24, 2014, https://www.scribd.com /doc/224332847/NYT-Innovation-Report-2014, p. 72.

7. BCG Global found that 70 percent of digital transformations fall short of their objectives, often with profound consequences. See Patrick Forth et al., "Flipping the

Odds of Digital Transformation Success," *BCG Global*, October 29, 2020, https://www
.bcg.com/publications/2020/increasing-odds-of-success-in-digital-transformation.
McKinsey's research found that more than 70 percent fail, and only 14 percent succeed in a
sustainable way. See Hortense de la Boutetière, Alberto Montagner, and Angelika Reich,
"Unlocking Success in Digital Transformations," *McKinsey & Company*, October 29, 2019,
https://www.mckinsey.com/business-functions/organization/our-insights/unlocking
-success-in-digital-transformations.

8. Steve Lohr, "G.E. to Spin off Its Digital Business," *New York Times*, December 13,
2018, https://www.nytimes.com/2018/12/13/business/ge-digital-spinoff.html.

9. Anand Birje and David Rogers, "Digital Acceleration for Business Resilience,"
HCL Technologies, 2021, https://www.hcltech.com/digital-analytics-services/campaign
/digital-acceleration-report-2021.

10. Lauren Forristal, "Disney+ Reaches 164.2m Subscribers as It Prepares for
Ad-Supported Tier Launch," *TechCrunch*, November 8, 2022, https://techcrunch.com
/2022/11/08/disney-reports-fourth-quarter-results-2022/.

11. CEO slide deck: https://businessleadersformichigan.com/wp-content/uploads
/2016/11/Patrick-Doyle-Presentation-FINAL.pdf highlights several of these innovations, plus:
Share price: $4.97 (2009) to $155.01 (2016). See Patrick Doyle, "Failure Is an Option—
Business Leaders for Michigan," *Business Leaders for Michigan*, November 2016, https://
businessleadersformichigan.com/wp-content/uploads/2016/11/Patrick-Doyle-Presentation-
FINAL.pdf.

12. Gabriel Snyder, "The *New York Times* Is Clawing Its Way into the Future," *Wired*,
February 12, 2017, https://www.wired.com/2017/02/new-york-times-digital-journalism/.

13. Sara Fischer, "*New York Times* Surpasses 10 Million Subscriptions," *Axios*,
February 2, 2022, https://www.axios.com/new-york-times-10-million-subscriptions
-eb401cfb-2135-4845-b873-8b3b5f7fd10d.html.

14. New York Times Company, "The New York Times Company 2021 Annual
Report," March 11, 2022, https://nytco-assets.nytimes.com/2022/03/The-New-York
-Times-Company-2021-Annual-Report.pdf.

15. This is a paraphrase of a saying that is famously misattributed to Darwin: "It is
not the strongest of the species that survives, nor the most intelligent. It is the one that
is most adaptable to change." This epigram does encapsulate one of the key insights of
Darwin's theory of natural selection, but it was never written by him! Rather, it began
as a portion of a 1963 speech by Leon C. Megginson that discussed Darwin's ideas;
Megginson's words were then repeated and condensed by various management writers
before becoming the popular saying misattributed to Darwin. A full explanation can be
found at https://quoteinvestigator.com/2014/05/04/adapt/.

2. DX and the Challenge of Innovation

1. Vijay Govindarajan and Anup Srivastava, "Strategy When Creative Destruction
Accelerates," Working Paper No. 2836135, Tuck School of Business, 2016, https://ssrn
.com/abstract=2836135 or http://dx.doi.org/10.2139/ssrn.2836135.

2. Todd Spangler, "Netflix Aims to Launch Cheaper, Ad-Supported Plan in Early 2023," *Yahoo! Finance*, July 19, 2022, https://finance.yahoo.com/news/netflix-aims-launch-cheaper-ad-203926425.html.

3. Sara Fischer, "Big Cuts Coming for CNN+ After Slow Start." *Axios*, April 12, 2022. https://www.axios.com/2022/04/12/cnn-plus-cuts-warner-brothers-discovery.

4. Jason Kilar, *Twitter*, March 29, 2022, 3:35 p.m., https://twitter.com/jasonkilar/status/1508890566276362241.

5. Lucia Moses et al., " 'Hubris. Nothing More.' Insiders Blame Jeff Zucker and Jason Kilar for the Rapid Demise of CNN+ as Warner Bros. Discovery Leadership Looks Forward.," *Business Insider*, April 12, 2022, https://www.businessinsider.com/cnn-plus-failure-blame-zucker-kilar-hubris-warner-bros-discovery-2022-4.

6. Michjael M. Grynbaum, John Koblin, and Benjamin Mullin, "CNN+ Streaming Service Will Shut Down Weeks After Its Start," *New York Times*, April 21, 2022, https://www.nytimes.com/2022/04/21/business/cnn-plus-shutting-down.html.

7. Ted Johnson and Dade Hayes, "CNN+ Debuts: Is It the Next News Innovation or Too Late to the Streaming Wars?," *Deadline*, March 28, 2022, https://deadline.com/2022/03/cnn-plus-launch-streaming-service-preview-1234987770/.

8. Alex Sherman, "CNN+ Struggles to Lure Viewers in Its Early Days, Drawing Fewer Than 10,000 Daily Users," *CNBC*, April 12, 2022, https://www.cnbc.com/2022/04/12/cnn-plus-low-viewership-numbers-warner-bros-discovery.html.

9. Austin Carr, "The Inside Story of Jeff Bezos's Fire Phone Debacle," *Fast Company*, January 6, 2015, https://www.fastcompany.com/3039887/under-fire. Sources in the article said that sales were in the tens of thousands of units before the company's radical price cut. The first such cut happened forty-five days after launch.

10. Benjamin Black, "EC2 Origins," *Benjamin Black Causes Trouble Here*, January 25, 2009, https://blog.b3k.us/2009/01/25/ec2-origins.html.

11. Rachel King, "Amazon Breaks out Cloud Results for First Time on Q1 Earnings Report," *ZDNET*, April 23, 2015, https://www.zdnet.com/article/amazon-breaks-out-cloud-results-for-first-time-on-q1-earnings-report/.

12. Todd Bishop, "Amazon Web Services Posts Record $13.5B in *Profits* for 2020 in Andy Jassy's Aws Swan Song," *GeekWire*, February 2, 2021, https://www.geekwire.com/2021/amazon-web-services-posts-record-13-5b-profits-2020-andy-jassys-aws-swan-song/.

13. Tom Huddleston, "Zoom's Founder Left a 6-Figure Job Because He Wasn't Happy—and Following His Heart Made Him a Billionaire," *CNBC*, August 21, 2019, https://www.cnbc.com/2019/08/21/zoom-founder-left-job-because-he-wasnt-happy-became-billionaire.html. In addition to this published account of Eric Yuan's departure, a former Cisco executive told me that Yuan had pitched his idea for Zoom to Cisco leaders, and the idea was shot down as too far from Cisco's enterprise focus.

14. Mansoor Iqbal, "Zoom Revenue and Usage Statistics (2022)," *Business of Apps*, June 30, 2022, https://www.businessofapps.com/data/zoom-statistics/, accessed December 14, 2022. March 2019 was 10 million daily meeting participants; March 2020 was 200 million.

15. Charles O'Reilly, Michael Tushman, and J. Bruce Herrald, "Organizational Ambidexterity: IBM and Emerging Business Opportunities," *California Management Review* (May 1, 2009), https://ssrn.com/abstract=1418194.

16. Malcolm Gladwell, "Creation Myth," *The New Yorker*, May 9, 2011, https://www.newyorker.com/magazine/2011/05/16/creation-myth.

17. Clayton M. Christensen, *The Innovator's Dilemma: When New Technologies Cause Great Firms to Fail* (Boston, MA: Harvard Business Review Press, 2016).

18. Theodore Levitt, "Marketing Myopia," *Harvard Business Review* 38, no. 4 (1960): 24–47. Still a classic more than fifty years later, the article is republished online at https://hbr.org/2004/07/marketing-myopia.

19. David L. Rogers, in *The Digital Transformation Playbook: Rethink Your Business for the Digital Age*(New York: Columbia University Press, 2016), 127.

20. "Harvard i-Lab: Fireside Chat with Michael Skok and Andy Jassy: The History of Amazon Web Services," *YouTube*, 2013, https://www.youtube.com/watch?v=d2dyGDqrXLo.

21. Julie Bort, "Amazon's Game-Changing Cloud Was Built by Some Guys in South Africa," *Business Insider*, March 28, 2012, https://archive.ph/20130119102209/http:/www.businessinsider.com/amazons-game-changing-cloud-was-built-by-some-guys-in-south-africa-2012-3. Longtime Amazon executive David Glick tells me that locating the EC2 team in Cape Town had a dual purpose: Pinkham, a South African national, was facing trouble renewing his U.S. work visa.

3. Step 1: Define a Shared Vision

1. Bill Ford, "A Future Beyond Traffic Gridlock," *TED Talk*, accessed December 14, 2022, https://www.ted.com/talks/bill_ford_a_future_beyond_traffic_gridlock.

2. Lucy Kueng, "Transformation Manifesto: 9 Priorities for Now," November 2, 2020, http://www.lucykung.com/latest-news/transformation-manifesto-9-priorities-for-now/.

3. In the memo, Stephen Elop relates a story about a worker on an oil platform in the North Sea awaking to find the entire platform on fire after an explosion. The memo is worth a read at; see Chris Ziegler, "Nokia CEO Stephen Elop Rallies Troops in Brutally Honest 'Burning Platform' Memo? (Update: It's Real!)," *Engadget*, February 8, 2011, https://www.engadget.com/2011-02-08-nokia-ceo-stephen-elop-rallies-troops-in-brutally-honest-burnin.html.

4. The theory of extrinsic motivation (based on external rewards) versus intrinsic motivation (based on the rewards of the work itself) comes from the self-determination theory (SDT) of motivation. A good overview of the work of Richard M. Ryan and Edward L. Deci can be found at Delia O'Hara, "The Intrinsic Motivation of Richard Ryan and Edward Deci," *American Psychological Association*, December 18, 2017, https://www.apa.org/members/content/intrinsic-motivation.

5. Ford, "A Future Beyond Traffic Gridlock."

6. Daniel Goleman defined six different leadership styles or roles that leaders could adopt and advocated developing the ability to combine them depending

on circumstance. But his empirical research found that the authoritative style—associated with using a narrative to align others with a vision—had the strongest positive impact of the six styles. See Daniel Goleman, "Leadership That Gets Results," *Harvard Business Review*, March-April 2000, https://hbr.org/2000/03/leadership-that-gets-results.

7. In McKinsey's study, the factor of a "clear change story" showed a 3.1 times spread between the 30 percent of companies that were successfully transforming and the 70 percent in its study that were not—the greatest difference among all the factors reported. See Hortense de la Boutetière, Alberto Montagner, and Angelika Reich, "Unlocking Success in Digital Transformations," *McKinsey & Company*, October 29, 2018, https://www.mckinsey.com/business-functions/organization/our-insights/unlocking-success-in-digital-transformations.

8. Satya Nadella et al., "Learning to Lead," in *Hit Refresh: The Quest to Rediscover Microsoft's Soul and Imagine a Better Future for Everyone* (New York: Harper Business, 2018), 62.

9. As Philip Bobbitt wrote, Parmenides' fallacy "occurs when one tries to assess a future state of affairs by measuring it against the present, as opposed to comparing it to other possible futures." Bobbitt first used the term in a 2003 op-ed for the *New York Times*; see Philip Bobbitt, "Today's War Is Against Tomorrow's Iraq," *New York Times*, March 10, 2003, https://www.nytimes.com/2003/03/10/opinion/today-s-war-is-against-tomorrow-s-iraq.html. He developed the concept in his later books, including *Terror and Consent: The Wars for the Twenty-First Century* (New York: Alfred A. Knopf, 2018) and *The Garments of Court and Palace: Machiavelli and the World That He Made* (New York: Grove Press, 2013). The fallacy has since been discussed in a business context by Clayton Christensen, Margie Warrell, and others.

10. This quote is widely attributed to President John Fitzgerald Kennedy, but I am unable to find the source or speech where he said it, including searching the online archive of the JFK Presidential Library at "Home: JFK Library," accessed December 14, 2022, https://www.jfklibrary.org/.

11. Dee-Ann Durbin and Tom Krisher, "Fields out at Ford; New CEO Hackett Known for Turnarounds." *Chicago Tribune*, June 4, 2018, https://www.chicagotribune.com/business/ct-ford-ceo-20170521-story.html.

12. Mark W. Johnson and Josh Suskewicz. *Lead from the Future: How to Turn Visionary Thinking into Breakthrough Growth* (Boston: Harvard Business Review Press, 2020), 210.

13. In a 1985 *Playboy* magazine interview, Steve Jobs describes the type of person who worked at Apple as "[s]omeone who really wants to get in a little over his head and make a dent in the universe." See David Scheff, "Steven Jobs Playboy Interview," *Playboy* (February 1985): 58.

14. "The CEO Test: Master the Challenges That Make or Break All Leaders," *YouTube*, 2021, https://www.youtube.com/watch?v=WXyFu53wMV8&list=PL38520A76CC5A4EE6&index=3.

15. John E. Doerr's book *Measure What Matters* provides an excellent deep dive into the practice of OKRs. See John E. Doerr, *Measure What Matters: OKRs, the Simple Idea That Drives 10x Growth* (London: Portfolio, 2018).

16. Doerr, *Measure What Matters*, 154–71.

17. D. E. Hunt, *Beginning with Ourselves: In Practice, Theory and Human Affairs* (Cambridge, MA: Brookline Books, 1987), 4, 30.

18. The term "business theory" is inspired by Todd Zenger's writing on the importance of each company having a "corporate theory"—although a business theory can be applied not just to a company but to any new strategy or change in resource allocation. See Todd Zenger, "What Is the Theory of Your Firm?," *Harvard Business Review* (June 2013): 126.

19. Mitchell Gordon, "Disney's Land: Walt's Profit Formula: Dream, Diversify—and Never Miss an Angle; Here's How His Divisions Complement Each Other," *Wall Street Journal*, February 4, 1958, p. 1

20. This was explained numerous times by Jeff Bezos, including in this interview: Jeff Bezos, "Interview with Adi Ignatius," *Harvard Business Review*, podcast audio, January 4, 2013, https://hbr.org/podcast/2013/01/jeff-bezos-on-leading-for-the. Bezos also discussed it in his 2008 letter to shareholders; see Jeff Bezos, "Letter to Amazon Shareholders," 2009, https://ir.aboutamazon.com/files/doc_financials/annual/Amazon_SH_Letter_2008.pdf.

21. Zenger, "What Is the Theory of Your Firm?," 126.

22. In 2021, National Commercial Bank merged with Samba Financial Group to become Saudi National Bank.

23. Bob Iger, interview with Kara Swisher, *Sway*, podcast audio, January 27, 2022, https://www.nytimes.com/2022/01/27/opinion/sway-kara-swisher-bob-iger.html?showTranscript=1.

24. Disney+ launched on November 12, 2019. Disney stock closed November 11 at 136.74. It closed November 13 at 148.72.

25. Bezos, "Interview with Adi Ignatius."

26. "Hackett CEO News Conference.mp4," *Dropbox*, accessed January 5, 2023, https://www.dropbox.com/s/k84legr519o0xpl/Hackett%20CEO%20News%20conference.mp4?dl=0&mod=article_inline. This quote occurs in the video at 17:10.

4. Step 2: Pick the Problems That Matter Most

1. Michael Porter, "What Is Strategy?," *Harvard Business Review* (November–December 1996): 60, https://hbr.org/1996/11/what-is-strategy.

2. Thomas Wedell-Wedellsborg, *What's Your Problem? To Solve Your Toughest Problems, Change the Problems You Solve* (Boston: Harvard Business Review Press, 2020).

3. Minda Zetlin, "This Video Is How Microsoft CEO Satya Nadella Introduced Himself to an Audience of 17,000 and It Was Perfect," *Inc.*, accessed December 16, 2022,

https://www.inc.com/minda-zetlin/satya-nadella-microsoft-xbox-adaptive-controller-super-bowl-video-disabled-gamers-owen-sirmons.html.

4. Kyle Evans, "Product Thinking vs. Project Thinking," *Medium* (Product Coalition, October 21, 2018), https://productcoalition.com/product-thinking-vs-project-thinking-380692a2d4e.

5. Among other places, this idea was prominently articulated in Amazon's 2008 shareholder letter; see Jeff Bezos, "2008 Letter to Amazon Shareholders," 2009, https://ir.aboutamazon.com/files/doc_financials/annual/Amazon_SH_Letter_2008.pdf.

6. Jeff Bezos, "Interview with Adi Ignatius," *Harvard Business Review*, podcast audio, January 4, 2013, https://hbr.org/podcast/2013/01/jeff-bezos-on-leading-for-the.

7. Another example comes from Mastercard Labs, which has a similar process for nurturing early ideas via its five-day "launchpad workshops," in which customers are brought in to help confirm their needs, pain points, and whether the proposed innovation offers real value.

8. Bezos, "2008 Letter to Amazon Shareholders."

9. This categorization is often credited to Kevin Fong, longtime managing partner at Mayfield Fund in Silicon Valley. One such source is Omer Khan, "Candy, Vitamin or Painkiller: Which One Is Your Product?," *SaaS Club*, accessed December 16, 2022, https://saasclub.io/candy-vitamin-painkiller-which-one-is-your-product/. Fong also described a third category, which he called "candy," for ideas that provided fleeting benefits; he did not like to invest in ideas from this third category.

10. Alexander Osterwalder et al., *Value Proposition Design: How to Create Products and Services Customers Want* (Hoboken, NJ: John Wiley, 2014).

11. Cited by early Uber investor Chris Sacca in 2015; see Chris Sacca, "Why I'd Never Want to Compete with Uber's Travis Kalanick," *Fortune*, February 4, 2015, https://fortune.com/2015/02/04/why-id-never-want-to-compete-with-ubers-travis-kalanick/.

12. Noriaki Kano et al., "Attractive Quality and Must-Be Quality," *Journal of the Japanese Society for Quality Control* 14, no. 2 (1984): 147–56, https://web.archive.org/web/20110813145926/http://ci.nii.ac.jp/Detail/detail.do?LOCALID=ART0003570680&lang=en. For a good summary of how the Kano model evolved, see "Kano Model: What Is the Kano Model? Definition and Overview of Kano," September 2, 2021, https://www.productplan.com/glossary/kano-model/.

13. Liz Tay, "Google Has Updated Its 9 Principles Of Innovation: Here They Are and the Products They Have Enabled," *Business Insider Australia*, November 19, 2013, https://www.businessinsider.com.au/google-has-updated-its-9-principles-of-innovation-here-they-are-and-the-products-they-have-enabled-2013-11.

14. John E. Doerr, *Measure What Matters: OKRs, the Simple Idea That Drives 10× Growth* (London: Portfolio, 2018), 127.

15. "From AT&T to Xerox: 90+ Corporate Innovation Labs: CB Insights," *CB Insights Research*, August 28, 2021, https://www.cbinsights.com/research/corporate-innovation-labs/.

16. Warren Berger, "The Secret Phrase Top Innovators Use," *Harvard Business Review* (September 12, 201), https://hbr.org/2012/09/the-secret-phrase-top-innovato.

17. Emily Chasan, "Don't Toss That Cup: McDonald's and Starbucks Are Developing Reusables," *Bloomberg.com*, February 18, 2020, https://www.bloomberg.com/news/articles/2020-02-18/reusable-coffee-cups-being-tested-for-mcdonald-s-and-starbucks.

18. Porter, "What Is Strategy?," 60.

19. "Steve Blank: The Key to Startup Success? 'Get Out of the Building.'" *Inc.*, accessed January 6, 2023, https://www.inc.com/steve-blank/key-to-success-getting-out-of-building.html.

20. Colin Bryar and Bill Carr, *Working Backwards* (New York: St. Martin's Press, 2021), 98–120.

21. David Leonhardt et al., "Journalism That Stands Apart" (New York: New York Times, 2017), Section: "The way we work: Every department should have a clear vision that is well understood by its staff."

22. Donald N. Sull, "Closing the Gap Between Strategy and Execution," *MIT Sloan Management Review* (July 1, 2007), https://sloanreview.mit.edu/article/closing-the-gap-between-strategy-and-execution/.

5. Step 3: Validate New Ventures

1. Sarah Nassauer, "WSJ News Exclusive: Walmart Scraps Plan to Have Robots Scan Shelves," *Wall Street Journal*, November 2, 2020, https://on.wsj.com/3c04VQF.

2. Tom Ward, "From Ground-Breaking to Breaking Ground: Walmart Begins to Scale Market Fulfillment Centers," Walmart Corporate, January 27, 2021, https://corporate.walmart.com/newsroom/2021/01/27/from-ground-breaking-to-breaking-ground-walmart-begins-to-scale-local-fulfillment-centers.

3. Melissa Repko, "Walmart Drew One in Four Dollars Spent on Click and Collect—with Room to Grow in 2022," *CNBC*, December 30, 2021, https://www.cnbc.com/2021/12/30/walmart-drew-one-in-four-dollars-on-click-and-collect-market-researcher.html.

4. Sarah Nassauer, "Walmart Pushes New Delivery Services for a Post-Pandemic World," *Wall Street Journal*, February 28, 2022, https://www.wsj.com/articles/walmart-pushes-new-delivery-services-for-a-post-pandemic-world-11645971260.

5. Dean Baquet, "The New York Times and Journalism's Future," presentation at the INMA World Conference of Media, New York, May 17, 2019.

6. Steve Blank, "No Plan Survives First Contact with Customers—Business Plans Versus Business Models," *SteveBlank.com*, April 8, 2010, https://steveblank.com/2010/04/08/no-plan-survives-first-contact-with-customers-%E2%80%93-business-plans-versus-business-models/.

7. Jonathan Becher, "RIP ROI: Time-to-Market Is the New Indicator of Success," *LinkedIn*, August 8, 2016, https://www.linkedin.com/pulse/rip-roi-time-to-market-new-indicator-success-jonathan-becher/.

8. Steven G. Blank and Bob Dorf, *The Startup Owner's Manual: The Step-by-Step Guide for Building a Great Company* (Pescadero, CA: K & S Ranch, 2012), 551.

9. Eric Ries, *The Lean Startup: How Constant Innovation Creates Radically Successful Businesses* (London: Penguin Business, 2019).

10. I am indebted to Bob Dorf's lectures in my classes at Columbia Business School for sharing this story of the origins of Diapers.com.

11. Marc Randolph, "Please Mr. Postman," in *That Will Never Work: The Birth of Netflix and the Amazing Life of an Idea* (New York: Back Bay Books, 2022), 24–37.

12. Eric Von Hippel, "Lead Users: A Source of Novel Product Concepts," *Management Science* 32 (1986): 791–806, doi:10.1287/mnsc.32.7.791.

13. The concept of product-market fit was developed and named by Andy Rachleff, who is currently the CEO and cofounder of Wealthfront and is a cofounder of Benchmark Capital. Steven G. Blank and Bob Dorf also use the term "problem/solution fit" in *The Startup Owner's Manual.*

14. Alberto Savoia, *The Right It: Why So Many Ideas Fail and How to Make Sure Yours Succeed* (New York: Harper One, 2019).

15. Tesla unveiled the new car on April 1, 2016, and had 200,000 orders in a little over twenty-four hours from customers who would not receive a car until late 2017 or 2018. See Chris Isidore, "Tesla Got 200,000 Orders for the Model 3 in about One Day," *CNNMoney*, April 1, 2016, https://money.cnn.com/2016/04/01/news/companies/tesla-model-3-stock-price/index.html.

16. Tim Harford, *Fifty Things That Made the Modern Economy* (London: Abacus, 2018).

17. Julie Jargon, "How Panera Solved Its 'Mosh Pit' Problem," *Wall Street Journal*, June 2, 2017, https://www.wsj.com/articles/how-panera-solved-its-mosh-pit-problem-1496395801.

18. Eric Ries, "Test," in *The Lean Startup: How Today's Entrepreneurs Use Continuous Innovation to Create Radically Successful Businesses* (New York Currency, 2017), 99–102.

19. In 2018, Reid Hoffman claimed that he coined this aphorism "more than a decade ago." See Reid Hoffman, "If There Aren't Any Typos in This Essay, We Launched Too Late!," *LinkedIn*, March 29, 2017, https://www.linkedin.com/pulse/arent-any-typos-essay-we-launched-too-late-reid-hoffman/.

20. Mark W. Johnson and Josh Suskewicz, "How to Jump-Start the Clean-Tech Economy," *Harvard Business Review* (November 2009): 87.

21. Clayton M. Christensen and Michael E. Raynor, *The Innovator's Solution: Creating and Sustaining Successful Growth* (Boston: Harvard Business School Press, 2003), 74–80, 96. Christensen and Raynor credit Richard Pedi with coining the phrase "jobs to be done," Anthony Ulwick with developing closely related concepts, and David Sundahl with assisting in their own formulation. The job-to-be-done concept has been further explored in various articles by Christensen with other coauthors.

22. David L. Rogers, in *The Digital Transformation Playbook: Rethink Your Business for the Digital Age* (New York: Columbia University Press, 2016), 56.

23. Geoffrey A. Moore, *Crossing the Chasm: Marketing and Selling Disruptive Products to Mainstream Customers* (New York: HarperBusiness, 2014).

24. Mark W. Johnson and Josh Suskewicz, "How to Jump-Start the Clean-Tech Economy," *Harvard Business Review* (November 2009): 87.

6. Step 4: Manage Growth at Scale

1. Penny Crosman, "Welcome to Open Mic Night at a Citi Fintech Unit," *American Banker*, November 22, 2017, https://www.americanbanker.com/news/welcome-to-open-mic-night-at-a-citi-fintech-unit.

2. An original source by Margaret Mead has not been found; the quote was first attributed to her by Donald Keys shortly after her death. See "Never Doubt That a Small Group of Thoughtful, Committed Citizens Can Change the World; Indeed, It's the Only Thing That Ever Has," *Quote Investigator*, November 12, 2017, https://quoteinvestigator.com/2017/11/12/change-world/.

3. J. Richard Hackman and Neil Vidmar, "Effects of Size and Task Type on Group Performance and Member Reactions," *Sociometry* 33, no. 1 (1970): 37–54, https://doi.org/10.2307/2786271.

4. Eric Ries, *The Startup Way: How Modern Companies Use Entrepreneurial Management to Transform Culture and Drive Long-Term Growth* (New York: Currency, 2017).

5. Mark Wilson, "Adobe's Kickbox: The Kit to Launch Your Next Big Idea," *Fast Company*, February 9, 2015, https://www.fastcompany.com/3042128/adobes-kickbox-the-kit-to-launch-your-next-big-idea.

6. Crosman, "Welcome to Open Mic Night at a Citi Fintech Unit."

7. Crosman, "Welcome to Open Mic Night at a Citi Fintech Unit."

8. Lucy Kueng, "Going Digital: A Roadmap for Organisational Transformation," *Reuters Institute for the Study of Journalism and University of Oxford*, November 2017, p. 16, https://reutersinstitute.politics.ox.ac.uk/sites/default/files/2017-11/Going%20Digital.pdf.

9. Mark W. Johnson and Josh Suskewicz. *Lead from the Future: How to Turn Visionary Thinking into Breakthrough Growth* (Boston: Harvard Business Review Press, 2020), 115.

10. Eric Ries, *The Startup Way: How Modern Companies Use Entrepreneurial Management to Transform Culture and Drive Long-Term Growth* (New York: Currency, 2017), 294.

11. Lucy Kueng, "Going Digital," 16.

12. Steven Levy, "Google Glass 2.0 Is a Startling Second Act," *Wired*, July 18, 2017, https://www.wired.com/story/google-glass-2-is-here/.

13. "NYT Innovation Report 2014," *Scribd*, March 24, 2014, https://www.scribd.com/doc/224332847/NYT-Innovation-Report-2014, p. 75.

14. Susan Wojcicki, "The Eight Pillars of Innovation," *Google*, July 2011, https://www.thinkwithgoogle.com/future-of-marketing/creativity/8-pillars-of-innovation/.

15. Alex Morrell, "We Spoke with Citi's Innovation Chief About Which Fintechs It Wants to Invest in, How Its Internal 'Shark Tank' Judges Know When to Kill an Idea, and Why Red Tape Helps Some Startups Flourish," *Business Insider*, February 8, 2019, https://www.businessinsider.com/vanessa-colella-citi-ventures-innovation-interview-2019-2.

16. Robert D. Hof, "Amazon's Risky Bet," *BusinessWeek*, November 13, 2006. The magazine's cover image can be seen at Jeff Bezos, *Twitter*, May 18, 2022, 3:11 p.m., https://twitter.com/jeffbezos/status/1527003895393812480.

17. For a good postmortem on the failed GE digital effort, see Alex Moazed, "Why GE Digital Failed," *Inc.*, accessed January 4, 2023, https://www.inc.com/alex-moazed /why-ge-digital-didnt-make-it-big.html. Another good analysis is Ted Mann and Thomas Gryta, "The Dimming of GE's Bold Digital Dreams," *Wall Street Journal*, July 18, 2020, https://www.wsj.com/articles/the-dimming-of-ges-bold-digital-dreams-11595044802 ?mod=djemalertNEWS.

18. Tenets are a set of principles that each team creates to guide its everyday decision making. The practice of tenets was first introduced at Amazon on a team led by my friend David Glick. During nearly twenty years at Amazon, Glick led many two-pizza teams in areas such as warehousing, logistics, pricing, and merchant fulfillment. When he was leading a team working on pricing, Glick met with Jeff Bezos to hash out the guiding strategy for their work. Bezos declared in the meeting, "We keep our prices very, very low because we think that earns customer trust, and over the long term, we take it as an article of faith that customer trust will drive long-term free cash flow." Glick wrote that down and captured four other ideas that seemed most central to the direction they had agreed on. He refined the wording, dubbed them his team's five tenets, and started putting them at the very top of every memo produced by his team as a reminder of what they were aiming for. After several monthly meetings, Bezos remarked, "I really like that this team has their tenets right at the top." Then he turned to his technical adviser and said "Ahmed, go make sure everybody does this!" And henceforth, 100,000 people at Amazon were told they had to define their own guiding tenets for decision making by their teams. "I got a lot of hate email," Glick said, "although they also asked me if I could send them my list of tenets."

7. Step 5: Grow Tech, Talent, and Culture

1. William Boston, "How Volkswagen's $50 Billion Plan to Beat Tesla Short-Circuited," *Wall Street Journal*, January 19, 2021, https://www.wsj.com/articles/how -volkswagens-50-billion-plan-to-beat-tesla-short-circuited-11611073974.

2. Boston, "How Volkswagen's $50 Billion Plan to Beat Tesla Short-Circuited."

3. Henry Man, "Volkswagen to Develop In-House Software for Next-Gen Cars," *CarExpert*, June 22, 2020, https://www.carexpert.com.au/car-news/volkswagen-to-develop -in-house-infotainment-software

4. Boston, "How Volkswagen's $50 Billion Plan to Beat Tesla Short-Circuited."

5. Herbert Diess, *LinkedIn*, February 2022, https://www.linkedin.com/posts /herbertdiess_i-am-happy-that-lynn-longo-as-our-new-cariad-activity-689893566 0502487040-h_zv.

6. Boston, "How Volkswagen's $50 Billion Plan to Beat Tesla Short-Circuited."

7. Jeff Lawson, *Ask Your Developer: How to Harness the Power of Software Developers and Win in the 21st Century* (New York: Harper Business, 2021), 3–4. Lawson cited Bezos as saying this at the first all-hands meeting he attended, after joining Amazon in September 2004.

8. Mark J. Greeven, Howard Yu, and Jialu Shan, "Why Companies Must Embrace Microservices and Modular Thinking," *MIT Sloan Management Review* (June 28, 2021), https://sloanreview.mit.edu/article/why-companies-must-embrace-microservices-and-modular-thinking.

9. Greeven, Yu, and Shan, "Why Companies Must Embrace Microservices."

10. This is my definition of technical debt, meant to be broad enough to capture the full range of the application of the idea today, which has grown far beyond "sloppy code." The idea dates back at least to 1980—when Meir Manny Lehman wrote, "As an evolving program is continually changed, its complexity . . . increases unless work is done to maintain or reduce it." See Meir Manny Lehman, "Laws of Software Evolution Revisited," in *Software Process Technology: 5th European Workshop, EWSPT '96, Nancy, France, October 9–11, 1996: Proceedings* (Berlin: Springer, 1996), 108–124. The metaphor of "debt" was later coined by Ward Cunningham, "The WyCash Portfolio Management System," March 26, 1992, http://c2.com/doc/oopsla92.html. Smart thinking includes Martin Fowler, "TechnicalDebt," May 21, 2019, https://martinfowler.com/bliki/TechnicalDebt.html.

11. Werner Vogels, "Modern Applications at AWS," *All Things Distributed*, August 28, 2019, https://www.allthingsdistributed.com/2019/08/modern-applications-at-aws.html.

12. The 2002 memo declaring Bezo's application programming interface (API) mandate is cherished legend, but no contemporary copies or accounts of it exist. A 2011 social media post from Amazon insider Steve Yegge attempted to paraphrase the original memo, saying that "[it] went something along these lines," but Yegge's own wording has since been repeated by others as the original memo itself. Yegge's post was on the now-defunct Google Plus but has been archived here: Steve Yegge, *Google Plus*, October 11, 2011, https://gist.github.com/chitchcock/1281611.

13. Vogels, "Modern Applications at AWS."

14. This account times the Netflix transition as happening in 2009–2011. shriram-venugopal, "The Story of Netflix and Microservices," *Geeks for Geeks*, May 17, 2020, https://www.geeksforgeeks.org/the-story-of-netflix-and-microservices/.

15. Joshua Benton, "The Leaked New York Times Innovation Report Is One of the Key Documents of This Media Age," *Nieman Lab*, May 15, 2014, https://www.niemanlab.org/2014/05/the-leaked-new-york-times-innovation-report-is-one-of-the-key-documents-of-this-media-age/.

16. For larger companies, a third option is to acquire a business with the capability you need. Thus, you will sometimes hear the choice framed as "build versus buy versus partner"—where "buy" means to acquire a firm, and "partner" means to buy services, components, or technology from an outside partner.

17. Lawson, *Ask Your Developer*, 4.

18. Angus Loten, "PepsiCo Bottles Tech Collaboration Effort into New Digital Hubs," *Wall Street Journal*, October 28, 2021, https://www.wsj.com/articles/pepsico-bottles-tech-collaboration-effort-into-new-digital-hubs-11635457546.

19. Boston, "How Volkswagen's $50 Billion Plan to Beat Tesla Short-Circuited."

20. Franklin Foer, "Jeff Bezos's Master Plan," *The Atlantic*, November 2019, https://www.theatlantic.com/magazine/archive/2019/11/what-jeff-bezos-wants/598363/.

21. The idea of the "T-shaped" person was espoused for consultants by McKinsey in the 1980s and later embraced in both agile software development and by design thinking firms like IDEO.

22. Benton, "The Leaked *New York Times Innovation Report* Is One of the Key Documents."

23. Aaron Aboagye, Ani Mukkavilli, and Jeremy Schneider, "Four Myths About Building a Software Business," *McKinsey & Company*, April 30, 2021, https://www.mckinsey.com/capabilities/mckinsey-digital/our-insights/four-myths-about-building-a-software-business.

24. Liad Agmon, "Dynamic Yield Joins the McDonald's Family," *Dynamic Yield*, accessed February 7, 2023, https://www.dynamicyield.com/blog/dynamic-yield-joins-mcdonalds/.

25. A study by McKinsey of 2,000 M&A transactions found that nondigital firms that began with an "anchor acquisitions" of a digital company worth $1 billion or more saw total returns to shareholders five times higher than those seen in nondigital companies that started with multiple smaller digital acquisitions. See Aboagye, Mukkavilli, and Schneider, "Four Myths About Building a Software Business."

26. Daniel Pink, *Drive: The Surprising Truth about What Motivates Us* (New York: Riverhead Books, 2013).

27. Satya Nadella, 2015 Microsoft shareholder meeting, https://www.youtube.com/watch?v=TDYAGKHFIjM.

28. Ann Rhoades, in *Built on Values: Creating an Enviable Culture That Outperforms the Competition* (San Francisco: Jossey-Bass, 2011), 19. Kelleher is not alone in thinking of culture in terms of norms of behavior. Leadership scholar John Kotter has defined company culture as a "group norms of behavior and the underlying shared values that help keep those norms in place." See John Kotter, "The Key to Changing Organizational Culture," *Forbes*, September 27, 2012, https://www.forbes.com/sites/johnkotter/2012/09/27/the-key-to-changing-organizational-culture/.

29. Ben Horowitz, *What You Do Is Who You Are: How to Create Your Business Culture* (New York: HarperBusiness, 2019), 2–3.

30. "Creating a Culture of Innovation," *Google*, accessed April 15, 2020, https://gsuite.google.co.in/intl/en_in/learn-more/creating_a_culture_of_innovation.html.

31. "Ten Things We Know to Be True," *Google*, accessed January 5, 2023, https://about.google/philosophy/.

32. Pauline Meyer, "Tesla Inc.'s Organizational Culture & Its Characteristics (Analysis)," *Panmore Institute*, February 22, 2019, http://panmore.com/tesla-motors-inc-organizational-culture-characteristics-analysis.

33. "Southwest Careers," *Southwest Airline*, accessed April 10, 2020, https://careers.southwestair.com/culture.

34. "Leadership Principles," *Amazon Jobs*, accessed January 5, 2023, https://www.amazon.jobs/content/en/our-workplace/leadership-principles.

35 Samir Lakhani, "Things I Liked About Amazon," *Medium*, August 28, 2017, https://medium.com/@samirlakhani/things-i-liked-about-amazon-4495ef06fbda.

36. Reed Hastings, "Freedom & Responsibility Culture (Version 1)," *Slideshare*, June 30, 2011, https://www.slideshare.net/reed2001/culture-2009.

37. "Netflix Culture—Seeking Excellence," *Netflix*, accessed January 5, 2023, https://jobs.netflix.com/culture.

38. Michael Lewis, "How Two Trailblazing Psychologists Turned the World of Decision Science Upside Down," *Vanity Fair*, November 14, 2016, https://www.vanityfair.com/news/2016/11/decision-science-daniel-kahneman-amos-tversky.

39. Krzysztof Majdan and Michael Wasowski, "We Sat Down with Microsoft's CEO to Discuss the Past, Present and Future of the Company," *Business Insider*, April 20, 2017, https://www.businessinsider.com/satya-nadella-microsoft-ceo-qa-2017-4. Satya Nadella called the same story Microsoft's 'creation myth' in Tim O'Reilly, "We Must Find a Grand Purpose for AI," *LinkedIn*, September 11, 2018, https://www.linkedin.com/pulse/conversation-satya-nadella-his-new-book-hit-refresh-tim-o-reilly/.

40. Minda Zetlin, "This Video Is How Microsoft CEO Satya Nadella Introduced Himself to an Audience of 17,000 and It Was Perfect," *Inc.*, March 30, 2019, https://www.inc.com/minda-zetlin/satya-nadella-microsoft-xbox-adaptive-controller-super-bowl-video-disabled-gamers-owen-sirmons.html.

41. Lucy Kueng. "Why Media Companies Need to Stop Focusing on Content," presentation at the INMA World Conference of Media, Washington, DC, May 17, 2018.

42. Robin D. Schatz, "How Blinds.com Searched Its Soul—and Found Home Depot," *Inc.*, May 2014, https://www.inc.com/magazine/201405/robin-schatz/how-blinds-com-acquired-by-home-depot.html.

43. Greylock, "Culture Is How You Act When No One Is Looking," *Medium*, June 1, 2017, https://news.greylock.com/culture-is-how-you-act-when-no-one-is-looking-f29d5dd16ecb.

44. Steven Kerr, "On the Folly of Rewarding A, While Hoping for B," *Academy of Management Journal* 18, no. 4 (1975): 769–83. Updated by the author in 1995: Steven Kerr, "On the Folly of Rewarding A, While Hoping for B," *Academy of Management Executive* 9, no. 1 (1995): 7–14, https://www.ou.edu/russell/UGcomp/Kerr.pdf

45. Ryan Felton, "Tesla Switching to 24/7 Shifts to Push for 6,000 Model 3s per Week by June, Elon Musk Says," *Jalopnik*, April 17, 2018, https://jalopnik.com/tesla-switching-to-24-7-shifts-to-push-for-6-000-model-1825335216.

46. "Netflix Culture—Seeking Excellence."

47. Jeffrey P. Bezos, "1997 Letter to Shareholders," 1998, https://s2.q4cdn.com/299287126/files/doc_financials/annual/Shareholderletter97.pdf.

48. This process of single-executive approval was described by Doug Herrington, senior vice president, North America consumer, Amazon while speaking at Princeton University's Keller Center. See: "Ten Rules of Innovating at Amazon," *Keller Center at Princeton University*, January 18, 2018, https://kellercenter.princeton.edu/stories/ten-rules-innovating-amazon.

Conclusion

1. Stanley A. McChrystal, David Silverman, Tantum Collins, and Chris Fussell, *Team of Teams* (London: Portfolio Penguin, 2015).

2. "Netflix Culture—Seeking Excellence," *Netflix*, accessed January 5, 2023, https://jobs.netflix.com/culture.

3. C. A. Bartlett and S. Ghoshal, "Changing the Role of Top Management: Beyond Strategy to Purpose," *Harvard Business Review* 72, no. 6 (November–December 1994): 79–88, https://hbr.org/1994/11/beyond-strategy-to-purpose

4. Jeff Bezos, "2013 Letter to Shareholders," 2014, https://ir.aboutamazon.com/files/doc_financials/annual/2013-Letter-to-Shareholders.pdf.

5. Lucy Kueng, "Why Media Companies Need to Stop Focusing on Content," presentation at the INMA World Conference of Media, Washington, DC, May 17, 2018.

6. Jeff Bezos, "2016 Letter to Amazon Shareholders," 2017, https://ir.aboutamazon.com/files/doc_financials/annual/2016-Letter-to-Shareholders.pdf.

7. This quote is popularly attributed to George Bernard Shaw—but there is no evidence. The earliest known source was in business writing: "The Biggest Problem in Communication Is the Illusion That It Has Taken Place," *Quote Investigator*, November 3, 2018, https://quoteinvestigator.com/2014/08/31/illusion/.

8. Alan Deutschman, *Walk the Walk: The #1 Rule for Real Leaders* (London: Portfolio, 2011), 158. He may be paraphrasing Wendy Kopp.

9. "Netflix Culture—Seeking Excellence," *Netflix*, accessed June 17, 2023, https://jobs.netflix.com/culture. https://jobs.netflix.com/culture. The origin of this quote is not completely clear and may be a paraphrase. See "Teach Them to Yearn for the Vast and Endless Sea," *Quote Investigator*, August 25, 2015, https://quoteinvestigator.com/2015/08/25/sea/.

10. First formulated in his 1970 essay, Robert K. Greenleaf, "The Servant as Leader," *Greenleaf Organization* (Cambridge, MA: Center for Applied Studies, 1970), which credits inspiration to Hermann Hesse's 1932 novel *Journey to the East*. Greenleaf expanded his thinking in 1977; see Robert Greenleaf, *Servant Leadership* (Mahwah, NJ: Paulist Press, 1977).

INDEX

Page numbers in *italics* represent figures or tables.

CARIAD, 221

causal theory, in Shared Vision Map, 80–81

CDO. *See* chief digital officers

CEOs, 47

challenge of proximity, 30, 40, 203

challenge of uncertainty, 29, 35, 37, 116

channel level, 98

Chase, 62

chief digital officers (CDO), 5, 47

Christensen, Clayton, 152

Cisco, 32

Citibank, 62, 101, 167, 168, 173, 177, 186; Discovery 10X, 131, 168, 185, 193, 218; innovation structures, *211*; P/O statements, *103*

CitiConnect for Blockchain, 168

Citi Ventures, 167

Citi Ventures Studio, 169

Cline, Patsy, 126

cloud computing, 26

CLV. *See* customer lifetime value

CMA CGM, 235

CNN, 62

CNN+, 28–29, 39

Colella, Vanessa, 131, 167, 169, 180, 186, 255

combinations, talent capabilities, 235–239

Comcast, 192

communication: of culture, 251–256, 258–259; in Culture-Process Map, 261; leadership and, 269

competition, 50; in Four Stages of Validation, 148–150

competitive differentiation, 153

Competitive Value Train, 52, 108

compliance, 171

composable technology, 232

consumable technology, 232

Cooper-Hewitt National Design Museum, 100

copper, 144

copycat products, 143

Corporate Innovation Stack, 212–217; innovation boards, 214–216; innovation structure, 212–214; innovation teams, 216–217; layers of, *212*

corporate VC, 206

cost/risk savings, 157

cost structure: in business validation, 158; of innovation, 145

COVID-19, 5, 119

Crossing the Chasm (Moore), 161

cultural principles; actionable, 258; in Culture-Process Map, 258; relatable, 258, tenets at Amazon, 293n18

cultural symbols, 251–256; in Culture-Process Map, 259

culture, 244, 262; at Amazon, 249–250, 256; as behavior, 247–251; communication of, 251–256, 258–259; defining, 249–251; at digital-native businesses, 255–256; in DX, 246–247, *251*; enabling, 254–256, 259–260; leadership and, 249; at Netflix, 250; at New York Times Company, 246–247; resource allocation and, 254; scaling, 254–255; at Tesla, 255–256

Culture-Process Map, 256–263, *257*; accountability in, 261; big three processes, 260; communication in, 261; communication of culture in, 258–259; culture enabling in, 259–260; data in, 261; incentives in, 260; metrics in, 260; principles in, 258; resource allocation in, 260; step 1, 257, 261; step 2, 257–258, 261; symbols in, 259; use of, 261–262; workspace in, 261

CUPID, 169

curiosity, 255

customer delight statement, 94

customer demand, 136

customer experience (CX), 71, 72

customer identification, in problem validation, 132–134

ABOUT THE AUTHOR

David Rogers is the world's leading expert on digital transformation, a member of the faculty at Columbia Business School, and the author of four previous books. His landmark bestseller, *The Digital Transformation Playbook*, was the first book on digital transformation and put the topic on the map. Rogers defined the discipline by arguing that digital transformation (DX) is not about technology; it is about strategy, leadership, and new ways of thinking. With this sequel, *The Digital Transformation Roadmap*, Rogers tackles the biggest barriers to DX success and offers a blueprint to rebuild any organization for continuous digital change.

Rogers has helped companies around the world transform their business for the digital age, working with senior leaders at corporations including Google, Microsoft, Citigroup, Visa, HSBC, Unilever, Procter & Gamble, Merck, GE, Toyota, Cartier, Pernod Ricard, China Eastern Airlines, NC Bank Saudi, and Acuity Insurance, among others.

Rogers regularly delivers keynote addresses at conferences on all six continents and has appeared on CNN, ABC News, CNBC, and Channel News Asia, and in the *New York Times*, the *Financial Times*, the *Wall Street Journal*, and *The Economist*.

At Columbia Business School, Rogers is faculty director of executive education programs on digital business strategy and on leading digital transformation. He has taught over 25,000 executives through his programs in New York City, in Silicon Valley, and online. His recent research has focused on new business models, innovating through experimentation, governance for growth, and barriers to change in digital transformation.

For new tools and content from David, visit www.davidrogers.digital.